Third Edition

Coaching Special Teams: By the Experts

Edited by
Earl Browning

COACHES
CHOICE™

ISBN: 978-1-60679-086-1
Library of Congress Control Number: 2010921279
Cover design: Brenden Murphy
Book layout: Brenden Murphy
Front cover photo: Brian Bahr/Getty Images

Coaches Choice
P.O. Box 1828
Monterey, CA 93942
www.coacheschoice.com

Contents

1

Making the Kicking Game Important

Frank Beamer
Virginia Tech
2000

I have always been a coach that believed in the importance of special teams. Everywhere I have coached, the head coach always stressed special teams. It was true with Mike Godfried, Bobby Ross, and Jerry Claiborne. They always stressed kicking. Then, when I got the head job at Murray State, it was obvious to me that the quickest way to win football games was with the kicking game. It has always been a part of me, and I have continued to stress it at Virginia Tech.

The first question we get about our kicking game is this: "How much time do you spend on the kicking game?" I am going to show you how much time we spend on the kicking game. We believe in making the kicking game important, and I will cover the things we do to make it important.

I want to show you a chart that we keep updated that illustrates the importance of field position. The essential nature of field position is just a fact about football.

Yardline	Chances of Scoring
-20	1 out of 30
-40	1 out of 8
50	1 out of 5
+40	1 out of 3
+20	1 out of 2
+10	1 out of 2

You can see your chances of scoring increase within a short number of yards. The best way to get field position is in the kicking game.

We are always talking about big-yardage plays. We are always talking about momentum plays. In the Sugar Bowl this past year, if Florida State had not blocked one of our punts, and if they had not run back the punt on us, I am not sure they would have beaten us. In the third quarter, when we made our comeback, we were establishing field position with punt returns. The kicking game was very evident in that championship game. It just makes that chart I showed you become more important because you increase your chances.

At Virginia Tech, we put an importance on the kicking game. I am going to go over some things that we do that may be a little different for what other teams do. There may be some teams that do it the same way we do.

Talking about being important reminds me of a story. The Pope was visiting this country one year. He called his chauffeur and told him to get his car ready, that he wanted to take a ride to see the countryside. The Pope came down to the car and told the chauffeur that he had decided he would drive today. The chauffeur asked him if he was sure that was what he wanted to do. He told the chauffeur that it would be an easy drive in the country where there would be very little traffic. The Pope got in the car and started driving out in the country. It was not long until a police officer pulled them over. He goes up to the limousine, and the Pope rolled his window down. He asked to see the license. The Pope obliged and gave him his license. The police officer goes back to his car and gets on the phone. He calls his supervisor. He told him he had pulled over a speeder, but he had a problem what to do about it. The chief asked him if he had pulled the mayor over? "No, sir! It is more important than that." The chief asked, "Do you have the governor?" "No, sir! It is more important than that." The chief asked, "Do you have the president?" "No, sir! I think it actually goes higher than that." Finally, the Chief asked him, "Who in the world *do* you have?" The officer responded, "I do not know who he is, but he has the Pope as his chauffeur." That was an important person in the back seat.

At Virginia Tech, we make the kicking game important. The first thing that happens with us is the fact that I am involved in the kicking game. I will tell you how this all came about. I came up as a defensive coach. I was a defensive coordinator most of the time when I was an assistant. When I got the head-coaching job at Murray, I spent all of my time on offense. I called all of the offensive plays. Then, when I got to Virginia Tech, I became involved in everything.

A few years later, we lost a couple of coaches. Before that, our position coaches handled their phase of the kicking game. After we lost those assistants, I started getting involved in the kicking game. Since that time, I have decided that I would not do it any other way now. You must have an offensive coordinator and a defensive coordinator that you believe in to do this. I have no problem with that phase. But, it allowed me to coach the special teams. Now I could get out of the way of the offense and defense.

As I see it now, it becomes very important for the kids to play on the special teams. They know how important it is to us. Just saying it is important is not getting it done. You have to show it is important.

So you will know what I am talking about, let me give you a couple of terms. Our Pride team is our punt team, our punt protection team, and our punt coverage team. Our punt block team and punt return team are called our Pride And Joy. I handled those two groups plus the kickoff coverage team. I have another coach that handles the kickoff return team, who has done it for a long period of time. If there was one area that I would take over, that would be it. I think the field goals and PATs—and blocks against those two teams—fit with the offense and defense. The things on those teams remain the same week to week. I think it sends a message to the team when the head coach is in charge of those special teams.

I think it is a more efficient way of operation to have the head coach in charge of the kicking game. Before we did it this way, I would always stress to the offensive and defensive coordinators to make sure they got their kicking game covered. But now what happens is this. Those guys go study the offense and defense and I go study the kicking game. By doing it this way, they get to spend more time on their area and the person working on the special teams get to spend more time on that phase of the game.

For example, I will spend at least four hours looking at the Pride and the Pride and Joy teams just looking for little things that will give us an edge. I look for things like this: some player may be mixed up on the protection. We may find one kicker that is a little slow on his steps. Another blocker may be creating too much space. How the personal protector blocks is another thing I look for. I spend at least four hours on this phase of the game. Not many assistant coaches are going to spend that much time on looking at the kicking game.

While the rest of the team is watching film on Sunday, I am working on the special teams. We will add a new rush every week. Each week we will do something a little different. Whatever the opponent that week sees from past games, they know they will see something a little different next week. The question will be, "Can they handle what we do different?" That is the issue.

When we start our practice I go down with the kicking teams. I go with the snappers, punters, and field-goal kickers. We have a competition every day. I think you have to put the field-goal kickers under the gun as much as you can. I work with them and we have competition every day. We work on the kickoffs and the onside kick. We work with the punters on the pooch kick. I think it helps to have someone with those guys to let them know it is an important part of the game.

We have our best players on our special teams. We have players that can do their very best. One reason for that may be because I am involved in the special teams. We try to convince them it will enhance their pro careers if they can play on special teams. If they have any ability in the kicking game, it may make a difference in being drafted or not, or on making the last cut. If they can protect the punter, cover in open field, or return punts it is an added benefit.

We never ask anyone to stay after practice or to come out early for the kicking game. We have our kicking game in the middle of practice. We never have them come out early or stay late as a punishment. A lot of teams will send their special teams out 20 minutes early. The other teams are not out early and to some it seems like punishment to send one group out early. We would never do that at Virginia Tech.

If you come to one of our practices, you would see that everything moves fast. We do not stand around during practice. Things move fast. When we do our special teams, everyone stops and we all come to one field and we do all of our kicking for that practice. It may be slow for some of the players in some ways, but it is another way of telling them the kicking game is important. I can tell you something about this part of practice. This is when I start getting cranked up. I get them moving and we get things done. It is an important period in that practice and the kids know it.

If we are working on conditioning drills, we will take our Pride And Joy teams and work on the punt return as far as a conditioning drill. I will promise you this; you will never see our Pride And Joy group walking off the field. They will run off the field before the other conditioning group. We have a drill where we work our Pride team against our Pride And Joy team. For conditioning that day, if they are in those groups, they get half of their sprints knocked off. We do this so the players will want to be on those teams. We do not want them to feel they have to do something extra to be on those teams.

We have special awards for offense, defense, and special teams. We have an award called the "big hit." Anytime the offense gets an award, the defense gets an award and the special teams get an award. That is just the way it is. The offense and defense selects their award winners in their meetings on Sunday. On Monday, we show the big hits in the kicking game to the entire team. Again, it is just another way of saying the kicking game is important.

We have goal charts. The offense, defense, and special teams all have goal charts. We have special team meetings. They stay on Monday and Friday for the meetings. On Monday, we show the film from the past Saturday's game. After the film, we go over what we are going to do for that week. On Friday, we go over all of the video each of the teams has been involved with in practice that week. Then we will show some video of the team we are getting ready to play. Those are some of the ways we try to make the kicking game more important.

Let me talk about goals. I do not like very many goals. If you get too many goals, they become too much. I like to keep goals simple and I like to make them obtainable. We like to make it a situation where we can say to the team if we make these goals we have a chance of winning.

Special Teams Goals – 1999
- *Pride (Punt)*
  - ✓ Allow no more than six yards per return.
  - ✓ Down punt inside 10-yard line.
- *Kickoff Coverage Team*
  - ✓ Average starting the opponent at the 20-yard line or less.
- *Pride and Joy (Punt return)*
  - ✓ Average 10 yards per punt return.
- *Punt Rush/Field Goal/PAT Rush Teams*
  - ✓ Block a punt, field goal, PAT, or force a bad kick every game.
- *Kickoff Return Team*
  - ✓ For 66 percent of the time, start our drive at the 28-yard line or beyond.
- *Field Goal/Extra Point Teams*
  - ✓ 100 percent on PAT attempts.
  - ✓ 66 percent (2 of 3) on field-goal attempts.
- *No Penalties or Mental Errors*
- *Hidden Yardage = +20 Yards*

We add up our kickoff return and our punt return yardage against our opponent. We want to end up with those 20 extra yards. That comes out to two first downs. We look for those hidden yards. If we can just start out 20 yards more upfield, we have a chance to be successful.

I am going to go over our practice schedule. There are some things here that I feel are very good. Eight years ago, we went 2-8-1 at Virginia Tech. After that season, I took a look at every single thing in our program. We started doing something different in our practice. I will show you some of those things that came about as I went to visit other coaches to find out how they did things and to compare them with what we were doing.

During that losing season eight years ago, we were ahead of six of those teams that we lost to in the fourth quarter. We were only down by six to twelve points to three other teams. So we had a chance to win nine football games. Instead we were 2-8-1. We were close, but we were just not getting the job done. So I will talk about some of the changes we made in our approach to practice.

As I said, we have a meeting on Monday with all of the team. We give the big hit awards to the offense, defense, and the kicking team. One of the things I was concerned with when we were 2-8-1 was the number of penalties we were getting. We used to run them after practice and give them punishment during the week. We tried a lot of things, but we were not getting any better. So we started showing the entire team all of our penalties in that meeting on Monday. You show that player blocking someone in the back to the entire squad; it makes an impression. That peer pressure is wonderful. It has really helped us. We have cut back on our penalties. We have really cut back on stupid penalties. I am talking about late hits and hits out-of-bounds. Those penalties will wear you out quicker than anything.

We show the penalties to the entire team. If they called a penalty and we do not agree with the call, we tell the team that. We will tell them the penalty should not have been called. Then I will tell them when a penalty should have been called. We go through each situation and we make those guys responsible for their action in front of their teammates.

I said we have our kicking game meetings on Monday. We go back and show the film of the game on Saturday. Then we give them a scouting report. People ask us about spending more time on the kicking game. We do not spend more time. We spend the same amount of time each week. Each team knows exactly how much time they have each week. I think having the practice schedule organized and making it more important is the key.

Monday Practice			
Period	Time	Minutes	Schedule
	5:10	10	Flex
1	5:20	5	Converge
2	5:25	5	Field Goal vs. Field Goal Rush
3	5:30	10	Individual
4	5:40	10	Skeleton vs. Varsity
5	5:50	5	Opt./Pride Protection
6	5:55	5	Inside – Pride Joy (Rush)
7	6:00	25	Team
8	6:25	10	Conditioning – Scrimmage
	6:35		Off the field

Here is one of the things that I like about our schedule. This is the way we start practice on Monday. After we have stretched and done our flexes, we go to our converge drill, which is offense against the defense. We come in and run screens, draws, reverses, and the halfback pass, and plays such as that. They are plays that either turn out real good or real bad. The thing I like about the drill is that it gives the offense time to work on those plays, and it gives the defense time to work against them, but another good point is that it starts out practice fast. It does not matter if you have won or lost, I want to start out practice fast. We flex, come together, and here we go. It is a fast-paced drill.

After the converge, we come together and we kick field goals against each other. One thing I like when we kick field goals is that we never rush the whole team. We only rush three men. But, the kicking team does not know which three men are going to rush. I do not like for everyone to rush on this drill in practice. One year, we lost a player to injury because we rushed everyone. We just keep it to three men.

We take five minutes on Monday and work on our Pride protection. We are a zone protection team. We want our guys working straight back. We put the Pride team with their backs to the camera. Then we put a light strip or a line straight back so they can see if they are working straight back. They can see it on the film.

We have the Pride and Joy guys over on the defensive side. We try to keep the two groups separated from each other because they work against each other a lot. The Pride linemen are big guys. They are tight ends, defensive ends, and big guys. On our punt blocking team we have all fast guys. We have the receivers, defensive backs, and linebackers. They have to be fast to get on the Pride and Joy team. We keep them separate so we can work against each other.

We run some of our punt rushes. We are in zone protection and it does not make any difference where they are coming from. If there is a special rush by the team that we are getting ready to play, we will run that against them.

Then we go to a five-minute period with our Pride and Joy team. We will go against the scout team here. Most teams protect their center one way or the other. We zone, so we just back him up. I get a scout team to run the punt against us. We work on our rush for that week. We will have two or three rushes each week.

That is all of the kicking we do on Monday. We do not stay late at night working on the schedule for the next day. If you stay late night after night, you get run down after awhile and you do not make good decisions. You are tired when you get to the game on Saturday. I made a conscious effort after that to get the details done, and get the work done, and then get home and get some rest. Then we could get something done the next day. Our staff has been together for a long time and we are not going to keep them late.

Tuesday Practice

Period	Time	Minutes	Schedule
	4:15	10	Flex
	4:25	4	Central meeting
1	4:29	9	Individual
2	4:38	9	Individual
3	4:47	9	Individual
4	4:56	9	Individual
5	5:05	10	Perimeter vs. Varsity three-on-three
6	5:16	10	One-on-one vs. Varsity, Middle vs. Varsity
7	5:25	10	Skeleton vs. Varsity – Pass Rush
8	5:35	10	Skeleton vs. Varsity, Pass Rush vs. Varsity
9	5:35	10	Team vs. Scouts (Blitz)
10	5:35	10	Kicking – Pride vs. Pride and Joy
			• Protect
			• Protect and Cover
			• Protect
			• Protect and Cover
			• Protect
			• Protect and Cover
11	6:05	10	Team vs. Varsity (Two Back - Play Action)
12	6:15	5	Team vs. Scouts (Short yardage)
	6:20	10	Conditioning – Pride and Joy (Return) – Deep Balls
	6:30		Off the field

After the season starts we never hit in practice. Let me tell you, Virginia Tech has always been a hard-nosed, tough football team. That is the type of kid we get at Tech. But, in that 2-8-1 year, we would get to the fourth quarter and we were soft. We could not finish it. So we made some changes and do not hit in practice like we use to.

On Tuesday, we have a perimeter period. I like this period. We have the tight ends, wide receivers, and backs going against the secondary. The secondary people are taking good angles to the football. They are not going to allow those long plays. On offense, we work the wide receivers on blocking. We tell the tailbacks they are never to run over a defender in this drill. We tell them we want to see some moves in the drill. It is a good period both ways. We tackle to the ground, particularly early in the year.

Then we come back and do a middle drill. It is seven-on-seven, offense versus defense. Nothing is fancy in this drill. We run isolation, sweeps, and kick-out plays. Again, we tackle to the ground. You hold your breath in this drill because you do not want to lose a player here. I think there is something about doing things full speed at least once a week. Since we started doing this, we have been a lot tougher especially in the fourth quarter.

Continuing on our Tuesday practice, we get to the special teams in period 10. Here again, we all come together on one field. There are some guys standing around. I do not care.

We work our Pride versus our Pride and Joy. The first thing we work on is protection. We will run the other team's rush. I usually put a towel on the ground at a certain point. If the rushers get to that towel, they can go ahead and block the kick. I do not want the rushers laying out. I do not want the punter getting hurt. It is full speed as far as protection and as far as rushing.

Next we work on protect and cover. First we snap the ball and punt it. We send the outside headhunters down to cover and send anyone responsible for the headhunters on the return. The deep back catches the ball and we check the first group down on the punt. Then we come back and punt it again and those guys are gone. Everyone that is remaining will go to his responsibility. I like this drill because with the headhunters out of the drill, it gives you a chance to see if your inside people have their lanes covered.

We will stay down at the end where we caught the punt and go the other way on the next punt. We protect on the first punt. Then we punt and cover on the second punt. We go back to the original position and punt and protect again. Then we punt again and cover. That gives us six reps with best versus best. It helps if you do not have the same people on the same teams.

Then at the end when we have conditioning, the Pride and Joy guys are only running half of those sprints. They are going to be off the field before the other guys that are doing conditioning.

| **Wednesday Practice** | | | |
Period	Time	Minutes	Schedule
	4:15	10	Flex
	4:25	4	Central Meeting
	4:29	5	Specials
1	4:34	9	Individual
2	4:43	9	Individual
3	4:52	9	Individual
4	5:01	10	Inside vs. Scouts
5	5:11	10	Pass Skeleton vs. Varsity (Scouts)
6	5:21	10	Pass Skeleton vs. Varsity
7	5:31	10	Kicking
			• Pride (Priority) vs. Pride and Joy (Rush)
			• Field Goals vs. Field Goal Rush
			• Pride and Joy (Return) vs. Pride
			• Onside Prevent
			• Pride vs. Pride and Joy
			• Field Goal vs. Scouts (Rush)
			• Punt Safe vs. Pride (Priority, Poocher)
			• Kickoff Return (Squib, Pooch)
8	5:41	9	Individual
9	5:50	10	Pub, Two-Deep (5 min); Blitz, Two-Deep (5 min)
10	6:00	10	Team vs. Scouts
11	6:10	10	Team vs. Varsity (third-and-long, no blitz)
12	6:20	5	Team vs. Scouts (field goals)
	6:25		Conditioning – (rocket, rainbow, lazer, scramble – perfect plays – deep balls)
	6:30		Off the field

Here is another thing that came from the revisions we made in our program eight years ago. Basically, we have two ways of punishing a player. We have reminders. This is where a player does 40 seconds of up-downs, then 20 seconds of rest, and you continue until you think the player is *reminded* of the violation. The other way is for serious offenses. We have Wednesday sunrise service. Our conditioning coach has it during the season. During the spring, the position coach is responsible for the sunrise service.

We decided eight years ago how we would handle discipline. We said, "If you screwed up, you are going to be punished." Sometimes it becomes a matter of who you screwed up for as far as your position coach. Some coaches may run the steps, another coach may give them up-downs. The punishment is not the issue. The issue is the fact that they screwed up. Our goal is to keep you from screwing up. "Do things right every time." Now, if a player screws up, he gets punished one way or the other. If it is sunrise service, we go on with it. We are not so concerned about the punishment end of it. I think that is important. I do not think that punishment is the issue. The important thing is not to screw up and that is the issue and to do things right.

Back to Wednesday's practice. Before we start with period 1, we have a special period. This is not so much for the punter and field-goal kicker as it is for the backups on our special teams. Sometimes those guys will go through a week's practice and not get any work. We work on all phases of the kicking game. We are spread out with each group working on a different phase.

We have the punters in one group with the punt return men at the other end. We have the snappers working with the punters. We have the field-goal kickers working at one area; I have the kickoff men working at another area. I take the guys that are on the return kickoff team fielding pooch kicks.

We have our punt block drill in another area. Everyone will be involved in the punt block. That includes the Pride and Joy players, and the people on defense that would be rushing on a punt safe situation. We use that if the ball is on our 40-yard line and we do not expect the punt. We like to work on a line on this drill. We want the ball on a line. We do that so the defenders can line up as close as they can on that line and know they are onside. We get a landmark back eight yards deep. I have a back up punter kicking in this drill. We are not going to take a chance with our starting punter.

The punter is going to make a soft kick. The defense is going to come to the landmark and take the ball off the punter's foot. We just go one at a time as the punter makes the soft kick. Everyone gets a chance to block a kick. You want them back where the punter is as much as you can get them so they will feel secure back there. When they get into a game they will know what it is like if you practice it in that manner.

We are still on that Wednesday practice schedule. Here is the kicking period. This is period 7. Everyone stops and comes to one field. The first thing is our Pride versus the Pride and Joy. The first kick is against a rush. If we do not block the punt, it is an automatic punt return one way or the other. Our punt team is covering. We have the whole operation in that drill. We will go downfield and touch the punt return man with two hands.

Next we go to our field goal versus field-goal rush. This is the period when I have the bullhorn and things really speed up. I go faster, talk louder, and we are really moving. It is a slow period because you are bringing people on and off he field but it is a fast-paced drill. Again, we only rush three players.

Then we go Pride and Joy versus Pride. This time we are working on the return.

The next thing we do is to work on receiving the onside kick. We have our Hands team on the field. I feel it is important to work on this every week. It comes down to this play a lot of the times. If you get it, fine, but you have to work on it. I like for those guys to get used to handling the ball on those kicks. If the ball is kicked high, we can call for the fair catch. If it is going out of bounds, we can knock it out of bounds. We do all of those things but we give them a chance to practice it during the week.

We come back with Pride versus Pride and Joy again. Then we go field goal versus field goal block. Usually we go against our team and not the scout team here.

Next we work on punt safe versus Pride. We put the ball on our 40-yard line and we are going to kick it inside our 10-yard line. Our defense will stay in the game and we put a man back at the 10-yard line. We work on this both ways.

Then we get our kickoff return team out there and we squib or pooch the ball to them. Those are the eight things we do in a 10-minute period.

Another thing we do. We work against our best a lot more now. We do not sit there and work against the scout team for 30 minutes. All we were getting by going periods 5, 6, and 7 was this: the scout team was getting a workout and we were knocking them off the ball four or five yards. We end up practicing bad habits. All it amounts to is an assignment check. You are not going to get better going against the scout team all of the time. What happens when you go good against good is that you get fundamentally better. You can improve as the season goes along. Sometimes the offense is not the same or the defense is not the same. But, to me, if you have rule blocking, this is one of the best things we do to improve our football team.

We go best against best for 10 minutes and come back the next period and go against the scout team. They are fresh and ready to go. Now you can work on special adjustments, blitzes, motion, and whatever you will be facing that week.

The next period we come back and go best against best again. Now we work on third-and-long. We make it a critical situation. We call out the down and distance. We run the play and see if we get the first down. We get some competition going. It is good against good.

Then we will come back and work against the scout team again and work on some other phase of the game. Most of the time, that will be goal-line offense and defense. By alternating against the scout team and best against best, you save your scout team, and you get better as the season goes along. When you work good people against good people, they just work harder. We never tackle them down to the ground. We do not tackle. We butt off, we do not chop block, and we do not block low during this period. The first three steps are full speed. You can get the game momentum when you do that.

Another thing we do on Wednesday is something we like. At the end of practice, we work on conditioning. I think there is a time when everyone should condition together. I think it is a part of football. You want everyone to go through something tough. We do not just run them for conditioning. We have a plan and everyone works on his aspect of the game. For example, with the quarterbacks we have we do not work on the scramble. We have an organized way of handling the situation. If you are a receiver and the quarterback starts running around, if you are running a short route you change the route when you see the quarterback scramble and go deep. If the receiver runs the out route and sees the quarterback scramble, he turns upfield. If he runs a deep post route and sees the quarterback scrambling, he comes back to the ball. We want an organized way for those receivers to do that. So we work on that drill. Everyone gets his running in during the drill.

Another thing we do for conditioning is to throw the deep balls. You cannot get enough of this drill. We like to use it for conditioning at times.

The kickoff team does not meet with the kicking team on Monday. We meet to start the practice on Thursday to go over what they are going to do. This is situation that we ask the group to do a little extra by having the kicking team meeting.

The first thing we do on Thursday is to work on kickoff returns. That stays pretty constant as far as how you are going to return the kick. There may be a couple of things that you change, but basically it stays the same.

Next we do kickoff coverage. Some changes occur here, but the basics do not change.

Then we have Pride and Joy. That is our punt block versus the scout team. If you are going to be a good punt blocking team, you have to give your people chances to work on it. This is what we do. We have the second punter back deep to work on the punt block. He has a soft football to punt. Again we have our Landmark set in front of the area where he will be kicking. The landmark is at eight yards from the center. The punter kicks the ball over that landmark. It can be a towel on the ground to mark the spot.

Thursday Practice			
Period	*Time*	*Minutes*	*Schedule*
	4:15	10	Flex
1	4:25	10	Kickoff Return
2	4:35	10	Kickoff Coverage (One) Lanes
3	4:45	5	Pride and Joy Rush
4	4:50	10	Offensive third-and-long, Skeleton vs. Scouts
5	5:00	5	Goal Line Pass, Skeleton vs. Scouts
6	5:05	5	Pride (Fake, Taking a Safety)
7	5:10	10	Two-Minute Drill vs. Varsity
8	5:20	10	Team (Clock) Dress Rehearsal
			• Defense – First Fourth Down (Punt Return of Punt Safe)
			• Offense – Barnyard (Five)
9	5:30	10	Team
10	5:40	10	Team
			• Field Goal (Two)
			• Field Goal Block (Two)
	5:50	5	Central meeting
	5:55		Off the field

We are always going to block by numbers. We number our players 1 through 10 from the left to our right. We will run this drill with only one half of the line rushing. I will call out the number of the defender that I want to make the block on the kick. The offense will let that man go free. However, everyone has to come off the ball expecting to block the kick. A lot of times, what happens on punt blocks is this: the rusher is slow coming off the ball and then he realizes that he is free. He comes after the punt but just misses it because he is too late. We want them coming off the ball expecting to make the block.

We ask the front line to pull the blockers on each side of the man we are sending after the block. When a rusher gets knocked off of his course we ask him to continue his rush on the outside. What happens is this. When you do get a block inside, the ball will come rolling out on the outside. Now they can pick the ball up and take it to the end zone. Also, one of these days the punter is going to pull the ball down and run with it. If that happens, we will have a man outside to make the tackle. That is why we want them to continue the rush when they are knocked off their rush lane. If they are blocked solid they need to stop and then start working outside.

Then we go to the other side of the line and do the same thing. We leave the center out of this drill. We want to give each of the rushers a chance to block the punt. After we block the kick, we start working to get the ball into the end zone. It goes fast but you are working on the principles of blocking the kick. We always expect to block the kick.

After a couple of periods, we come to period 6 and have our Pride period. If we are going to use a fake kick that week, we will work on it at this time. We do work on taking a safety, but most of the time we do that on Friday. We usually work on something special during this session.

The next session is our two-minute session. We are in shorts and do not have contact. We allow the quarterback to take his five steps and throw the ball. Sometimes when you are in pads, the quarterback has a hard time getting the ball off. We work on the fundamentals of the two-minute offense. We go 1's against 1's, both offensive and defensively. We stress that we are working on the fundamentals. We do not stress who wins or who loses. I think it is very important to practice these situations as much as you can. Again, stress the fundamentals. Go over details such as when the clock starts, how to save time, killing the ball, and other situations. If we get to the 20-yard line and the situation calls for a field goal, we will kick it. That is a good time to let that field-goal kicker get experience. The defense gets to work on the field-goal block. We go two series on this and then they are out.

We work on our team offense and defense. We are going up and down the field with the different teams. If we call for the field-goal block team, they come on the field immediately. When we call a team out, they go on the field. We practice this a lot. We had better not have a penalty for too many people on the field and we do not want to end up with not enough men on the field. We work on getting the different teams on and off the field.

One thing we do now I got from Bobby Ross when he was with the San Diego Chargers. It was right after they had made the NFL playoffs. He told me one of the best things they did was to take the best plays of the last game and show them to the team before the next game. We started doing that. We show the film on Friday night. You will never see a play in the film that is not a good play. We make the session fun for the players. The players will cheer and yell and carry on. It is a good session for us. You can ask our players what is one of the things they enjoy about football at Tech and they will tell you it is Friday Night Video.

The basis for the film is that it is all positive plays. We may add some funny clips in the film. But every play that they see is a great play by their teammates from the previous week. We do it win or lose. I think this is a good thing. Sometimes when you lose, you need that more than you do when you win. I believe it is important what people think when it comes to winning.

Friday Practice

Time	Schedule
4:00	Flex in Groups
4:10	Individual
4:15	Central Meeting
4:20	

Pride
- Poocher (vs. Punt Safe)
- Kicking out
- Kick at Five Seconds
- 11-Man Rush
- Take safety

Kickoff Return
- Pop up
- Ball blocked (behind or past line of scrimmage)
- "Peter" or "Short" vs. Return
- Kicker loses protection
- Block kick close to line of scrimmage
- Fake

Field-Goal Rush
- Jump
- Ball blocked (behind or past line of scrimmage)

Field Goal
- Jump on ball
- Cover

Kickoff Coverage
- Squib
- Onside
- After 15-yard penalty
- After a safety

Punt Safe

Onside Prevent

4:35	Break to Offense - Defense
4:55	Off the field

Friday is really a big kicking day. We go out and break a sweat. We go over different situations in the kicking game. We will punt from the 10-yard line and from the one-yard line. We want to make sure we do not have any problems in this area. We work against the 11-man rush where we just want the punter to take a rocker step and kick the ball. We work on taking a safety with our punt team. We will block you up front and have the punter run out of the end zone.

When we work on our Pride and Joy, we line up and tell them this punt is going to be blocked. The punter catches the ball and then throws it down on one side or the other. He may throw the ball on the other side of the line of scrimmage. If it is behind the line of scrimmage, we are going to try to get it into the end zone. If it is on the other side of the line of scrimmage, we are going get away from the ball. The ruling is the same on a field goal. We work on the short punt. We do not want the short punt coming down and hitting one of our linemen. That is what we do with Pride and Joy.

Next we work on field-goal blocks. We do the same thing here that we did on the punt. We tell them the field-goal try is going to be a blocked kick. The center snaps the ball and the holder will throw the ball down. If the ball goes behind the line of scrimmage, we pick it up. If it is beyond the line of scrimmage, we stay away from it. We work on this every week.

Then we work on kicking field goals. If it is a long attempt, we want to make sure we cover.

We work on the kickoff coverage. We work on the squib, onside, a kick after a penalty, and kicking after a safety.

Then we go to our punt safe drill. After that we work on the onside prevent team. Those are the things we work on for Friday. Basically this is our schedule for the week.

Some other thoughts I have on the kicking game. Most of these things apply mostly to the college level. I would strive to have at least two snappers, two kickers, and two holders. In 1992, we went down to Southern Miss and our first field-goal kicker got hurt. We had to bring in our second kicker. He kicked two field goals and we won the game. That started us on a winning streak and we have gone to seven straight bowl games. I have often wondered what would have happened if we had not had another field-goal kicker. To me, it is important to work not only the starter but also the backup player.

A lot of teams do not give scholarships to kickers. They want to have them walk on and try out. I feel if the kicker is good enough, you give him a scholarship.

I think it is important to develop depth in the kicking game, not only in college but in high school as well. This is true with punters, kickers, and snappers.

If I am hiring coaches, I always ask about special teams experience. If they have special teams experience, it is a plus for me. I have coaches on our staff that can sit down and talk about special teams and it is a good discussion because the coaches know what they are talking about.

We say this: a kick is coached by one person. I know the fundamentals of kicking. But I do not mess with our kickers. I think the punter needs to go to only one guy. If that guy knows his swing and style, that is the only guy he should go to. My point is that only one coach should be with the kicker. If he does not have a guy to go to them, you may be able to help him.

I think catching the punts is the same thing. I think it is the toughest thing to do in college and high school football. The more you can work on this, the better off you are. Usually the punt return man is the player that catches most of them in practice.

We want our kickers to be team players. We want them to do everything the rest of the team does. We do not have a different set of rules for the kickers. The conditioning is the same and they follow the same rules. They are regular members of our team. On Saturday morning, we go for a walk before the game to stretch them out. I walk with the kickers. I do not worry about it when things are going good, I worry about it when things are not going so well. I think they must fit into your team. The more they fit in, it is easier to get them through the bad times. If they miss a kick they are part of the team. You are not going to grab them by the throat. I think it is important that your specialists are treated the same as the rest of the team.

We have a Pride and Joy meeting just before the pre-game meal. We ask them if they have any questions. We block a lot of punts. We usually have everyone covered. We have someone responsible for every man. It takes on a great deal of importance because it is the last thing we do before the pre-game meal. We review all of their assignments in the meeting.

I am going to cover one additional thing before I stop. This started with Mike Godfried when we were together at Murray State. We have a session on the last Saturday before our opening game. We have about 80 play situations we go over. It used to be about 70 situations but it has increased to about 80 plays now. We have a scrimmage with all of the unusual things that happen in a game. We have all of these situations that could take place in a game. It covers everything you can think of. Everyone will tell you they cover these situations, but I think it is good to physically go through these situations on the field.

When we started doing all of these different situations, we realized most of them are related to the kicking game. When we come on the field we have one player calling out Pride and Joy. When we say Pride and Joy, you better be out there. If you have everyone screaming when they come off the field, you can't tell what is being said, so we have one player calling out the team that is going on the field. We have only one player calling out the teams. Then if something happens, I am going back to that one guy.

Another situation we cover in this session is when we score and go for two points on the PAT. If we score on defense, we make sure the players do not come on the field or off the field until they know if we are going for one or two points.

We go through all the rules that we must cover related to those special situations. For example, if a kick is blocked when we are kicking from our five-yard line, we tell the kicker to kick the ball out of the end zone and take a safety rather than giving them ball inside the five-yard line.

On our Pride situations, we cover what to do if the punt is blocked. If it is blocked and the ball is behind the line of scrimmage, we can advance the ball. We try to pick it up and run with it. We do not want them to throw the ball because we probably have players downfield.

We cover those situations that are unusual. One more situation we cover is the field goal fire. If we get a bad snap, we call "fire." We work on that situation. We work on the third-down field goal. If we block the kick we are going to get on the ball. We do not want the kicking team to fall on it and get another kick. If we get a bad snap on a field-goal try with eight seconds left, we will throw it at the feet of the upback and kick it on fourth down.

It has been good being with you and I hope I see you in Blacksburg. Thanks very much.

2

Punt-Return and Punt-Block Schemes

Frank Beamer
Virginia Tech
2006

I want to thank Nike for the opportunity to speak here today. Their people treat us great. I have been impressed with the personnel they have and the way they do business. Bill Kellar has headed up the program for us and has been a good friend to high school and college football.

If you have heard me talk before I think you will find some new wrinkles and ideas in the topic. I really believe the quickest way to win a football game is through the kicking game. There is no question in my mind. I coached in high school for a number of years and have watched it for a long time.

If I were coaching in high school, I would wear out the preparation in the kicking game. I watch a lot of tape on high school teams and I see a bunch of shaky long snappers. If you can block kicks, you have an advantage against that type of snapper.

If you find a team that is not settled as to how they protect the punt, you have an advantage. You may think the kicking game is boring. However, I can guarantee it is without a doubt the quickest way to get you beat or win a game for you.

The chart I am going to show you is all about percentages and makes perfect sense to me. If you won any money in the casino last night, you probably understand percentages. If a team takes over on their own 20-yard line, they have a one out of 30 chance of scoring. If they take over on their own 40-yard line, the chance of scoring is one out of eight. However, if they get 10 more yards on the punt return and move the possession up to the 50-yard line, they have a one out of five chance to score.

In the kicking game, we always talk about big plays and momentum gains. There is a lot of yardage involved with the kicking game. If you block a field goal and return it for a touchdown, that is a difference of 10 points. The difference is the three they did not get and the seven you got.

Coaches think we spend a lot of time practicing the kicking game. I do not think that is true at all. What we do with the kicking game is make it important. The most important thing to making the kicking game successful is to have the head coach involved. I worked and played under some excellent kicking-team coaches. I played and coached for Jerry Claiborne, I worked for Bobby Ross and Mike Gottfried, just to mention a few. I have always been around some good kicking coaches.

When I became a head coach, I emphasized that part of the game. I knew how important it was. I always had a coach that headed up our kicking teams. I was always involved with the offense and defense. However, the head coaching duties took me away from that type of planning. When I lost a couple of assistant coaches that were involved with the kicking game, I decided to take over that portion of the game myself. What I found was it helped our overall operation.

When the head coach is actively involved in the kicking game, the players become more inclined to become a part of it. That fact helps with the success of that part of the game.

Having the kicking game as my responsibility is the most efficient way to run our operation. Bud Foster used to have the punt-protection team. He is now our defensive coordinator. Before Bud could work on his defensive plans, he had to get the punt-protection scheme ready. Now I take the kicking game and he can concentrate on the defensive responsibility he has.

I spend hours studying the opponent's punt-blocking assignments. I want to know the way they protect and if there is a weak link in their protection. I look at when and how they snap the ball. The secret is that I spend the time instead of one of my offensive or defensive coaches. I have a new punt rush prepared for each game. It takes time to get that all done.

The first four periods of our practice each day have to do with kicking. The periods are five minutes in length for a total of 20 minutes in all. We start out with a field-goal competition. We have players kicking field goals competing against one another. That is one of the toughest plays in football. Coming off the bench to kick a field goal or catch a punt has a lot of pressure attached to it. The more times you can put these players in pressure situations that count, the better prepared they are to handle the pressure. It is difficult to come off the sideline and kick a field goal to determine the result of the game. It amounts to only one play. Working through the competition in practice helps in preparation for the games.

I time the punters' hang time and the time it takes to get the snap. We practice kicking directional and pooch kicks. Any time you can kick a team inside the 10-yard line is a big play in a football game. If you can start a team inside their 10-yard line, the percentages against them scoring really go up. We also compete with our kickoff men. We want to see which one can kick the ball the deepest and who can keep it in the air the longest.

This happens every day, and I can see all kinds of benefits from that part of the game. One of the points I use in finding players for special-team work is the benefits that can come from it. The last five or six spots on a pro rooster are filled with players who can play on special teams. We tell our players that if they do something well in the college kicking game, they may be helping themselves at the next level. We had one of our former players quoted as saying the reason he made the Washington Redskins was his ability to play special teams.

Those types of statements really help boost your players' attitudes about playing special teams. You need your best players playing on those teams. You cannot take a substitute and block kicks. It will not happen. It takes a good athlete with speed and height. He has to bend his body and get his arms out. You cannot block kicks with average people. You must get your best people into that part of the game.

Never come before practice or stay after practice to practice kicking. If you do, you punish those players who play on special teams. When you do your kicking drills outside the realm of practice, you reinforce the fact that kicking is not as important as offense or defense.

We stop practice right in the middle and bring everyone to one field. If you came to a practice at Virginia Tech, you see everyone moving around. We do not have players standing around doing nothing. We practice with a fast tempo. All of a sudden we stop that tempo and bring everyone together for a kicking drill.

That immediately tells everyone that this phase of the game is important. If we stop our practice and everyone is looking at what is going on, it has to be important. I think that is the way you must approach it.

We also use our punt-return game as our conditioning period. While everyone else is conditioning, our punt-return team is practicing the returns. They have to do it perfectly for one to count. I promise you, the return team will finish its conditioning before everyone else. The punt-return players are running off the field while the conditioning people are still working. There are advantages to playing on these teams.

On Tuesday, in the middle of practice we practice our punt team against our punt-block team. The players on these teams work extremely hard. If they work hard in this drill, there will be less work for them at the end of practice. Give your players privileges for playing on those teams. The players watching may begin to think they would like to be on one of those teams.

Everyone pays lip service to the importance of the kicking game, but you have to show your players you mean it. Give them the same awards as you do offensive or defensive players. If you have an "offensive player of the game," you need a "special teams player of the game." If you give awards for big hits, make sure you include the special teams play in that area.

When we give offensive and defensive awards, we do it in their meetings. When we give special team awards, we do it in front of the team. There are generally offensive and defensive players on those teams. In addition, it is another chance to praise those players.

When you do your goal charts for your locker room, make sure there are special team goal charts as well. We want to make sure the goals are not too complicated. Sometimes the goals are so complicated they lose emphasis. Our goals have a basic theme of, "Did you get the job done or not?"

We have simple goals. The punt-coverage team strives to allow no more than six yards per return and to down a punt inside the 10-yard-line. The kickoff-coverage team goal is to force the offense to start behind the 20-yard line. The goal for the punt-return team is to average 10 yards on a punt return. On our punt- and kick-block team, we want to block a kick or force a bad kick.

Forcing the bad kick is the particular statistic missed on most occasions. If the punting team gets off a 20-yard punt instead of a 40-yard punt, that amounts to two first downs. That is a lot of yardage when it comes to big plays. If you look at defensive goals, most of the time they have "allow no big plays" as one of their goals. They define big plays as 15-yard runs and 20-yard passes. It is the same thing with the bad kick. It is the hidden yardage in the kicking game that adds up to big gains.

Our goal for our kickoff-return team is to start at the 20-yard line. On extra point and field goals, we want to be 100 percent on the extra points and 67 percent on the field goals. We want no penalties or mental errors in the kicking game. This goal is the one I like the most. We want our punt-return and kickoff-return teams to gain an advantage of 20 yards over their opponent's kickoff- and punt-return teams.

On Monday, we go over game planning in offensive and defensive meetings. The same should hold true for special teams. They should watch films of their play and corrections made. They get a game plan in the kicking game for the upcoming opponent during their meeting. On Friday, we do the same thing, with the teams evaluating their week's practice and looking forward to the game.

We strive to have entirely different personnel on our punt-protection team and our punt-block team. We may have one or two players we need on both, but we try to prevent that from happening. The reason for that is the ability to work against each other at practice. That is a big advantage because we work good on good.

The next day we watch the tape of that competition in the meetings and learn from it. The blocked punt is probably the biggest play in college football as a momentum turner. It generally leads to points on the scoreboard or at least a drastic change in field position.

We have a section in our game preparation called "Pride and Joy." This involves the new punt-block scheme, the return, and the fakes in the kicking game. The "Joy" personnel consists of our punt-block team and the "Pride" personnel is the punt-protection team. Before our pregame meal, we have a 10-minute session with "Pride and Joy." In that session, we go over who is responsible for the fakes in all phases of the kicking game.

I want to go through the way we practice. When we start Monday, we go a shorter period than other days. We go over the scouting report before we get on the field. In Monday's practice I like to get out and start practice fast. It does not matter whether we won or lost, I want the tempo upbeat. We work the offense and defense on plays that are big plays one way or the other.

We run screens, reverses, halfback passes, and big-play type of plays. We get the offense going against the defense for about five plays. From there, we go to a field-goal and field goal–block team for one kick. That builds confidence in the kicker, knowing he can perform under pressure.

We put our punt-protection team with their backs to the camera and work on that scheme for five minutes. We block any special punt-block scheme the opponent might have installed.

We put in our new "Pride and Joy" punt block for the week. Our punt-protection team works against our "Pride and Joy" personnel in some instances. That is what we do on Monday.

On Tuesday, in the middle of practice we stop practice and bring our team together. We have our punt-protection team against our punt-block team. I like to practice this way. The first thing we do is set up a rush scheme. It may be the one I use in the upcoming game or one we have used before.

We do not physically block any kicks during this part of the drill. I give them landmarks to rush through, but no kick blocking. We go through the rush and protection scheme and punt the ball.

The next phase is punt and cover. I like to break up the coverage and concentrate on the coverage in piecemeal segments. If we have a return left, I send the headhunters and anyone assigned to block them. The headhunters are the wide players on the coverage team. On the left return, we double-team the left headhunter and single-block the right headhunter.

We have a punt return man catching the ball, the two headhunters, and the three blockers going in this portion of the drill. It is easier to show the responsibilities and correct the mistakes when you have only a few bodies going in the drill. Doing the drill this way isolates the action and you can see more. We go through the coverage and return three times using the part method.

On Wednesday, we have a specialty period. That period is not so much for your first kickers and catchers, but the reserve and back-up kickers and snappers. We want to give the back-up players time to work on their skills. We have our pooch kickers working with the player who might return those types of kicks. We have punters kicking to the return players.

I want players going down under the punt to make the punt return man make a move after catching the ball. They do not tackle the return man. They simply try to touch him, which gives him the added pressure of the coverage coming down on him. I do not want the return man to catch the ball and throw it back. I want him to concentrate on the catch and make a move as if he were going into a wall. If the return is a side return, I want him catching the punt, taking a hard step up the middle, and breaking outside. He does the opposite thing on a middle return.

In another area of the field, we have kickoff and kickoff-return personnel working in that phase of the game. I want the catchers to simulate game situations when they catch the ball. This is not a lollygag part of practice. We want game situation and intense concentration in each phase of the game.

In another area of the field, we work on punt blocking. I will talk about that part of the game later in detail.

In the middle of practice that day we have a kicking drill. We bring everyone together in the middle of the field and give out the helmet covers for our kicking opponents. We wear maroon and white jerseys in practice. The special teams have people wearing both jerseys on them. Therefore, when we go to a kicking period, we use blue helmet covers to designate the opponents. It takes less time to get them on than a scrimmage vest.

During this period we bring our kick-block and punt-protection teams together and work. During this period, if we can block the punt, we do. This is a live punt-block period. The next thing is field-goal and the field goal–block team. We run them on and off the field in a high-tempo movement. We want it fast.

"Pride and Joy" is our punt-block team. We have running backs and receivers as part of this team. Andre Davis, who is with New England as a wide receiver, was one of our "Pride and Joy" personnel. He blocked two kicks at Boston College on a Thursday night on ESPN. The personnel on this team includes the best players we have available who can block kicks. They are not necessarily defensive personnel.

Our first punt-protection team could be tight ends or defensive ends. We have the best people available for that team. Our first punt-protection team and punt-block team go against each other. We put the blue helmet covers on the "Pride and Joy" personnel.

After that, we practice the onside kick–prevention game. During that period we look and practice against all kinds of different onside kicks. When it comes to this part of the game, we have to get the ball. We practice hard at this phase because the results usually determine the outcome of the game.

We come back with the punt and punt-block teams again. From there, we go to the field-goal and field goal–block teams again. Then we practice a punt safe kick. That is a situation where the defense is not sure the punting team will punt the ball. We keep our defense in the game and put a return man deep to receive the ball around the 10-yard line. We also practice the other side of the situation and kick the ball inside the 10-yard line.

We work on returning the crazy kickoffs. The squib and pooch kicks are the ones most teams use. We do all this kicking within a 10-minute period and do it at a fast tempo. Getting the teams on and off the field is part of the drill. We want them moving when they go on or come off the field. The blocking in the drills is full speed and it is live. However, we do not tackle live. We look up the runner and butt him.

On Thursday, we start with kickoff returns. It is basic and we do the same thing every week. We make sure we get the numbering of the opponent's kick personnel during this period. That is a 10-minute period. The kickoff-coverage team remains very consistent from week to week. However, I have four headhunters covering on the team, which I move around each week. We spend 10 minutes doing that part of the kicking period.

The "Pride and Joy" spends five minutes on a block at this time. We work them against the scout team. The Pride team is next in the progression of kicking. We like to install a fake every week with the punt team. We practice the fake, pooch, and playing our headhunters in a tight formation.

We have to practice that because of the way we protect the kick. We man protect to one side and zone protect to the other, depending on the rush scheme we face. When the headhunters come to the inside, they become part of the protection scheme. They need to know the scheme we use. The headhunter on the zone side blocks zone and the headhunter on the man side blocks man.

In our offensive team period, we practice a couple of field goals and during the defensive team period, we practice a couple of field-goal blocks. The last thing we do is practice kicking the field goal with the clock running down. We must get on the field, set the team, and kick the field goal while the clock is running out. If you do not practice those situations, you cannot execute them when you need them.

Here we use man blocking to the kicking team's right and zone blocking to the left (Figure 2-1). The blocking back blocks the number 1 man from the center. The right guard blocks the number 2 rusher, the right tackle blocks the number 3 rusher, and the wingback blocks the number 4 rusher. When we punt the ball, we kick it to the man-blocking side. We kick that way because the blockers make contact with the rushers, knock them off their stride, and release in the coverage.

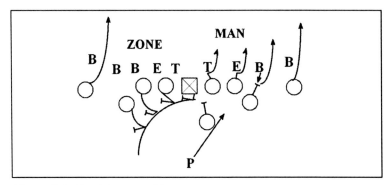

Figure 2-1. Punt to man side

The zone blocking side gives ground in their scheme. They cannot cover immediately and must drop in their protection. If the punter kicks the ball toward that side, the coverage is not as good. The headhunter to the man side releases outside and the headhunter to the zone side releases inside.

On the overload side we zone block and man block the other side. In theory, if the zone side stays solid, the rushers have to come outside to get to the ball. Since we are kicking away from that rush line, we should get the kick off.

For many years, we were a zone-protection scheme. However, when you zone protect, the coverage has a hard time releasing to cover the kick. In addition, when you zone protect, you need bigger players to match up with the rushers. Consequently, the bigger players do not run as fast as the smaller ones. That gives the good punt return man an advantage. That is why we went to a man-protection side in our scheme.

Our guards and tackles are tight-end and defensive-end type personnel. They are bigger bodies that can get their hands on the defender and get through them. The wingbacks may be back-up linebackers. However, they are the most dependable players you have on the team. The headhunters are fast receiver-types or maybe defensive backs. The personal protector has to be a quarterback-type in a linebacker's body. He has to be a smart player. He makes all the calls, talks, and keeps people under control.

We align with our inside foot forward in the stance. As we step, we shuffle inside. To the zone side, we want to form a wall. The center snaps the ball and takes a shuffle-set back to his zone side. The guard next to him shuffles inside and back on him and sets. The tackle outside the guard takes a couple more shuffle steps back and is deeper than the guard as he sets. The wingback is off the ball in his alignment, but still gives ground to form the wall. They protect with the inside arm and look outside.

They protect the inside with their arm, but they are responsible for the outside gap. They take anyone coming into that gap. To the man blocking side, the technique is the same for all three of the blockers. They take one shuffle step, face up on the defender, make him redirect his charge, and release. They take the best possible release they can get. We would prefer to release outside if we can get that release.

On Friday, this is break-a-sweat day. We check our special teams for the first-line players and back-up players. We bring the Pride team out and pooch the ball into the 10-yard line area with the safe punt scheme. We practice kicking out of the end zone. The personal protector has to move his alignment up to account for the reduced yardage we have to kick the ball. If he tries to align at his regular depth, he gets the ball up his butt.

We practice kicking the ball at three seconds. In the fourth quarter if we are ahead, we want to take time off the clock. We practice snapping the ball with three second left on the play clock. If we have to punt on the last play of the game against an 11-man rush, the punter takes a rocker step and kicks.

We practice taking a safety. We may substitute the quarterback for the punter. We let him take the snap and at the last second step out of the back of the end zone and not take a hit.

On the kickoff return, we practice all the different kinds of kicks. We practice all the quirky things that could happen in a game. We practice how to handle the blocked kick. If we block the kick behind the line of scrimmage, we want to get it to the end zone. We cover kicks after a safety as part of this period. We do not want something to happen in the game that we have not practiced. We have to cover all the fakes that could come in the kicking game.

On our kickoff team, we practice the squib and onside kicks. We practice kicking off after a 15-yard penalty against the other team. We try to kick the ball as high as we can to the one-yard line. We also practice the kickoff after a safety. All this occurs in a 15-minute period.

I want to get into blocking kicks. We have a drill we use to find our punt blockers. If they turn their head or close their eyes, they cannot block a punt. We give them two shots at the ball. If they do either one of those things we send them packing.

Not everyone can block a kick. I look for players with great speed, quickness, and a knack for blocking the ball. The longer and taller they are the better I like them. The quicker the player can go from point A to point B and the further he can reach out at the end makes the difference.

The biggest thing in blocking kicks is the landmark. If a team kicks at nine yards, my landmark is seven and half yards. We are very exact on that distance. The body has to go through the landmark, not on a collision path with the punter. We want our hands to the sides of our bodies to keep the body away from the punter's leg. If the punter is a right-footed kicker, a rusher coming from the left side reaches his hands to the left of his body to stay away from the punter's leg as he comes through the landmark.

Finding the landmark of the opposing punter is my job. That comes from film study. Most of the time it is the same spot every week. I do not like players leaving their feet because they have no control of where they will land. However, if they do leave their feet at the last second and have a good rush line, it is alright with me. What we have to prevent is them leaving their feet and coming down on the punter.

The proper angle for the block is not a straight line. If the protection is zone, the rusher has to clear the outside of the zone and bend in to the landmark. The only time you come on a straight line is when the protection misses an assignment.

If the punt rusher is knocked off his course more than one step, he stops and makes sure the ball is kicked. It only takes one person to block a punt. If the rusher is knocked off his course, I want him out of the way. We only want one player free in the punt block scheme. If you break two players loose, they will try to avoid each other, miss the kick, and probably rough the punter.

We never take a personal protector and push him back. We pull him out of the way. That clears the area for another rusher. If the area through the landmark is clear and the rusher does not have to dodge players, he can block the kick. Every rusher leaves the line of scrimmage thinking he will come free. When he is knocked off his course, he stops and clears the area by getting outside.

By releasing outside, the rusher puts himself in a position to tackle the punter. If the punter realizes the punt will be blocked if he kicks it, he pulls it back and starts to run. He runs into the rusher who was knocked off course. If the punter kicks the ball and it is blocked, we are in position to take it to the end zone.

The punt-block scheme and return scheme should look the same. The punting team should not be able to tell if you are blocking the kick or returning the ball. We want to get as close to the ball as possible. We want our hands on the ball and our heads behind our hands. Keying the ball and getting a jump is critical in blocking the punt. Usually when you miss the block, it is only by inches. If we can figure how to make up the distance, we can get the block.

The rusher cannot wait to see if he is open before he accelerates. He has to come out of his stance as quickly as possible. The last movement is to stretch the hands out. Do not run with the hands out. At the last second, the hands are extended to the foot of the punter. They have to look at the ball to block it.

If the blocked ball crosses the line of scrimmage, get away from it. If it stays behind the line of scrimmage get it to the end zone. If the rushers do not practice what to do after the punt block, they will jump on the ball. We blocked four punts one year and did not score with any of them. It did not make sense to me. When you block a punt, you have the advantage in numbers. There always seems to be four of your players and one or two of theirs. Whichever player is closest to the ball takes his time and picks it up. Everyone else turns and blocks the other color jersey. We rehearse so we do not have two players trying to recover the ball.

In the punt-block drill, we use a snapper and a punter. We take air out of the ball so it does not hurt the rushers' hands. We snap the ball to the back-up punter. He punts the ball at three-quarters speed. We practice punt blocking with all our players. The man on the headhunter is also a rusher. We mark the point at which the punter will launch the ball for that week. In this case, it is eight yards.

The blocker coming off the headhunter comes down the line of scrimmage with his shoulders square. That way you can tell he is onside and he can see the ball, plant his foot, and go to the ball. If he comes at an angle, he may get offside.

We bring the rushers in rapid order, one after the other. They use the techniques for the landmark and block the kick. The next drill we use involves the scout punt team (Figure 2-2). We align in our punt-block scheme. I designate the blocking assignments for the scout team line. In each case, I leave one rusher unblocked and he blocks the kick. When the kick is blocked, we react and get the ball into the end zone.

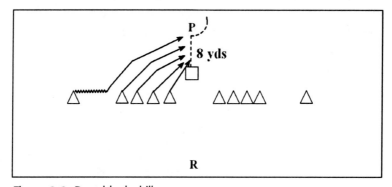

Figure 2-2. Punt block drill

The punt-rush team does not know who will be unblocked. Everyone comes off the ball as if he will come free. They react to the blocks and play their roles. We do this several times, changing the free rusher every time. We go half line at a time. We do the same thing to the other side.

I want to show you our typical rush formation and talk about the personnel (Figure 2-3). We align with 10 men on the line of scrimmage. We have a basic 5-5 alignment on either side of the center. The number 1, 2, 3, 4, 7, 8, 9, and 10 rushers are defensive-back or running-back types of players. We have two defensive-back types defending the headhunters as they come downfield. The 2 technique players or number 5 and number 6 rushers are defensive ends. We felt we needed bigger players on the inside.

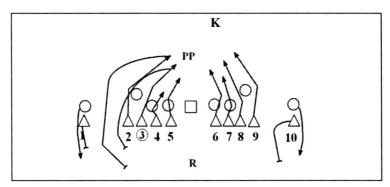

Figure 2-3. Punt block/return formation

If the protection is a zone scheme, I want the number 5 rusher to force the offensive guard's block by attacking his outside shoulder. If I can do that, I have three rushers on two blockers to the outside. I want to put my tallest, quickest rusher in the number 3 position coming inside the wingback.

The coaching points for the inside rushers are to come off low and turn their shoulders sideways. If we stay square on the zone blocker, it gives him more surface to block. We want to turn and get small. The number 4 rusher takes off on an outside rush on the tackle and jumps inside. He turns his shoulders and gets small. Once he clears the blocker, he bends to the landmark.

The number 3 rusher fires low and hard upfield until he clears the tackle. At that point, he bends hard inside for the landmark. The number 2 rusher picks a point one step outside the wingback's block. That means one step outside a point where the wingback can get his hands on the rusher. Once he clears the blocker, he bends inside to the landmark. If the rusher gets past his landmark, I want him to stop his rush. All that can happen when a rusher passes his landmark is roughing the kicker. The right side does the same rush with their corresponding players. That is our full rush with a return right.

The return right or left comes out of the full rush. The wall may not be clearly defined, which is not all bad. That prevents the kick-coverage team from totally identifying the return. A cluster of blockers downfield can spring the kick return man.

On the return left, we want a series of double teams (Figure 2-4). We want to keep the headhunters from getting downfield instead of simply directing them outside or inside. The number 7 rusher doubles the left headhunter blocker. He may leave the line of scrimmage a little early to get into position. The number 9 rusher comes through from the right to force the kick. If he comes clear, he goes for the landmark to block the kick. However, he has to make sure the blocker is not releasing on a pass to that side.

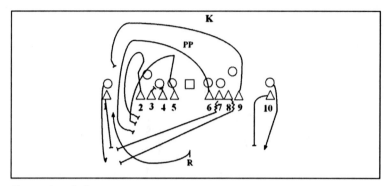

Figure 2-4. Left return

We want to rough up the headhunter and keep him from getting downfield. The only thing you cannot do is let him split the double-team. If he is outside keep him outside. If he is inside, block him inside, but do not let him split that block.

We double-team the left tackle with the number 3 and 4 rushers. They get shoulder to shoulder and block him. If he comes outside, the number 3 rusher takes him and the number 4 rusher circles outside and gets back on him. If he goes inside, the number 4 rusher takes him and number 3 rusher falls back inside and blocks him. The tackle had better not make the play on the return. However, we have to use common sense with the block. If we get down the field and one of the blockers has the tackle blocked, the other blocker can get in the wall and get ready to block someone else.

We want to create a gap between the wingback and the tackle coming down the field. The number 2 rusher makes the wingback stay on him and if he clears, he goes for the block. If he does not clear, he sets the wall. The inside rushers fire into the guards and keep coming upfield. I want them to occupy the personal protector to keep him from going outside if one of the rushers comes clean.

After they do that, they get into the wall. The number 8 rusher comes to the middle of the field and blocks the first threat coming down the middle. He secures the catch of the return man. We want him 25 yards down the field.

If the ball is in the middle of the field, the wall is set at the top of the numbers. If the ball is on the hash mark, the wall sets a couple yards outside the other hash. The wider we can set it the better we are.

We can put a wrinkle into this return by using a reverse (Figure 2-5). The blocking is the same as the left return. The difference is the number 8 rusher, instead of blocking the first threat down the middle of the field, becomes the reverse runner. He starts his angle as he would on the return left. The kick return man catches the ball and starts right with the ball. He reverses the ball to the number 8 rusher and he returns left.

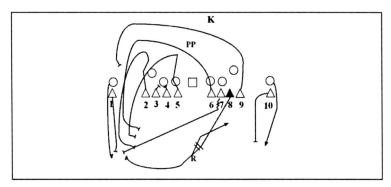

Figure 2-5. Reverse left

It keeps the same techniques for the return team and gives misdirection to the play.

Sometimes we cannot predict where the punter will kick the ball. If the ball is coming down the middle, we are fine with the rules for the left return. However, if I cannot tell where the ball is going, I need to double on both sides. I always want to double the headhunter to the side of the return. However, if the ball is on the right hash mark and we have a return left into the wide side of the field, the most dangerous headhunter is the one coming down the right side of the field.

That is the one I want to double because we have space going to the left to make the move on the headhunter coming to that side. We have a chance to run inside or outside of him because of the width of the field. If I cannot predict the position of the kick, I call return left double (Figure 2-6). When we do that, the number 4 and number 7 rushers are the double-team players.

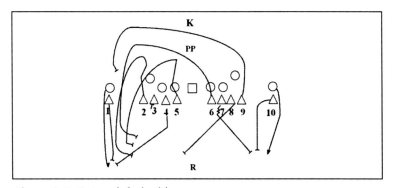

Figure 2-6. Return left double

Everything is the same except for the double to both sides and the single block on the tackle by the number 3 rusher. When we return the ball to the outside, the return man has to start forward before he breaks outside. The further the return man can take the ball upfield, the better the chance of getting a good side return.

I have made up my mind to reduce the number of schemes we have in the punt return. I want to solidify the personnel on the teams and work on a couple of returns and perfect the techniques on those returns. I am guilty of changing things because they look good on the blackboard. If you do that from week to week, you do not execute as well. The deal is to execute. The secret to a good return is to make the alignments of the rushers look like the block alignment.

We have three basic alignments we use in the punt-block schemes. We do that to keep the kicking team off balance. If they can predict exactly where you will line up, it makes you vulnerable to the fake.

Our punter launches the ball at 10 yards from the line of scrimmage. We align at 13 yards. The snap comes back in 1.7 seconds and the punt comes out in 1.9. We never want the punt coming out over 2.2 seconds. I guess the average time is 2.0 seconds.

Any questions? Fellows, I have enjoyed being with you and I hope you come to Blacksburg to see us. Thank you.

3

Techniques for the Two-Step Punter

Mike Bellotti
University of Oregon
1998

Let me talk about punting. I have some goals listed, and I will cover each of those. This year we had 61 punts. We averaged 40.4 yards per attempt on those punts. We averaged a net of 38.2 after the punt return. We had 15 punts down inside the 20-yard line. We gave up 52 yards returned by punts in our first game. In the rest of the season we gave up 56 yards on punt returns.

We use the directional punt. I think it is a big weapon. We feel that is a very important aspect of the game. It requires more from your punter. He must be more accurate and more deliberate. He must sacrifice some distance to be accurate because he is kicking at an angle. We follow a very simple rule: if we break the huddle on the right hash, we will kick the ball to the other side to the right numbers. If we are on the left side it is the same thing; we kick it to the left numbers. If we are in the middle of the field, we started out kicking the ball to the left side because the ball tends to tail to the left side of the punter. However, our punter was kicking across his body most of the time. We actually offset the punter by having him square his shoulders in the direction he wanted to kick. We think this helps the centers as well. If we are going to kick the ball to the left side, then we tell the center to snap the ball to the inside of the punter's right hip. As the punter kicks, he should be behind the apex of the protection and 10 yards back from the snap.

Our first goal is to get the ball off in 2.2 seconds. Sometimes we are 2.1 or 2.3. That is realistic. We have good snappers. You do not have to have great snappers, but you must have a good long snapper. We may move our punter up to 14 yards at times. I think that is a unique thing about a two-step punter. I will talk about the whole ball of wax if I have time.

We want the hang time to be 4.5 seconds. You should demand one second for every 10 yards the ball is punted. If the punter kicks it 30 yards and you get down the field in 3.0, you want 3.0 hang time. If he kicks it 40 yards, you want 4.0 hang time. Do not tell the punter to kick the ball as far as he can. Tell the kicker to kick the ball as high as he can. At our level, there are several teams that can take that punt back on you. We want to maximize our distance and get down the field. We can do that by stretching the hang time. If we want to average 40 yards per punt, we will have to average 4.5 on our hang time. Now, we do not have all of the guys on the punt team who can run the 40 in 4.5. But you must understand that the higher we hang the punt, the more time we have to get down under it and cover it.

Let me say this: we do not want any punts blocked. Now, as an offensive coach, the fewer defensive people I have on the punt team the better. I want to minimize the number of people who can put pressure on the punter. We use the spread punt formation. Let me cover that formation. The guards have their inside foot at the heel of the center. The guard's depth is about six inches. We want the tackle's inside shoulder parallel with the guards. They are to be one half a chicken's wing length from the guard. This way, they do not have a rule that they must touch elbows. That is how they get their alignment. The wings are about two yards off of the ball and just outside the tackles. Our personal protector is on the right side of a right-footed punter about five or six yards deep. His inside leg is on the outside leg of our guard. If we are kicking at an angle, we will move the personal protector just a little. That is a very standard thing that we must communicate to him. This is what we look like.

Our punter is back 15 yards. His heels are at 15 yards. Again, we can offset the punter and kick it to our left or right. Generally we tell him to kick through the A gap. We tell him to kick through the guard. That is all we tell him. That will generally put the ball at the numbers. That is where we want the ball, between the hash mark at the numbers.

I have shown you just a basic coverage. We try to keep five-yard lanes as we go down the field. Our guys on the outside are "free hitters." They are going to the ball. Their only rule is to keep outside leverage to the ball. They will take a shot at the return man if they can. Everyone else keeps the five yards spacing down the field.

Let me talk about the technique at the line of scrimmage for a second. First is stance. The feet should be shoulder-width apart. We want the inside foot up and the outside foot back. We are staggered slightly from the heel to the toe. We want to start out with our eyes up. When the ball is snapped I want to take a kick-step and slide. The big thing is this: as we come back, we do not want to open the hips. We kick-step and slide. We do not want to lean back and we do not want to open our hips. We poke to the inside with the inside thumb up. We poke to the inside and punch with the outside. We will drop to a depth of four to five yards. We must drop back in a straight line. We must not get wider. Understand this, we are protecting a point 10 yards behind the center. Regardless where we are punting the ball, that is where the punter is supposed to be. The kicker's toes should come through the 10-yard area behind the center. We zone protect. We are responsible for the area from my inside foot to the outside foot of the person next to me. We have not had a punt blocked in three years. We have had a couple of punts that were close to being blocked. We have been lucky in that we had a very athletic punter and he could get the ball off very quickly.

We want our eyes straight ahead. You must see the ball out of the corner of your eyes. The ball is the trigger. We work on different drills on getting off on the snap of the ball. The center snaps the ball when he is ready.

We want the blockers to bend at the waist and knees. We want to look from the inside out and we want to look for loopers and blitzers coming back inside. You are waiting for people coming to you. We want to eliminate the false step by grounding your weight on the balls of your feet. The weight should be on the balls of your feet rather than your heels. We do not want them rocking back on their heels. We want to push back off of the balls of the feet. We want the thumb up. That is a power position. We find that will bend the arm quicker. The one concept of zone protection is this: we stay together, step together, and vision together. When we are dropping, we should have the 10-yard area that we are protecting.

The punter is offset at a depth of 15 yards. His weight is balanced and he is in a staggered stance. He is toe-to-instep when he is receiving the football with his left foot slightly in front. Our hands are loosely framing our target. We want the punter to relax with his hands rather than giving a target. There are a lot of drills you can use to teach this. We say the location of the ball is the right hip of the punter. That is for a right-footed punter. We would like for everything to be in a straight line. When the ball is coming back on the snap, we want a hard focus on the football. We want a soft focus on the rush. In fact, we tell our quarterbacks that we want a hard focus on the receiver and a soft focus on the defense. His primary focus must be on the football when he is punting. He must feel breakage or seam moves. Once he receives the snap, his weight must shift to the right foot so he can punt on two steps.

Let me talk about the catch. We want the ball caught in this manner. The left hand is forward and the right hand is back. A lot of people hold the football like they are going to shake hands. There are a lot of different schools of thought on this. Some people hold the ball with their hands under the ball, and some like to hold the ball with their fingers on the top of the ball. I like the shake-your-hand method the best. I think the majority of your fingers should be on the top panel of the football. The reason I say that is because when I drop this ball with my hands under the ball it has a tendency to drop forward. If I drop it with my hands on top the ball has a tendency to come back to me. We want the ball with the nose up. We want to make contact with the ball about knee height. We want to line up the inside of the ball with the inside of your kicking foot. We line up the center top half of the ball on the top half of the foot. The ball is going to extend about two to three inches beyond your toe. We are going to kick the ball off of the top right-hand side of the foot.

The laces must be upright. Some people like to put their thumb on the lace on the top of the football. It must be something your punter feels comfortable with. Once he has done that, his first step is a balanced step. That stride is like a walking motion. It is only two or three feet. It is just like he is walking motion. He is only going to take a two- to three-foot step, and that is all. He wants to keep everything in a straight-ahead manner. As he steps forward, he carries the ball from the elbow to waist high. He does not want to take the ball up high and then bring it down. We do not want him to take the ball outside the body. Everything should be in front of him in a controlled manner. His shoulders should be parallel to the line of scrimmage. His posture should be tall with a slight forward lean. We do not want him to lean back and we do not want him to hunch over. He wants to stay upright with his body in a walking manner.

The second step is a longer step. It is a five- to six-foot step for a normal punter. I do not want to have a heel plant. I do not want to overstride to a point where I can't accelerate through the football. I can power through and lock my leg behind me. If you overstride, you lose hip drive. We want the hip cocked so we can get that extra drive going up through the football.

Let me make one point. I have looked at a lot of film of punters. You do not want the punter swinging through with a straight leg. We do not want to extend the leg too soon because the hip muscles can move the leg a lot faster if he uses hip movement in the kick. Just prior to the contact, we want complete extension.

The swing path is from the inside to the outside of the foot. If they have problems, this tells them to place the ball over there. We talk about placing the ball on the inside of the knee or on the outside of the knee based on the swing plant of their foot. When I coach the punter, I stand to the side and slightly behind to his right foot. I want to see where the ball goes, but as he goes away from me I can watch the swing of the leg.

We talk a lot about the release. All we are doing on the release is straightening the arm. When you release the ball all you do is let go of the ball. I let go with my fingers. We do not tip the ball; we just drop it. There is little or no wrist action. The drop should be done in a manner that allows the nose or front point of the ball to stay level, or slightly down and in, toward the midline of the body. The laces of the football are at the punter's right shoulder, or kicking side. Generally we keep the ball level to the ground and point it in the direction we want the ball to go.

The contact point should be about knee high. The contact should be made on the top of the right side of the punter's foot with the ankle not flat. The foot should be tilted a little. If the punter kicks through the ball, it will have a natural spin on it. If you tell your punter to kick across the ball, they actually lose power. We want them to kick straight through the football. The worse thing he can do is to put the ball across the top part of his foot. If he kicks the ball on the down side, he may get a spiral, but the ball will not turn over and he will lose distance. The long axis of the ball should be in line or turned inside 10 to 15 degrees and across the midline of the foot. The inside edge of the ball will line up with, or it will overlap the inside edge of the punter's foot. On contact we want the foot and the ball to be parallel to the ground so we have two flat surfaces, which gives us a flat surface and gives us maximum contact and force. If the ball is dropped too far forward, it will end up being an end over end kick. The most important aspect of punting is developing a consistent drop that places the ball on the punter's foot the same way every time.

If we are kicking with the wind, we raise our contact point a little. I want to kick the ball higher to let the wind take it. We kick from a point as high as the middle of the thigh. If we are kicking into the wind, we lower our contact point by keeping the ball low.

I want to talk about follow through and hip rotation. We do not want the hips to rotate until the ball is kicked. If I want to rotate at the hip, I turn my foot inward. That changes your contact point. First, you must make sure the punter is kicking through the ball and then the rotation occurs after the ball is kicked. The foot should follow through above the kicker's head. If a punter does not have the flexibility to allow the foot to come up on the kicking side, it will come up across the face and end up on the opposite side of the head.

Let me make some general points. The punter must keep his body mechanics upright and in line. I can't emphasize this enough. Most kids want to drop down, and then they want to raise the ball up, or they want to lean back. If they do that they lose all of the hip drive and power.

Here are some warm-up drills for our punters. Everything we do with the punters we try to do on lines. When they are warming up, or just playing catch, we try to keep it on a line. When we work out, we want to make sure we do not overload one muscle. What we do with one foot, we do with the other foot. This is for muscle balance and so they don't pull a muscle. We do a lot of stretching exercises and a lot of flexibility work.

General Keys

- Keep body mechanics upright and in line.
- Utilize a relaxed, walking manner.
- Develop ballhandling skills and consistent drop.
- Establish proper ball placement on the foot.
- Improve the hip drive.
- Perfect the leg swing and follow-through.

4

Making Big Plays on the Kickoff

Jeff Bower
University of Southern Mississippi
2005

It is great to be here. I want to thank Larry Blackman and the Nike staff for inviting me to speak at this clinic. I have just completed my 14th year as head coach at Southern Miss. In current times, it is a little unusual for a coach in major college to hold one position that long. I feel very fortunate to be a part of this program.

It is good to be here and have the opportunity to speak to you about the kicking game. I want to talk about the kickoff return today. Most coaches do not like to talk about the kicking game. As a head football coach, I love to talk about it.

When I became the head coach at Southern Miss, the first couple of years I coordinated the offense. However, I began to realize the importance of the kicking game. I dropped the offensive coordinator's job and became a receivers coach so I could hire a full-time kicking game coordinator. In the organization of a staff, you generally have five offensive coaches and four defensive coaches. By hiring a special teams coordinator, it eliminated a coach on the offensive side of the ball. That is the reason I started coaching the wide receivers.

After a few years of coaching the wide receivers, I felt I needed to get more involved with the entire program. I think a lot of coaches pay lip service to the importance of special teams. They tell you how important it is, but never spend the time working on that part of the game. We believe in the importance of the kicking game and devote the time to accomplish our goals.

We feel the kicking game is as important as the offensive and defensive phases of the game. We have an award system within our football team. We give helmet awards every week for performance on offense, defense, and the kicking game. The offensive players have an opportunity to get two helmet decals each week. They can get them for winning the game or grading out with a high percentage on performance. On special teams, the players have the opportunity to receive five awards for each special team.

We spend a lot of time selling our players on the importance of special teams. We talk about that more than any other phase of the game. Over the years, we have been good in our special team play.

I played quarterback and coached the offensive side of the ball my entire career. I never played defense or coached on that side of the ball, but I believe you win with great defense and having a sound kicking game.

Special teams can do so many things for you in relationship to field position and making big plays. The kicking game leads to so many things that can make the difference in a football game.

We have been fortunate to win a lot of games and some championships at Southern Miss. I attribute those championships to the type of defense we play. If you know anything about Southern Miss, you know we play strong defense. We have a tradition of being good on defense.

Since 1999, we have allowed the fewest number of touchdowns by any Division I football team. The Miami Hurricanes are second, Oklahoma is third, and Kansas State is fourth. We have been good on defense, but our special teams have been responsible for just as many wins. I cannot tell you the number of games that have been turned around because of the play of the special teams.

Those types of plays do not have to be touchdown plays. They are plays that have turned the momentum of a football game. I feel that big plays in the kicking game and forcing turnovers are the biggest momentum changers in college football. That is why we spend so much time working on the game and trying to sell it to our players.

We lost our special teams coordinator and did not replace him with a full-time coordinator. Our outside linebacker coach has put together everything related to our kicking game. He has done an outstanding job of coordinating all aspects in each phase of the game. He oversees all the special teams. We have a coach who is the head coach of each phase of the game. The head coach for each phase has designated coaches to assist him.

We have more coaches and players than the high school coach has available to him. We break our staff up so that the majority of coaches that have players on a particular special team will be involved as assistant coaches in that phase. We free up as many coaches as possible to assist with special teams during that part of practice. The position coaches are still working with their players during special teams practice. They can continue to work with the players on individual and fundamental skills during the special teams period.

We try not to involve any coach in more than two special teams. We know there are certain positions that put more players on certain special teams than others. Tight ends, linebackers, and safeties are the types of players that will end up on special teams. They are the athletes with the bigger bodies and speed that most special teams need.

We get our graduate assistant coaches heavily involved with our special teams work. The NCAA only allows two GAs on the field and they are important to our program. They coach specific positions in our special team phase.

We are strapped for time because of NCAA rules governing practice. We have a difficult time getting meeting, practice, and video time for our players. We get our afternoon practices under way around 2:00 PM and our study halls begin at 6:00 PM. That gives us a limited amount of time to practice and allow the players to eat before they report to nightly study hall. That challenges us to get quality meeting time, practice time, and meaningful video time for our players.

We encourage our players to come by in their free time to watch video. I do not think you can get enough of that aspect of football. With the technology available, it is easy to get a great deal of teaching done through video. That gives your players something extra to get ready to compete on Saturdays.

According to NCAA rules, you have to take one day off during the week. Sunday is our mandatory day off. Our game plan for the following football game is done by Monday afternoon. We will meet and practice all phases of the special teams game plan Monday afternoon. It is a basic introduction and scouting report of how we want to attack each phase of the kicking game.

On Tuesday, we emphasize our punt protection and punt coverage team. We have a team meeting before practice with those teams. We emphasize the points covered in that meeting in special teams practice that day. We also meet with our punt block and return teams on Tuesday.

On Wednesday, we meet with our punt protection team again and our kickoff return team. On Thursday, we meet with all four of those phases before practice.

Our field goal and field-goal block teams practice for five minutes each day after our stretching period. The skills involved in field-goal blocking do not change from game to game and require less teaching time. We work both phases at the same time.

We have our first field-goal team going against our first field-goal block team on one hash mark and the two's going against the two's on the other hash. We alternate between the two teams and go rapid fire with their repetitions at varied distances. After we get into the season, we limit the repetitions to about four kicks in that period.

We feel like we slight our kickoff coverage team. However, we get quality reps in spring and pre-season practices to keep us sharp. Kickoff coverage does not change from week to week. Kickoff coverage is the phase of the game that has landmarks on the field and teaches assignments that do not change. We kick the ball from the left hash mark and our coverage remains constant. We get good work on the kickoff coverage on Monday and Thursday. If we feel we need additional work in this phase, we do it during conditioning period on Tuesday and Wednesday.

Unless you show your players the commitment and importance of the kicking game, you will not get results from this area. Whenever we have a special team meeting, the head special teams coach is not the only one who attends the session. Every coach assisting in that phase is at the meeting.

In our kickoff return meeting, in addition to the head coach, we had a coach with the return personnel. We had one coach assigned to the wedge personnel. We had two coaches assigned to our front five players. Each coach has his players surrounding him and goes over each assignment and adjustment they need to execute the return.

We make teaching tapes for these teams. We have about 25 players in these meetings. We want our players to know this meeting is as important as any offensive or defensive team meeting.

We have a pecking order as to what starter we want on certain special teams. We put our best players on our punt protection and coverage. We want starters on our special teams. If you only involve back-up personnel on your special teams, it de-emphasizes the importance of that phase of the game. We have a rule that a starter on offense or defense cannot be involved on more than two special teams. However, on occasion we break that rule in certain circumstances. If you have a redshirt freshman or sophomore, you do not want to put too much on his plate. If he is learning an offensive or defensive position, more than two special teams will affect his level of play.

The more experienced player can play more special teams for you. However, you do not want a guy on the field who is fatigued. At the same time, you have to consider how many plays the player is playing and whether he has a competent back-up at his position. However, we are like you in that we want to play as many players as we can to help us win a football game. If we play two sets of linebackers, we can involve the starting linebacker in more than two special teams.

Punt protection and coverage is our number one priority in our kicking game. The kickoff return is the next most important phase. If you can return the ball outside the

30-yard line, the kickoff return gives you the opportunity to establish field position and make first downs.

The kickoff return is an opportunity for a big play. It is a better situation than a punt return. There are too many variables in the punting game. Punters are using all kinds of methods to prevent the punt return. They angle the punt out of bounds, kick away from the return man, hang the ball high, and use the rugby punt. Returning the kickoff has a better chance of getting a big play.

The third priority to our special teams approach is punt return and block. The kickoff coverage team is next on our list of importance. In this phase of the game, all you need is a bunch of guys who are relentless in their effort to get down the field as fast as they can. There are techniques involved, but the biggest thing is effort and speed. It is the phase where you can be more repetitious in your teaching because you can control where the kick goes.

I want to talk about the kickoff return as to the X's and O's of how we run it. However, before I get to that I want to show you how we teach our players in respect to the kicking game.

As a head coach, I have to make a decision about our spring practice and game. If you go through spring practice and never work on the kicking game, that sends a bad message to your team. We need to work our young players in that phase of the game to see what they can do. In our spring game, we run every phase of the kicking game live except the punt block.

We conduct live kicking drills during preseason to help with the selection of our special teams. We try to create the best competition for our players that we can. We use our best personnel against our best personnel. We try to find out as much as we can about our personnel.

We are not involved in schemes. I am a great believer in simplicity. I know high school coaches know that as well as anyone. You are working with less time, players, and coaches on the field. You cannot confuse your players, especially in the kicking game.

In the kicking game, we want to be simple and repetitious. We want a chance to get good at what we do. The kickoff return is like an offensive play. If the defense changes, the offensive blocking scheme changes. We do not see many kickoffs down the middle of the football field. Teams are kicking into the corners and into the boundaries. If you have an excellent return game, you get squib and pooch kicks.

We want to be simple in our return but we want to devise a system to be effective when the kicking team squibs or pooch kicks the ball. If the kicking team skies or squibs the ball, we have to catch it at different points on the field. When the kicking team kicks the ball deep, it is in the air from 3.6 to 4.0 seconds. Everything on the return times up for a kick that is in the air at least 3.6 seconds.

When the kicking team skies the ball to around the 30-yard line, we find it destroyed our deep return timing. We have to develop a return that can still create good field position and give us a chance for the big play.

I want to take you through some of the basic things we do from a coaching standpoint. This material came out of the playbook from last year. Generally, there are no offensive linemen on a kickoff return team.

We have our offensive line coach coaching the front five on the return with a graduate assistant. The next level of the return team is the right and left end. The tight end coach coaches them. The next tier is the wing player. They are safety or defensive back types of players coached by the secondary coach. The wide receiver coach coaches the return players. We have an upback, who is primarily a communicator, and a deep back, who returns everything he can reach. We free all these coaches up during the special team period, which allows them to coach their positions.

When we have our kick return meeting, we include the scout kickoff team. I want the scout team aware of what they are supposed to do. I want them to give us the best possible look and make it as realistic as they can.

We had to answer a number of questions about the kickoff return. The first question deals with the kicker. We have to know from what position he is kicking the ball and how high and deep it goes. We want to know from what point he kicks the ball and the tendencies that go with those types of kicks.

We want to know who the safety is on the return. Does the coverage team twist their alignments as they cover? If they do, when does the twist occur? Do we have to change or renumber the coverage team as they come down? We want to know where the kickoff team is vulnerable in their coverage. We want to identify their best coverage men.

We look for tips as to alignment of the coverage team or kicker positioning as to where the ball is kicked. We may wait until the kicker approaches the ball to call the direction of our return.

We have established goals for our kickoff return team. Our goals are as follows:

- Win
- Score
- Ball security/great effort
- Average start after KOR = 30 yards line or greater
- Average KOR = 23 yards or greater
- Big returns/30 yards or greater

The team will be composed of players that give great effort and expect to win every opportunity that is presented to them! With the high expectations resulting in great productivity, this unit will help our football team win the field position battle. Three words this unit will live by are: *house, squeeze*, and *finish*.

There are some general rules about the kickoff return. We never want to block below the waist or in the back of the opponent. A cover man may not low block any wedge or double-team player. The defender must attack the return team above the waist.

Once the ball travels 10 yards, it is legal for the kickoff team to touch and recover the ball. After the kick, we may step into the 10-yard zone, but once we touch the ball, it is a free ball. If a kick travels out of bounds, we have three options. We may take the ball where it goes out of bounds, penalize the kicking team five yards and make them re-kick, or take possession at our 35-yard line. Anyone can fair catch a kickoff; however, if the ball hits the ground, the ball is a free ball.

The kick return man has rules that govern his play. If the catch momentum carries the return man into the end zone, he does not have to bring the ball out. If the return man muffs the ball in the field of play and it rolls into the end zone, he does not have to bring the ball out. However, he must recover the ball.

If you mutt a kick in the end zone, you must cover the ball and get down. If the return man catches the ball in the end zone and any part of his body crosses the goal line, he must bring the ball out. If he catches the ball in the field of play and retreats into the end zone, he must bring the ball out. A ball fumbled from the field of play into the end zone must be run out.

In the kickoff return game we have important principles we pass on to our team. The first thing is communication within the team. The upback is in charge of all communications. The team wants to field all kicks.

We have blocking principles we teach our return personnel. We want them to square up on the opponent whenever possible. Keeping the eyes below the defender's eyes allows for a great fit. We want to get a standoff in the block and let the return man go by.

The return team needs to have awareness of what the kickoff team is doing. A change in the direction of the kick can many times be detected at pre-snap. During pre-game warm-up, we answer many of the questions we have about the kickoff.

The scheme has to be simple but good. We use a system that will allow us to have two double-team blocks with a trap block. We use a call system that will allow us to change the players we double-team.

On our returns, we have to ID the coverage personnel. We will always ID five right defenders and five left defenders. The kicker will never be identified. We designate the five right defenders as R1-R5. The R1 will be the widest defender on the right side. We number the defenders on the left side the same way with the L1 defender being the widest to the left side. We still ID 5R's and 5L's even if the kicking team is a 6-4 look in their alignment to the ball. If they have six defenders on one side of the ball and four defenders on the other side, both 5R and 5L would be on the same side of the ball. If the coverage team uses a stack front, we ID the coverage personnel according to how they fill their lanes as they cover the kick.

This is an example of how we scout the kickoff. This comes from our last ball game against California. We had 68 total kicks to scout. They had no squib kicks, eight skied kicks, and no on-sides kicks. They were 50-50 on placement of the ball. They kicked to the right middle or left middle. The kicker kicked the ball to an average of the 1.5-yard line. If the ball was sky kicked the average was to the 28-yard line.

If the ball is sky-kicked inside the 35-yard line, there is an opportunity to get a good return. Of course, that depends upon the height of the kick. The hang time of their kickoff was between 3.6 and 3.95 seconds. We want to know that because of the trap return we use in our scheme. The widest two defenders away from the trap-blocking scheme are not blocked. That means the more hang time the kicker has on the ball, the more of a factor the outside defenders have on the return.

They varied their alignment from a 5-5 to a 6-4 in defenders-to-the-ball relationship. They used the stack techniques and twist techniques, usually between the number two and three defenders. From these tendencies, we draw up our return schemes.

We found that the kicker aligned five yards deep when he sky-kicked the ball. When he approached from eight yards, he kicked the ball deep. We adjusted our return from the sideline on the kicker's depth. We had the team watch us for the signal and they adjusted their depths and angles on their blocks according to the type of kick.

The position of the return man and upback depends on the kicker. If they kick the ball from the left middle position on the field, the return man is four to five yards inside the right hash mark on the goal line. The upback aligns four to five yards inside the left hash mark on the 10-yard line.

If you have a lot of success returning the football, teams will give you something else. That is why we believe in simplicity in the return game. If the defense will not kick the ball to you, it is a credit to what you have done in the return game.

Before I get into the return, let me show you the types of personnel we plug into our kickoff return team. Our left tackle is a back-up cornerback. He has good speed and he is a bit bigger than the other corners. The tackles on the kickoff team have to be able to run. If the return is set away from them, they have a longer run to get to their position. These players have to be fast but they do not have to be the most physical players on the team. They have to use leverage and run the defender by the return man.

The left guard is the starting middle linebacker. He is more physical because he usually takes on another linebacker on the coverage team. His back-up is also a linebacker.

The center on the return is our weakside, all-American linebacker. He has probably thetoughest job on the return unit. Backing him up is a 230-pound fullback who is very athletic.

The right guard is a back-up running back. He is very athletic and what we call a special team guru. He plays many of our special teams. He was an outside linebacker before we moved him to running back.

The right tackle is another cornerback. He has to have more speed and probably is less physical than the guards and center.

Our left end is our starting wide receiver. In fact, the ends and wing players are all receivers, tight ends, or running backs. They are more skilled people with good hands. We have a linebacker or two mixed into this group of athletes. The return man is our starting corner.

In the spring and fall, we use the first five minutes after stretching period to work on our individual special team drills. We have two Jugs machines we use as kicking devices. We have the punt receivers in one area of the field and kickoff receiver in another. We can use a punter but the Jugs machine is more consistent and we can get more reps. On another area of the field we have our snappers and holders working on their individual skills. We also work on the squib and sky kicks during this period. In five minutes, we can get a tremendous amount of reps. It is amazing how many players you can develop in the return game. When our freshmen come in, we try everyone out to see what they can do.

The first kickoff return is what we refer to as Right-43 (Figure 4-1). The right and left returns are exactly alike in their rules. The defender double-teamed by the front five is R4. The RT and RG will carry out the double-team. The front five not involved in the double-team will block L5, L4, and L3.

The defender double-teamed by the end and wing player is R3. The double-team on R3 will be carried out by the backside end and wing. The LE and LW double-team R3. The number 43 tells us the right 3 and 4 coverage man will be double-teamed.

The playside end will execute the trap block. The RE will trap block R5 as he comes down the field. The playside wing will execute the kick-outblock. He will kick out R2. The upback secures the fielding of the ball by the return man. He fits the return man into the seam of the return and blocks the most dangerous man.

The 43-Left is the same return to the left side. We can adjust the double-teams, trap, and kick-out blocks by changing the numbers of the return. If we call Right–32, we double-team R3 and R2 and trap R4. In the Right-32, the playside wing will kick out the R1 man.

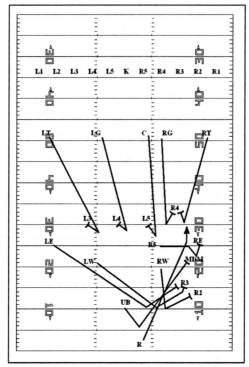

Figure 4-1. Right-43

Our alignment and stance for the kickoff return will remain consistent. With the ball in the middle of the field, the tackles align at the top of the numbers. The guards line up on the hash marks. The center is two yards to either side of the kicker. In their stance, their front foot is on the 48-yard line and the back foot is on the 49-yard line. They tilt at a 45-degree angle facing the ball. The center lines up square with his heels on the 49-yard line.

The ends align at the 25-yard line at the top of the numbers. The wings line up on the 20-yard line on the hash marks. The upback aligns at the 10-yard line in the middle of the field or aligns by the game plan. The return back aligns on the goal line or according to the game plan. If they kick the ball from the hash mark, the team moves two to three yards accordingly.

We have particular mechanics for blocking. At the kick of the ball, the front five men involved with man blocking techniques turn to the inside. They drop to the 27-yard line. At the 35-yard line, they make a half-turn to check their count on the men they are blocking. They are blocking L5, L4, and L3. They plant their foot at the 27-yard line and engage the defenders while traveling uphill. They fit their blocks on the defenders and work their leverage for the return.

The front five, who are involved in the double-team, turn inside as the ball is kicked. They retreat to the 30-yard line and get hip to hip. The guard is the post man on the double-team and sets square on the R4 defender. He calls either "in" or "out" to use the leverage of the defender to their advantage. The tackle is the drive man and drives the near pec of the defender with his hands and shoulder.

The playside end performs the trap block. He takes a subtle drop and traps the defender at the 25-yard line. He has to be patient and hide as the defender comes down. This is probably the hardest block. He is coming from the outside and blocking the R5 coverage man as he comes down the field. However, this is an opportunity to really light someone up if the defender does not see him coming.

We refer to the next block as the "train." The train includes the kick-out block by the playside wing and the double-team block by the backside end and wing. The playside wing will set the train 10 to 12 yards in front of the return man. He is blocking R2 out. If the ball is kicked to the sideline, he sets the train at the top of the numbers.

The backside wing and end go to the train. The playside wing kicks out the appropriate defender and the backside end and wing execute the double-team block on R3. They use the proper mechanics for double-team.

The upback is the communicator. He calls "you" or "me" and points to the return man. He sets eight yards over the return man and verifies that he has caught the ball. He leads the return man into the fit of the double-team and kick-out block. If there is a defender coming from outside the return, he has to block him to ensure the return man gets into the seam. If there is no one behind the return, he blocks the most dangerous man.

The return man catches the ball in the soft spot between the bottom of his shoulder pads and the waist. He wants to catch the ball moving downhill with his hips and shoulders square. He wants to catch the ball off-center, not in the chest. We want him to keep the leg to the side of the return back as he catches the ball. We never want him to go any further than the top of the boundary ticks on a sideline kick.

If the ball is kicked short, the upback will call "short" (Figure 4-2). We define a short kick as a ball that does not travel past the 15-yard line and stays between the hash marks. The front five drop to the 37-yard line instead of the 27-yard line. All other blocks in the return move up 10 yards. The train is set eight to ten yards in front of the return man.

If we have called our Right-43 and the ball is skied to the right or left, we call "sky" and we go to our sky return. We define the sky kick as a short kick greater than or equal to the 20-yard line (Figure 4-3). When the ball is skied, the playside tackle, guard, and center whip their heads toward the sideline and run outside. They block the playside one, two, and four coverage men respectively.

We assign the backside wing to the playside number-five coverage defender. The backside end has the backside number-five coverage defender. The backside guard and tackle block the backside four and three defenders. If the playside wing does not catch the ball, he double-teams the playside number-three defender with the playside end. The upback catches the ball if he can and returns up the sideline.

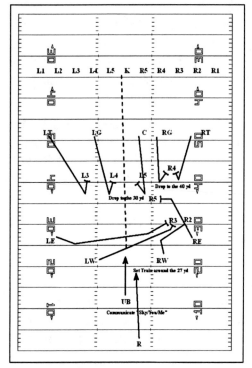

Figure 4-2. Short return

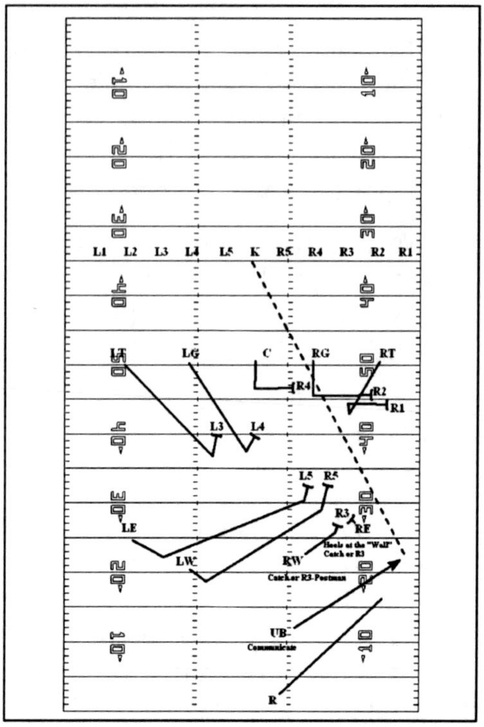

Figure 4-3. Sky return

When we get the sky kick, we want to get a hat on a hat and get upfield with the ball. We want something positive to come from the return.

Another special situation occurs on the squib kick. The squib kick by definition is a kick that hits the ground quickly or is kicked on the ground. If the ball is a line drive kick that carries deep, we run our regular return. On the squib kick, we call "wedge" (Figure 4-4).

When we make the wedge call, the playside tackle and guard block the playside two and three defenders. The center, backside guard, and tackle block the backside five, four, and three defenders. They drop 12 yards and try to ID their blocking assignments. If they cannot ID their blocks, they block area.

The closest non-return man sets the wedge with the remaining ends and wing players. They set the wedge and get hip-to-hip eight yards in front of the return man. The return man fields the kick cleanly and keeps his knees off the ground. He makes a "go" call for the wedge as he approaches it.

If the squib kick angles toward the sideline, the rules remain the same (Figure 4-5). The players forming the wedge have to hurry to get into formation, but the return is the same.

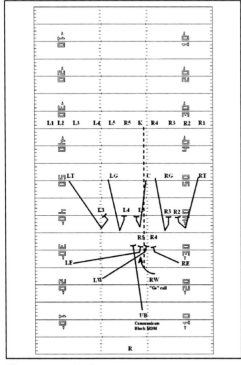
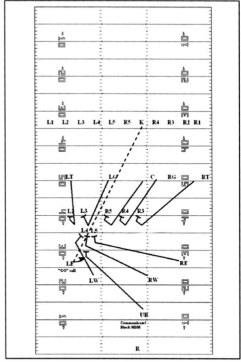

Figure 4-4. Wedge   Figure 4-5. Sideline wedge

If we have to make a fair catch, we have a simple rule for the fair catch. If the defenders are within five yards, we give a "Peter" call, make the signal, and catch the ball. If the defenders are not within five yards, we field, squeeze, and return.

We call the last return "Fisher Left." We use this return as a last-second attempt or as a gadget (Figure 4-6). The front five influence the drop and set a wall down the left sideline. The left tackle starts the wall and sets it at the top of the numbers. The ends move their alignment up to the 33- or 35-yard line. The left end influences in his drop and peels down the sideline to receive the lateral. The right end influence drops and goes to block the safety. The wings set a wedge eight yards over the ball and protect. If the kickoff team kicks the ball to the upback, he gets it to the return man and fits into the wedge. If the ball goes to the return man, the upback sets the wedge over the ball at eight yards. The return man sells the return to the right and throws the ball back left to the left end. He has to make sure it is a lateral or backward pass.

That is all the time I have. I see a bunch of high school coaches out there today. I hope you got something out of this. I want to take two minutes to harp on something that has just come up in high school football. We have just finished recruiting and I have seen something take place in the state that I have never seen before. There were fewer qualifiers for athletic scholarships in the state of Mississippi than ever before. To qualify for an athletic scholarship the athlete must have 14 core credits and a 2.5 GPA with test scores. If you have a freshman, by the time he is a senior he must have 16 core classes in addition to the GPA and test scores.

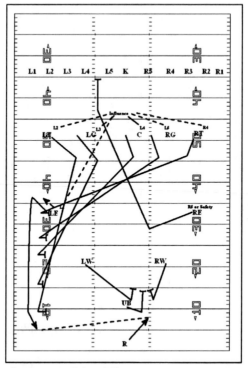

Figure 4-6. Fisher left

That has become a major problem not just in Mississippi but all over the southeastern section of the country. Mississippi has the lowest average A.C.T. test scores in the country and has the lowest percentage of students taking college prep classes.

This is something we all have to work on to correct. It takes mom and dad, counselors, teachers, coaches, and the NCAA to start to get the kids a better education. Mississippi is a great state for high school football. I have seen more quality athletes in this state this year than I have ever seen before. We want to recruit the state of Mississippi because it is in our backyard. We want Mississippi to continue to put out quality student-athletes.

I want to talk about Southern Miss for just a second. We have done many good things here. We have just completed our eleventh straight winning season. We are one of eight schools out of 117 that have had 11 straight winning seasons. We just finished playing our seventh bowl game in the last eight years. We have won four championships in the nine years Conference U.S.A. has been in existence. There are only three schools in the last nine years that have won four or more championships. Those schools are Miami of Florida, Florida State, and Marshall.

We have done a lot of good things, but the thing I am most proud of is our graduation rate. Southern Miss has the highest graduation rate in our conference. We are enjoying success on the field but more importantly, we are graduating our student-athletes. They are getting an education. That really makes me feel good. Next year we will have 50 percent of our seniors either going to graduate school or getting a double major.

I appreciate you being here and listening to my lecture. If we can do anything for you, please call on us. I wish you the best for next year and please do everything you possibly can to help your athletes in the classroom. Thank you very much. It is a pleasure to be here.

5

Motivating the Special Teams

Frank Gansz
Detroit Lions
1991

What we try to do with the kicking game in every phase is to try to get an edge on the other team. On every single snap, we are trying to get an edge on the opponent. We want to work our personnel so that we can take advantage of anything the opponents may do wrong. In every meeting, every walk-through, every practice, and every scrimmage all of our players know we are trying to get an advantage on our opponents. What it can lead to is big plays from your kicking game. It starts out with fielding the ball cleanly or staying onside. It is painstaking attention to details when you have all of your men working together to get that one clear-cut objective, which is to gain the advantage. We want that small win which takes place on one of those six or seven snaps which can change a game around. We think they are there in the kicking game every week if we work hard and play together. That is the key to success in the kicking game. You have to be committed to helping your team win.

The next thing is one play and out. The kicking game is different from the offense or defense. On offense you can fumble the ball on first down, recover it, and on second down you can get a first down or touchdown. The same thing can happen on defense. The defense can give up a big play or two, but if they hold after that for three plays they have done their job. That is not the case in the kicking game. Your people have to develop the special team mentality of one play and out. I believe you have to drill it that way. They have to believe that if they get the one play and out, they are going to gain an advantage. You have to do it in your walk-through and simulations to build that attitude. This is something you have to continually put in front of them. You have to coach them, teach them, and communicate it to them endlessly. I think this helps you avoid the breakdowns that can occur in the kicking game. We talk all the time about getting the edge in the kicking game. However, if we are not getting the edge, we are giving the opponent the edge.

In order for us to develop that special-team mentality we have to develop strength in every area. If you don't have a good punter or punt returner, then you have a weakness in some area. You have to develop those talents with what you have. For instance, your punt returner may not be the fastest guy in the world, but he can be secure. Being secure does not always mean mishandling a kick. You could have a short returner who doesn't make the proper call on a short punt. If the ball bounces into one of your players because that returner didn't make a poison or peter call—those calls tell everyone to get away from the ball—if he doesn't make those calls and the punting team recovers the ball, he has let his team down. Everyone has to develop the techniques, skills, and talent that will keep you from beating yourself. You have to teach that returner to be secure. He may not catch all the punts, but he can make the proper calls to keep everyone else from making mistakes.

You have to take advantage of any opponent's weakness. They may have a problem in protection or coverage. If a team returns the ball up the sideline, we will work all week on taking that away from them. Kick the ball away from that return man. If he would happen to fumble or mishandle the return, that could be the one big play in the game to turn the advantage to you. You can go back to your players again and again basing your relationship on your ability to communicate trust to them. When things you work on in practice turn out to be the game-turner, your players begin to believe in you more. What you say and what happens are exactly the same. The most important thing you have in the kicking game is that your players trust you. If you, as the coach, have a weakness in a certain area, tell your players about it. If you can establish a high level of trust in your team and constantly get better in that area in practice, you can motivate them. The trust between coach and player is the most important thing in coaching.

The next thing is step-by-step progression. You have to explain to your players that it takes time to develop. They are not going to be where you want them all at once. Success is the progressive realization of a goal. It will not happen right now in the kicking game. You have to make a staff commitment to make it happen. Even if you are to where you want to be you have to continue to work on it. They will get better. When that happens, they start to trust you. This helps them perform at their highest level.

The last thing in the introduction is quality work. Quality work is doing your very best. But that is not good enough. We talk about it all of the time with the Lions. We want to play at our highest level for 16 games. We do not worry about what happened last week or the week before. We want to look at it this way. You do your best, but you have to become better. It is a commitment to ongoing skill development. I tell my players it is the same for me. I have to model that. I have to show them that I am trying to get better and trying to get them better. If you have an athlete who plays his best game ever in the first game, don't let him sit on his one-game laurels. Make him work to the best of his ability. Don't put limitations on the athletes. If you refuse to accept limitations, they will continue to get better and better.

What I am going to try to give you is information that you can use. Not just good information, but this is going to get pretty basic. I read the newspaper this morning. There was a lot of information in that paper, but not a lot that I could use. When we get our team together at the beginning of the week, everything I tell them is something they can use. I am going to start with what I think is the most important thing and carry it from there. This is kind of a shotgun approach. The most important thing in the kicking game is kick protection. That is the most important facet: protection of the punt, field goal, and point-after. The most important play in the game is the punt. If you can be secure in your protection and average 35 yards per punt all year long, you will gain an advantage. If you check your records and come up with a number for your net punt average, where the offense doesn't score when you punt that distance, you can build some goals. If you can sell that difference to the team, it can make a difference. You will find you will be getting an edge on a team if he breaks down just one time. If they have a bad snap or a bad punt, your team will understand that breakdown. They will go on the field and take advantage of it.

I will start with the long snapper. There are some things that are very important in coaching the long snapper. The first thing is the grip on the ball. He has to grip it with a light fingertip grip. The second thing is the flat back. If the back rounds or hunches up, the snap will be erratic. You want to keep the ball coming back to the punter in good weather and bad weather the same way. The hard thing for the long snapper is the snap into the wind. We want the shoulder firm, back flat, and the hips down. If the hips start to round and the legs become straight, the snap will be erratic. The hands come through the legs with speed. The right hand is the snap hand and the left hand is the guide hand. Keep a light touch on the ball. The elbows have to stay in and finish with the hands to the target. These techniques will let you correct an error a man is making in a game or practice.

The second area is coaching the punter. If there is one important word in coaching the punter, it is contact. Making good contact with the ball is the most important thing the punter can do. Let me cover some techniques for the punter. For the right-footed kicker, he wants to field the ball over his right side. He should concentrate on the point of the ball prior to the snap. He has to make adjustments to the ball as it is in the air. If the ball is off target and he doesn't adjust to the flight of the ball, he has trouble after he catches the ball. If he reaches up to catch the ball, he has to bring it back down and he is out of rhythm. He has to move his feet while the ball is in the air so that when he fields the ball he is over his right side with the ball. As he catches the ball, he wants to do it cleanly. If he catches it heavy-handed, it throws off his timing. We want the kick off in 1.3 seconds after he catches the ball. The whole operation time is 0.8 seconds for the snapper and the 1.3 seconds for the punter.

We like a two-step punter. He wants a slight stagger with the right foot in front of the left. We talk about weight and balance in the kicking game all the time. We start from the ground up. The punter has to control his feet first before he can punt the ball. The punter catches the ball over the right side because he is going to punt the ball with the right foot and drop the ball on the right side. We describe the drop as not a push or drop, but a placement of the ball. We want a light touch on the ball. When the kicker punts the ball, all he does is open the fingers. He doesn't push the ball or drop it. He doesn't fly the elbow out or bring the wrist in. He holds the ball out about 90 degrees. This builds in consistency into the drop. The punter imagines the ball being cut off in the lace area. There is no forward part of the ball or backward part. He wants to hit the ball in the fat part of the ball to the front of the ball in a crossing motion. We want the mass of the foot to make contact with the mass of the ball. We want the ball to be dropped slightly in and slightly down. The contact will be made slightly below the knee. We want good control on the left foot on the ground. He finishes with the right foot up over the right side. This allows the punter to stay square and hit through the ball. We don't want a glancing blow. We want to hit from the base of the laces to the front of the laces. Just imagine there is no front or rear to the ball. Don't let them try to kill the ball until they get into the groove. Make them concentrate on making contact with the fat part of the ball in good balance. If you want more hang time, hold the ball a little higher. If you need a line-drive kick, hold the ball a little lower.

One little drill we do with our punter is to get him on one knee. We have someone spin him a ball. He catches it, takes his time and drops the ball straight to the ground. The ball should actually turn to the right a little. Being on a knee, he is closer to the ground and he can isolate on seeing the drop of the ball. We are looking for 4.3 seconds of hang time on the punt. Of course, if we can get better, we will take it.

Don't let your guys overkick in practice or warm-up. When your punters are hitting the ball good, they want to stay out there and punt longer. What they do is kick themselves through the high performance area. They will only have 12 to 15 punts like that. How many of you have seen your punter kick great in pre-game and then go out in the game and can't hit one good punt? I make my punters quit when they start hitting the ball solid. It is very important to make the punter keep his head down through contact.

Let me get into punt protection. Our punt protection is from the two split ends' look. I am not going to tell you that this technique is the best way to protect a punter. You know what you have to accomplish with your protection. This is the one we use the most. We have the right and left tackles off of the ball. The reason for that is the upfield rush we get from people in our league. With the speed of the people coming off of the corners, we have to back up our tackles to give them a chance. The technique of protecting the punt is very important. We cannot go downfield with our interior people until the ball is kicked. If we are blocking an eight-man front with three deep receivers, we man block. With the ends split, they take a defender with them. Everyone else blocks man-on-man. That would work fine if the defense would rush straight ahead. However, it does not happen that way. The defense will cross and stunt to try to block the punt. Because of that, we have to line up in a zone scheme and finish off with man blocking. The reason we like man blocking is because it is the best way to protect. The athletes in the NFL can cover that nine-yard distance to the block spot in a hurry. A guy like Noga, who plays for us, is so quick in this area that you have to finish him off with a drive block to keep him from coming through. We drop back off of the ball at the snap and protect inside. We are not going to let anyone come inside. When we drop inside, we finish off in man blocking on anyone coming inside. We are going to finish with the helmet on the torso of the man that is rushing. We want the firm finish because it keeps the protection unit close to the line of scrimmage.

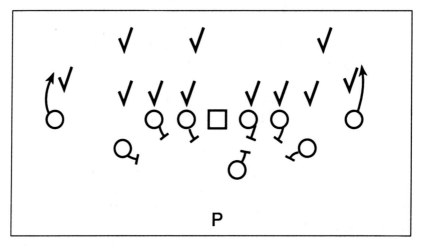

The next protection is against a nine-man rush. We still split the ends so they are responsible for the rusher who must cover them. We still line up in the man-to-man protection, which means that the personal protector is responsible for the fifth man wherever he goes. The blocking scheme is the same for the eight-man rush except the personal protector has to pick up the extra man in the nine-man rush.

The next protection is the 10-man balanced protection. When this happens and you have a center who can't block, you have to bring one of your split ends in. We have a tackle make a technique call. He calls out "double bump." The punter is instructed to punt away from the double bump. If you have a good coverage man, a man that the defense likes to double-team, then split the other end. If the defense gives us a double on a split end, we split the other end. If they only have single coverage on the split end, then that only accounts for one man that you have to block. The three inside men to the split end take the 2, 3, and 4 rushers to that side. The personal protector takes the 5 man to the side of the split end. When the personal protector comes out over the ball, he calls his block by jersey number. The slotback to either side calls out the number so they know who has the double bump. Everyone away from the call takes his man from the inside out. The last man or slot has the double bump. The way he does it is to take the first and most dangerous threat. He takes the inside charger off of his stride with a firm inside hand. He puts his helmet on the torso of the outside charger.

The next protection is the 10-man overload. When you work on your punt protection, do it in the middle of practice as a surprise. Make the situation like it would be in a game situation. Give them the confidence that they need. This puts the punt team in a manufactured pressure situation. They will want to do it. And, you will see them start to get better and start to go up that ladder of success with step-by-step progression. Against the 10-man overload, we still split the end. That takes one defender. If they don't cover him we can still protect using a double bump on both sides. The personal protector takes the fifth man to the side you want to kick to. He makes his call and the slot makes his calls. Everyone then begins to take his man with inside-out responsibility. The last man on the line of scrimmage gets the double bump. The blocker we use in the double bump blocking scheme is a bigger, faster athlete. We would use linebacker personnel in these spots. When we punt the ball, we want to punt into the single coverage man so he can go down and get the big hit. The return man has to field the ball on an angle. He can't get square on the ball and you stand a good chance of getting the big hit and the turnover.

The next thing I want to touch on is our coverage on the punt. This is one of the most important phases of the game. What we like to do is first cover the field and then cover the ball. The center goes directly to the ball. The guards or the two men on either side of the center start down the pro hash mark. The pro hash marks are six yards apart. The next guys go down the college hash marks, which are about five yards outside the pro hash marks. The next men fan out and go down the numbers, which are about 12 yards from the sidelines. The split end goes directly to the ball and the personal protector goes to the ball. The coverage fans out over the field with four men going to the ball. The most important thing the coverage team has to do is compress the ball. They have to fan out to cover the field but as they come down to cover the ball you should almost see the protection unit in formation at the ball. We want no holes in the coverage. If one man doesn't get down the field, it is like running into a

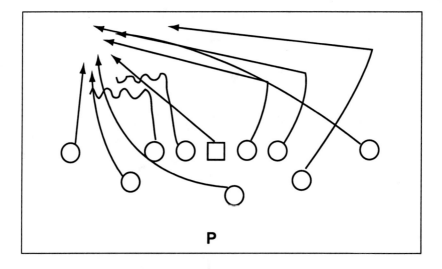

P

bubble linebacker. That gives you big problems. They have to go down in relative position. The right-side people have to stay on the right side of the ball in coverage and the left-side people have to stay on the left side of the ball. If one of your coverage men crosses over, he leaves a hole in the coverage and cuts off one of his guys coming down on the other side. One of the things we work on every day in practice is coming to a torso position in the tackle. That is keeping your head up and wrapping up with your arms. The coverage of the punt goes back to fundamental tackling. We work on it every day.

We have been very pleased with our return game. We have a wall return and a middle return. Everything we do comes off of those two returns. Let me cover the wall return with two split ends coming in coverage. We double both wide men. The end on the wallside forces the coverage men into a wider than normal coverage lane. The players over the guard and tackle hold up the men they are aligned on. The backside guard and tackle set the wall. The backside end forces the kick. The returner in the wall return is not trying to get to the boundary. He wants to take the ball upfield as soon as he can. He is looking for the seam of the wall and the forced wide coverage man. This is our base return.

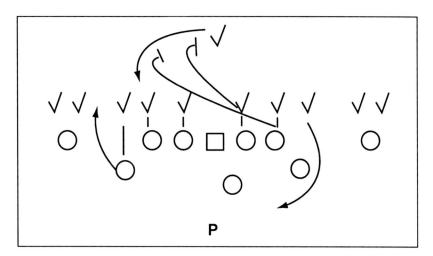

We can do something off of this look. The two men whom we are doubling are turned over to one man. The other two guys come to the inside and rover around. We are still running the return to the right but we have a different look. This also gives us a safe defense against a team who may try to run the ball from punt formation. We let them to play the slot blockers man-to-man and the end can go upfield and contain.

With the base wall return, we can run stunts with our interior line. If we find a weak blocker in the slot, the outside rusher can hard-charge up the field and make a move to come back inside for the block. This gives us the combination block from the left side and return to the right.

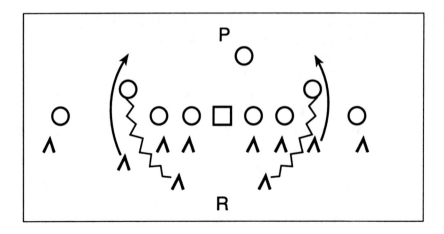

Let me draw up the wall left return. When you draw up a return you need to think about the opponent. We want to know how the weak coverage people are. We have to have a game plan to give to our team on Monday. Once the team starts to believe in you and the ideas you bring into that meeting, you can hear a pin drop. They will get out their pencils and notebooks. What you are telling them works. You are giving them information that they can use to accomplish what they want. That is to win games and have fun. Two years ago we had Benny Blades and Ray Crockett. Green Bay had a kick coverage man named Carl Bland. He was killing everyone on kick coverage. I told our men we were going to catch the ball in the end zone and if we have to we will return it. We caught one on the two-yard line and brought it back to the 30-yard line. We came within a whisker of breaking it. In order to do that you have to go against many of the things people have told you to do in the kicking game. But we felt we could return the ball.

This is how we got it done. We game plan the opponents. We manufacture the game situation. We go over each detail. After all, we are going to run a simple scheme and work on execution. We do not set the wall the same way every time. The wall-setters use a technique we call stalk blocking. It is like playing one-on-one in basketball. We want to stalk the defender, keeping the body between the ball and the defender. We want to position the blocker away from where we are going to return the ball. When the defender changes feet, we are all over them. We are just like a chicken on a June bug. In practice I have to call them off. We gear our players for one play and out. We want to get one hit and get off of the field.

Let me cover a simple thing with the middle return. We find out who is making the tackles and make sure we block him. The interior linemen turn out on the punt coverage team. One of the outside men, depending on which way you call the return, comes in and traps the center. This is a simple return right up the middle. The key to any return is the stalk block. The real key is to avoid the penalty. You can have the best return, but one clip and they bring it all back. The big thing is playing with discipline.

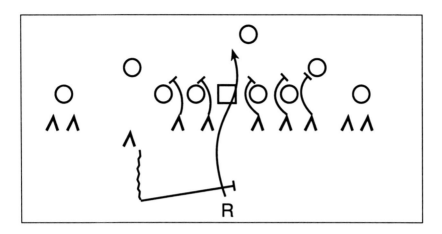

Next is one block scheme on the punt game. Albert Lewis has taken this part of our game to another level. We get into an overload to the left. We put Lewis at the right end. We drive the inside two people outside through the punt team. Lewis loops to the inside and straight up the middle. We absorb the personal protector with the overload. Albert Lewis has such great quickness he is coming in the A gap to the ball. We run our returns off of that look. The punt team doesn't know if we are blocking or returning.

I want to cover a kickoff coverage against a three-man wedge with three deep men. We have a kicker with five men on each side of him.

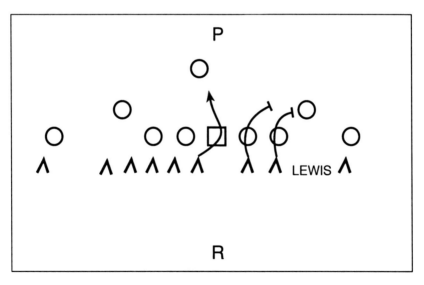

We want to kick the ball where they don't want it. If they have a great returner, we don't want to kick the ball to him. We want the returners to have a problem fielding the ball. Games have been lost on missed communications by the return men. We have kicked the ball right between two guys just waiting for them to run together trying to field the ball. We number our coverage team from the kicker to the sideline. The 1's are next to the kicker, and the 5's are against the sideline. When we cover against a three-man wedge, our 1's attack the shoulders of the middle wedge blocker. Our 2's attack the inside shoulder of the outside wedge blockers. Our 3's attack the outside shoulder of the outside wedge blockers. We are going to go to where you want to return based on your blockers.

The front five on the return team are blocking from left to right, numbers 2, 1, 1, 2, 3 on the coverage. That means our 1's, 2's, and 3's are going to have to defeat the front 5 and at the same time pick up their landmarks on the wedge blocker. They have to compress the ball with the left-side coverage staying on the left side of the ball and the right side staying on the right.

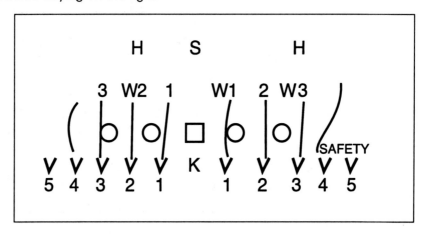

We go to the four-man wedge next. The kick return team has to defend the huddle of the kickoff team and then defend the field. The Chicago Bears came out in a bunched-up huddle on us all year. We had to defend the huddle first. As they spread out, we had to defend the field. As we cover the kick, we want to cut the field down as we run down the field. We want to have a relationship where we are about two to three yards apart at the opponent's 30-yard line.

Let me show you a return that people run against us. The outside man on the front line and the outside wedge block will double-team our 3. The second man drops and blocks 2. The middle man drops and blocks the left 1. The offside drops and blocks 1 and 2 respectively. The two middle wedge blockers double-team the onside 4. The outside wedge blocker to the off side comes back through the middle and seals back against the offside 3. The back who doesn't catch the ball comes into the alley behind the double-teams and blocks 5. They have a double-team on 3 and 4 and everyone else blocked. The way we would defeat this is to send 3 and 4 on the inside and outside shoulder of the outside wedge blockers. The 1's and 2's are on the inside and outside shoulders of the inside wedge blockers. We are going to cover the field, defend their wedge-blocking scheme and get to the ball. Every team you play has a return-blocking scheme. The key is to prepare in practice for that scheme. You coach your scout team to run the return better than your opponent. Then you work on coverage and correct your mistakes. We drill and drill and then correct the mistakes. Guys in the NFL hate it when a guy who is not getting the job done is not getting corrected. They may not say anything but they hate it. You have to show your players that problems are going to be addressed.

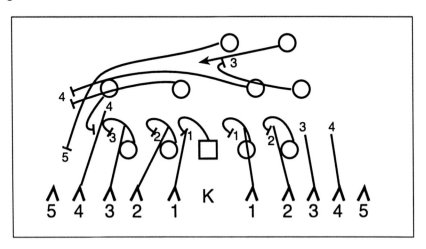

The best return we have had is our sideline return. We use a three-man wedge. The reason for that is I don't want any mishandled kicked balls on our end of the field. There is nothing that can put your team on a down quicker than a mishandled ball that goes out of bounds at the five-yard line. We must protect the field. That is why we use a three deep to handle the ball. With a two-deep scheme it puts pressure on those deep men to run to the sideline to field the ball.

We are going to drop in relationship to the football. We have had success running the ball out of the end zone when it was six yards deep. Our frontline people are going to drop back keeping their man between them and the ball. They are going to spring back, turn with their weight over their feet, and keep moving. We have a motion problem. The coverage is flying down the field. If the blockers are stopped, the coverage will fly right by them. The outside men on the front line take the 3 man to the side of the return. He stays between him and the ball until he stops him. At that point he attacks his outside shoulder. The other four men on the front line are going to do the same thing taking their men. They take the 2, 1, 1, and 2. The outside wedge man is going to widen to influence the number 4 man to get wider. Then he is going to go back inside and double on the 3 man. The middle wedge man and the on halfbacks form a diamond on the return. We could blindfold these men and they would get into their position.

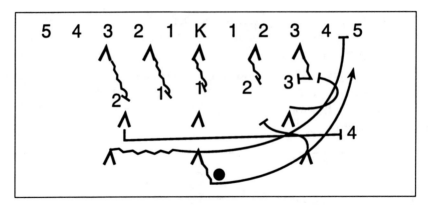

The last thing I want to cover is the protection on our field goals and point-after-touchdowns. The main thing is to get your big people in the game. This is a personnel game. It is going to be zone protection. This allows you to get your big people on the field. The holder is seven-and-a-half yards deep. If we think there is going to be a hard rush we may put him back eight yards.

The time to snap the ball and get off the kick is 1.3 seconds for the total operation. We get shoe-to-shoe and interlock our feet on the center. The center has to bridge as he snaps the ball. If he fires out, there will be a hole. The line must rise with power and stay on the same relative plane. The key to protection on the field goal is there is not separation in techniques. There is no one firing out or falling back. They are all tight and in line together.

The wingback protects to the inside and actually lays out up the field to protect the corner. The kicker wants to kick the ball at the base of the laces on the back of the ball. The plant foot of the kicker will vary depending on the height of the kicker. Once you find out where the plant foot is for the most accuracy for the kicker, keep it the same. As the kicker plants his left foot, we want him to have a firm left side. He has to keep his weight on the left side and stay firm. We want him to finish to the target.

Some things that can cause kickers problems are the right and left hash marks. When the right-footed kicker has to kick from the right hash mark, it is not the same as kicking from the middle of the field, or the left hash mark. The angle to the ball is different and he has to readjust his approach a little. That is where he must spend the most time practicing.

In conclusion I want to say this. I tell my guys that they have to learn to communicate with their team members and me. They have to know what they need from their teammates and me to perform at their highest level. It takes tough, unreasonable communications sometimes to get to the highest level in a high-performance business such as football. I think communication has to start with the people who are coaching and they have to learn how to develop powerful and productive relationships. All this has to be modeled from the people that are coaching.

6

The Winning Edge in the Kicking Game

Jerry Glanville
Portland State University
2009

It is a real pleasure to be here. Thanks for having me. Is there anyone in the room attending their first clinic? I was coaching in Ohio, and this clinic was the second clinic I ever attended. They held it at the Brown Hotel at that time. I was a high school football coach at the time. Roy Kidd was the coach at Eastern Kentucky University. He had an opening on his staff and was going to interview me that night at 8:00.

I was sitting on a couch in the hotel lobby talking football with some other coaches. Nick Dennis, the head coach at Western Kentucky University, walked up. He told me he wanted to interview me for a job. I told him I was supposed to interview with Eastern Kentucky. He told me he wanted to hire me right then and there. I was so excited because at the second clinic I had ever attended, I got a college coaching job.

In Cincinnati, I was making $4,800 a year and got a college job at Western Kentucky making $125 a month. It was great to step up to a big college job (laughs). Western Kentucky was always very good to me. They changed who I was, and we had all kinds of success.

While I was at Western, we never lost a game. We had one tie but no losses. Bud Carson, who was the head coach at Georgia Tech, called me. He told me he wanted to interview me at the national coaches conference for a job with them. We set the interview up for a Wednesday. I did not know where the national clinic was being held. As it turned out, it was in New York City. That was in 1966. My roommate at Western was Joe Bugel. We made $125 a month and were paid on the 30th of each month. By the 5th of the next month, we were broke. We had all this money, so we both got dates and tried to act like a big shot.

When I found out the conference was in New York, I did not know how I was going to get there. I did not have a car, so I hitchhiked from Bowling Green to New York for the interview. I did the interview, but did not get the job.

Just about the time you go to a clinic and think you did not learn anything, something good happens to you. Today, this lecture is going to change where you coach, how you coach, and how your team plays.

Every coach that you know talks about special teams. Most of them pay lip service to special teams and do not give a damn about it. I was at Georgia Tech under Pepper Rogers for six years. I recruited Louisville in those days. We beat Notre Dame, back when they could beat somebody, with Louisville players. I remember when Notre Dame could play. My goal when I took the Portland State job was to win more games than Notre Dame. If I can win two or three a year, I will be okay. The bottom line on special team is a lot of lip service.

While I was at Georgia Tech, a coach named George Allen called. He wanted me to interview for a job as the first special teams coach in the NFL. I went in and talked to Coach Rogers. I told him I had to go for an interview with the Washington Redskins. He jumped up, pounded the table, and said I better get the job. He told me if I went to Washington for the interview, I was fired from this job. He was the new coach, and we had only had just finished spring practice. That was all I needed anyway. I told him I would rather sell shoes than work for him, and I went for the interview.

Little did I know, George Allen was a bigger joke than Pepper Rogers. When I got there, he interviewed me on the practice field. He asked me if I saw the small stand of woods by the practice field. He told me we started work at 6:00, but before I came to work, he wanted me to chop down two trees. I told him if he had my airline ticket, I would be on my way back home.

I left and went home. Pepper was not kidding, and I was fired at Georgia Tech. Every time you get fired, the best thing that could happen to you is right around the corner. I was sitting home without a job when the phone rang. It was the Detroit Lions. I went for an interview. Two days after the interview, the coach dropped dead of a heart attack while cutting the grass. They named Rick Forzano as head coach. He called and told me he wanted to hire me, but did not know how to deal with Georgia Tech. I told him not to worry, and I would handle that situation. He did not know I did not have a job. I told him I was on the way to the Lions.

Do not worry about not having a job. The way you coach and the way you present yourself will take care of those kinds of situations. Just keep doing what you believe in, and do it the way it has to be done.

Special teams are not given the attention by any coach in America the way it should be. I have had many special teams coaches. The first special teams coach I ever hired was Bill Belichick. I paid him $15,000. He is making $6 million now. People asked me what I thought when I hired him for $15,000. I told them I overpaid him. He was not worth it because he did not know the special teams. I hired Nick Saban, and the list goes on and on. Bobby April, the special teams coach for the Buffalo Bills, worked for me. My special teams coach at Portland State is Bobby April, Jr. He started with me when he was nine years old. He knows the important of the kicking game.

I interviewed a coach for a special teams job. I wanted to know what his overall goal was. He told me eventually he would like to become the offensive line coach. Do you think he had a snowball's chance in hell to be my special teams coach? I ask him why he wanted to take a demotion. Why would he come in as a special teams coach and become an offensive line coach? Special teams have to be the priority for the special teams coach.

The way to become a dominant team is stop paying lip service to special teams and become dominant in that part of the game. Every day in practice, we go over two phases in the kicking game. It may be kickoff and kickoff return on one day, and two other phases on the next day. Write this next statement down, and you will become a different football team. When we have two-a-days, the morning practice has an hour-and-a-half of kicking drills. After the kicking session of practice, we have 30 minutes remaining. That is not lip service. I have done that everywhere I have been. I have been at the Falcons, Lions, Bills, Oilers, Georgia Tech, and countless other places. That is getting it done and teaching it.

When you put in an offensive play, you do not go to practice and run the play in a team drill first. You break the play down in its separate units and teach the individual skills involved in the play. You have to do the same thing in the kicking game. We break down all segments of the game and work on them individually.

If you come to our practices, you will see players working on individual blocks on the kickoff. You will see the wedge blockers working 3-on-3, sifting out the twists and turns of the coverage. We do those things for weeks before we bring it together as a team. You have to commit the time to be what you want to be, not the lip service.

The last 30 minutes of the morning practice is devoted to the freshmen. I just sat in 30 living rooms with 30 moms and dads and signed 30 new freshmen. I would do this if I went back to high school coaching. In the last 30 minutes of that practice, every freshmen on our team moves to first string. If I signed a center, he is the starting center. What does that cause? This year, Portland State started 17 freshmen. You cannot do that if you set them on the sideline and hope they grow up. If you are hoping they will get better and do not work with them, you will soon forget them. You will find yourself looking at a player who has been with you for three years and still cannot play.

I always wear all black. That is an attitude. Special teams are all about attitude. Black is not even a color. It is the absence of all color. At Portland, we wear all black even though our colors are green. It is all about attitude. There is a third-string center who can be a star on special teams. I have a player by the name of Matt Ford, a chicken has bigger legs, but he wants to play. You have to get the third-stringer to change. We are going to change it to the point where he wins game for you. His mother came down from the stands, doing what I call an "O.W." She was "openly weeping" because her son helped us win a game. It was like Dick Vermeil the night he retired. He was weeping like a baby.

There is a way to get those third-stringers to play well enough to help you win. One day a week, we pull power sleds. Those are the sleds you load with weight and pull them around. I make every starter on the team play one special team. I have done that since the Detroit Lions in 1974. That makes your starting offense and defense part of the special teams. It becomes a team concept. We do not have an indoor facility, but we have sleds.

One day a week, we make them pull 14 percent of their body weight on the sleds. If you get too much weight on the sled, they lose their running form. We have found that 14 percent is about the right ratio. I stood there two days ago and watched Matt, my third-stringer, pull that sled. I know who will not quit in a ball game, and I am sure his mother will cry again because this kid will help us.

One day a week, we do plyometrics for our third-string special-team members. One day a week, we do the stadium steps for the third-string special-teamers. At our stadium, you cannot see the top. If those special-teamers have to crawl on all fours to get to the top, they will do it. Those players will not let you down on the kickoff against your big rival. The fourth day, we do hurdle exercises to work the hip-flexor muscles. We work them four days a week.

We do those things because these players have to come to balance before contact. I did not say break down. We want full-speed contact, and it is no fair to dodge. They do not break down, but they come to balance. There is a thin line between those two items. The point is: they have to be killers and love contact.

Our team votes each year for the MVP on special teams. At Portland State, we have two fullbacks who could not play for you coaches in high school. I lied. They could play for a good high school football team. They battled it out for the MVP of our special teams. We have the best field-goal kicker in the history of the school. He did not get one vote. Our kickoff-return player was fourth in the nation and was voted the MVP in the Big Sky Conference on special teams. He did not get a vote.

Why did that happen? Special teams are about kicking someone's butt. It is not about running around and looking good. When we score a touchdown on special teams, we replay it three times to show the blocks, not the runner. That is the attitude of a special-team member. Our two fullbacks who cannot play dead battled it out for special-team player of the year. We gave each one of them one carry at the fullback position, and that was probably too many.

These players are not on scholarship, but they help you win. I have sat in 30 living rooms this year and guaranteed moms and dads that their sons were going to start in the opening game of the season against the Rose Bowl champions. At the time, I thought Oregon State was going to win the PAC-10 championship. We open up with them next year. The players on the kickoff or kickoff-return teams are the starters. Only in scrimmages do the offensive or defensive teams get to start.

In our weight room, we do not allow any harassment for not being strong. There is no crime for being weak. The crime is if that player does not try to improve. I got Matt Ford up to a 140-pound bench press, and he is winning game for us. A player in your school right now can help you. People ignore them and do not know they are on the team.

Look around on Monday, when you get back to school. You will find some player who has been there for every activity you have had in football. But he has never been in a game. I guarantee you if you get him on the sled, stadium steps, and plyometrics, he will help you.

If you are a 5.4 runner and do these three things, you will improve to 5.2. If you are 4.9, it will get you to 4.7. In the state of Texas, they still run Jerry Glanville's program and have been running it since 1970. This program gets players faster and makes them more powerful. Everybody on your team will get faster.

Do any of you know Bobby Dodd, or is everyone here too young to know him? When you win the coach of the year award, it is named for Bobby Dodd. I coached for Bobby Dodd before I went on to coach on my own. Bobby called me one day and told me I was the luckiest coach he had ever seen in football. He told me in the last three years, we won 17 games at Houston on the last drive of the game. I told him I loved him and he was a great coach, but I was not lucky. We were fast. There are no lucky plays for a short, fat, dumpy guy.

To play football, your players have to run. Get your players going, and get the attitude right. Those third-stringers know you care about them and recognize what they are doing. I promise you these are players who cannot play but overachieve every day. These players who play on your special teams have an assignment. The assignment for every player is to be very physical. We want them to come after the opponent and set the stage for the game. You cannot set the stage on offense or defense as quickly as you can in the kicking game. In the kicking game, you can set the stage about who you are and what you want to be. This is our identity, and it is very important to me.

I am going to start off with the kickoff team. I watch high school films every day. There is a kickoff return on every film. The reason for the returns is the coverage team is defending the entire field. The field is too wide to defend. When we cover a kickoff, we cover only from the goalpost to the boundary. The most important thing in that theory is to have a good kicker. To cover only half the field, the football must be placed from the numbers to the boundary. We want to pin the return team into the corner of the field and blow them up.

Coach the kicker to place the ball where you want it on the field. The approach run to the ball is six steps, not 10 yards. The only time we allow a kicker to take a 10-yard run to the ball is with the wind at his back. With the wind at his back, we think we can kick the ball through the end zone. We only take a 10-step approach when we kick the ball down the middle. If they take the 10-step run-up, trying to kick the ball outside the numbers, they will kick it out-of-bounds more times than not. We do not kick the ball down the middle unless there is a penalty. If they move the ball up 15 yards, we will kick it down the middle.

I have coached for 42 years, and I have done this all my life. This coverage will work in high school, college, or pros. When we huddle before the kickoff, we call "corner left, wiggle right." Wiggle is an important term in the coverage scheme. As the coverage team comes down the field, all the players have to wiggle around the blocks to the same side. If one player wiggles around the block to the right and the next player goes around to the left, there is a big hole in the coverage. Wiggle means all the coverage team is avoiding blocks the same way. We practice that individually. The players use the same leg, rip arm, and dip as they come down the field.

When I first got into football, we had wedge busters. The rules do not let you bust the wedge any more. We have two players attacking the wedge. We call the technique "high yucca." Whichever player gets to the wedge first, goes up and over the wedge. That is an attitude for your coverage team. They go airborne into the wedge. We do it every time there is a wedge. Players who cannot play are taking two and three blockers out of the return scheme. Those players cannot play a lick. But, never tell the player that.

There are two things I am coaching these players who cannot play. "False praise cheapens plays." There is no false praise, but there is coaching and teaching. The only jobs I get are bad jobs; the colleges come to me. I do not go to them looking for that job. I have never had a good job in my life. Do not go looking for a good job. The good jobs are all taken. You have to get a bad job and change it. I told the president of the college, I will be the best teacher on campus. Coach means teacher.

If you coach with me, it will be different. If a player swears on the practice field, he is done for the day. I send them home. When I walked in to Portland State, the hair on my arms stood up. Everything was M.F. If you swear on a practice field where Jerry Glanville coaches, you are done for the day. If you are an assistant coach and get after a player and curse him, you are fired. Our job is not browbeating, harassing, and cursing; it is teaching. You teach it and teach it and teach it some more. If you do that, it will change your entire team and how you coach your players.

Your players did not get false praise, but they did not get cursed either. When the player does a good job, you tell him. However, do not give him five "'atta boys" when he deserves one.

On kickoff-coverage team, we align five coverage defenders from the hash mark to the sideline of the side we intend to kick the ball (Figure 6-1). We number the player on either side of the ball 1 through 5. We align both the #1 runners on either side of the same hash mark. They are our "high yucca" players. Whichever one of them gets to the wedge first gets airborne and goes over the top of the wedge. In Hawaii, they would show it on the JumboTron™ about four times. The entire stadium would get excited and on their feet by the time the player got to the sideline.

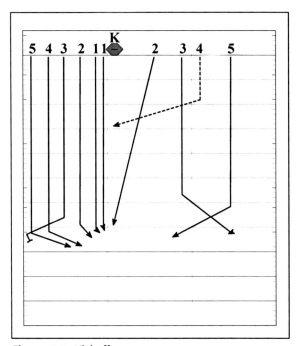

Figure 6-1. Kickoff coverage

The #3 defender on either side is the outside contain man. We designate the safety man. In the diagram, the safety is the wideside #4 defender. To confuse the return, we may use defenders running from one side of the coverage line and looping to the other side on their run up to the ball.

In 1970, we ran this coverage against the San Francisco 49ers. We call it the "West Coast twist," and it still works (Figure 6-2). The #1 runners coming down the middle of the coverage twist their paths when they get 20 yards into their runs. We run an X-cross between the #4 and #5 runners on the outside. When you cover kickoffs, you cannot stay in lanes because the lanes are moving. You have to converge and kill people. On this coverage, we kick the ball down the middle. If we kick it down the middle, we have a penalty to move the ball up, or we have the wind at our backs.

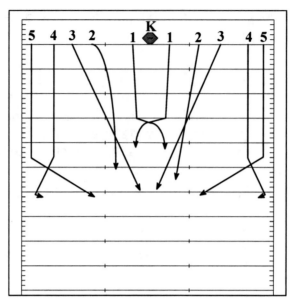

Figure 6-2. West coast twist

If you want to be a better coach tomorrow, pay attention to these points about the kickoff return. This will win you one more game next season (Figure 6-3). The number-one rule about the kickoff return has to do with playing on the road. When we play on the road, we will accept no penalties on the kickoff return. If you get a penalty on a kickoff return on the road, you get your butt kicked and lose the game. Every player on my team knows if it happens, I may go crazy. You cannot have a penalty on the road because if the offense cannot move the ball, they will give the ball up in a position where the opponent will score. We were fourth in the nation and led the league in kickoff returns.

We emphasize the double-team block between the outside blocker on the front line to the side of the return and the outside blocker at the 35-yard line. We double-team the best coverage player on the opponent's team. One player on the opponent's kickoff team makes 80 percent of the tackles. When that player plays us, he does not make tackles.

The second thing that makes you successful on the kickoff return is to play the play longer than the opponent. The officials will be spotting the ball, and the offense will be coming on the field, and we are still double-teaming their stud out-of-bounds. Play the play longer, and you will be a good football team.

We have three players in our wedge. They have to sift the defenders and block the #3 coverage runner. They end up blocking two in most cases. We usually end up with a 2-on-1 block in the wedge.

On the kickoff, the return player who does not get the ball is extremely important. He enters the wedge area first. The rule for the non-ballcarrier is to block the defender that could tackle him. If the defender cannot tackle him, he does not block him. It is that simple. We watch for that in the team meeting and emphasize that point. We stand up in the chair and cheer when he does it right.

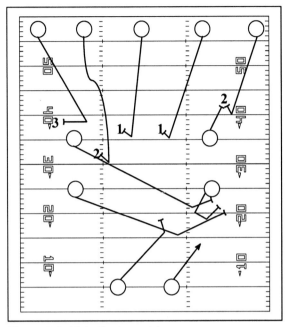

Figure 6-3. Kickoff return side

His second rule is never chase a missed block. If the off back misses his block, he cannot turn and chase him into the pile or the wedge. If he turns and chases, he makes it worse and ends up hitting the defender in the back. He needs to block someone else.

If the ball is kicked away from the callside, the return man takes it up that sideline. The three-man wedge tries to get to that side and help.

If a team kicks the ball down the middle of the field, we run a return with a cross blocks in the middle. I have run this return since I was at Western Kentucky. We cross block on the #1 runners coming down the middle. We use the guard positions on the front line to perform the cross block.

The next thing I want to talk about is extra-point and field-goal block. We hold every record with every team I coached in blocking points and field goals. The coaching staff from Bucknell University in Pennsylvania told me they showed all my field-goal blocks to their team. They said they had never seen anything like it. That was astounding to me.

The extra-point and field-goal block is the only play in my coaching career that I do not grade. If you ask any of my players about that situation, they will tell you it is between the player and God.

Montana in the Big Sky Conference is the team to beat. They have won the championship the last 10 years. They kick the crap out of everyone. We played them and were ahead by the score 9-5. They average 42 points a game. The only reason we could lose this game was because our goalie dies. They had a 14-play drive and scored and went ahead 11-9. They line up for the extra point. We blocked the point and ran it back for a two-point conversion.

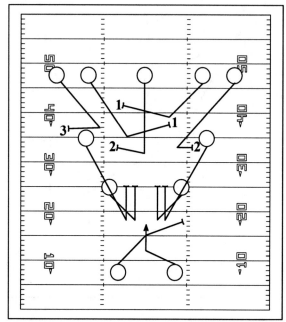

Figure 6-4. Kickoff cross block

The reason we blocked the point is inside the players. That effort is totally individual within the player. It defines who their parents were. It defines how the player grew up. Extra points are huge in a football game. There are more games lost by one point than won by 50. This type of effort is what the game of football is about and what is inside of you. If you want to go to a field-goal-block meeting, here is the New Testament.

When you talk about Solomon and the Proverbs, God told him he could have anything he wanted. He did not choose gold or silver; he chose wisdom. Proverbs is all about what is inside of men. They ask who you are and how important it is. People ask me how we practice this. It is not about schemes. We block kicks better than anyone in football.

This type of effort will win you games. We have won games we had no right to win. I will show you some of the things we do. When we come off the edge, the corner is the "skinner" (Figure 6-5). The strong safety is the "jumper." The skinner dips his shoulder, stays on his feet, and comes around the horn of the wing man. The jumper comes between the end and wing player. He puts his hands on the backs of the tight end and the wingback. He jumps through the crease between the end and wing and pulls his legs through with his hands.

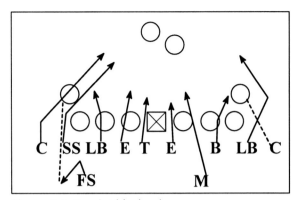

Figure 6-5. X-point block edge

When we tell one of our secondary players they have to be in coverage, it kills them. They feel they have nothing to do with the play and want to rush the kick.

On a field-goal block, if the ball crosses the line of scrimmage, get away from it. I have a young team. I have 46 freshmen, and 17 of them play. That is like having a carload of hemorrhoids. If we block an extra point, pick it up and try to score.

The next block is "4-on-2." We load the middle of the formation with two linemen on each guard (Figure 6-6). They get shoulder-to-shoulder, look for penetration, and get the hands up. The get-off is the important thing in this block. It is nothing great as far as a scheme, but it is the effort that is the emphasis. I started doing this with the Detroit Lions, and I have done it ever since.

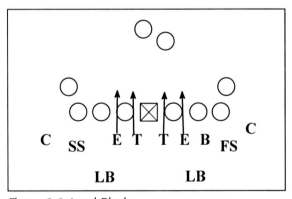

Figure 6-6. Load Block

You cannot cover the punt if the punter cannot directional punt. You do that so one end has an outside release. The defense is taught not to let outside coverage people inside. We punt the ball to the outside. That means we have a free runner going to the ball (Figure 6-7). When we punt the ball, we punt from a spread alignment with three big people as the personal protector for the punter. The middle man in the wall allows the ball to come through the wall and hinges back to fill the hole.

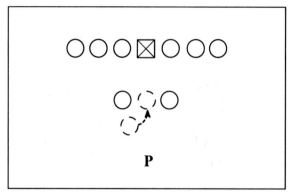
Figure 6-7. Punt formation

The punter reads the outside defender into the boundary side. If he does not come and peels back for a return, the punter can run the ball to that side. The punter has the right to run the football out of punt formation if he sees the contain player peel back to block.

We do not allow anything but successful fakes, and we do not call any of them. This is a good rule to write down. Anything that you invent after midnight, throw it out. Do not put that in your offense. I invented the fake punt at about one o'clock in the morning. It was a stupid idea, but I thought you'd get a kick out of it. The snap goes to the middle man in the protection wall. He runs to the outside with an option to pitch the ball to the punter.

There are no punt returns in this lecture. Why would you let a punter feel good about one play? After the punt, we want punter to be glad he got the punt off. We come after every punt. We may never get close to blocking a punt, but we are coming. We played Green Bay in Atlanta. They had the game won, and all they had to do was get the punt off. They had punted the ball eight times already. This was their ninth punt. We did not block the punt; the punter dropped the ball. He dropped the ball because the pressure keeps coming on every punt.

We do have a punt return. The record holder in the NFL for punt returns for a year is Dick Jauron. He averaged 17 yards per punt return when I was with Detroit. He may be the only guy I can beat in a race. He went to the Pro Bowl when Mike Ditka was coaching the game. Mike called me and wanted to know who the player I sent to the game was. He told me he could not play. He led the entire league in the punt return, and we did not call one return the entire season. That was in 1974. We tried to block every punt. People did not cover the kicks; they protected the punter.

On special teams, find the player who sets the other team's tempo. You want to take their tempo away from them. Everyone said when we played defense, we got penalized a lot. Jerry Glanville's team on defense never got penalized on third down with two minutes to go. On first and second downs, we went after you. Never get penalized on the kickoff return when you are on the road. That backs you up and the crowd becomes a factor. You end up punting the ball from deep in your own end. That gives the offense the ball well inside your territory. The offense generally gets a score from that field position.

Thanks for having me. Win some games, and let me hear from you.

Punt Return and Kickoff Return

Bobby Johnson
Vanderbilt University
2004

It is an honor for me to be here, and it humbles me to be talking about Vanderbilt football. I obviously don't have all the answers. If I did, we would have beaten some of the teams we lost to this year. We are working on our program, trying to get better. We are excited about Vanderbilt and the opportunity we have. We realize Vanderbilt is a top-20 academic institution and plays football in the SEC. There are not many schools that have that combination.

The attendance here at this clinic makes a great statement for the game of football. In the middle of February, we have a room full of people trying to get better at what we do. I just want to ask you one question. Do you all know it is Valentines Day? My wife asked me what we were doing for Valentines' Day. I told her I was going to Louisville to do a football clinic. That didn't go over too well.

My topic today is about our kicking game. Before we get started on that, I would like to talk to you about our overall philosophy. I have been where you are, and know what you are thinking when the head coach starts out talking about philosophy. I didn't want to hear it. But this fits in with my talk today.

We have a very simple philosophy at Vanderbilt; don't beat yourself. We play in a league with teams that have great athletes and great coaches. If we tried to do what everyone else in this league was doing with their athletes, we would be in trouble. We are trying to make sure we don't help the other team. The kicking game fits into that train of thought.

There are things that you can do to keep from beating yourself. The first thing is to control the football. If you give Florida the football a bunch of times, they are going to put points on the scoreboard. We think the best way to control the ball is to run it. We want to do well on first down so we can have some manageable third downs. If we end up in third-and-six or more, we are going to be in big trouble.

I have seen teams control the football by using the controlled passing game, but we don't try that. However, if you control the football, you have a chance to be in the game in the fourth quarter.

The second thing we try to do is minimize turnovers. Turnovers are a part of the game, but there are some turnovers that are worse than others. When people are playing hard and running backs are trying to get that extra yards, the ball is going to get knocked out. But when you have blocked kicks and interceptions, I believe that is one of the biggest momentum builders in a football game.

The third thing is to minimize penalties. When I was head coach at Furman in the Southern Conference, we were the least penalized team in the conference just about every year. Basically, we were able to do that by avoiding postscrimmage penalties. Those are penalties that are selfish acts by your players. They hit someone out of bounds or after the whistle blows, which is a useless act. If you can eliminate those types of penalties, there is a good chance you will win the penalty battle every week. The past two years we have been at Vanderbilt, we have been the least penalized team in the conference. I don't know if it is the job we do coaching, or the referees just feel sorry for us.

The fourth thing is to be sound on defense. We say being sound on defense means not giving up the big play. At Furman, before becoming head coach, I was the defensive coordinator. We won seven conference championships, and in most of those years we led the league in defense. In 1988, when we won the national championship, we led the nation in defense. Every year, fans and alumni wanted to know why we didn't blitz more. The answer is simple. When you put yourself in a position to give up the big play, it is going to happen. That is true when you are playing teams with athletes better than yours. That was the case at Furman, and right now we are facing the same problem at Vanderbilt.

The fifth thing is to be sound in the kicking game. That is my topic today. The schemes I am going to cover today are our punt and kick-off return schemes. They are different than what you normally see. I think they will work for you to have a sound kicking game.

To be sound in the kicking game, you must avoid the big plays against you. When we are in a kicking situation, the other team has the opportunity to score. I am going to place a lot of emphasis on that part of the game. When you punt the ball, the defense can block the kick or return the kick and get the ball in the end zone. On the kickoff return, the offense can return the ball for a touchdown. I am going to spend most of my time and focus on those two aspects of the kicking game.

When we are taking possession of the ball, I spend less time and focus on those teams. Our punt return and kick-off return teams do not receive the same focus as the other special teams. We want to make sure we don't have the ball returned against us for a big gain.

A blocked kick really excites the fans and turns the momentum of a game. How many times have you seen a team line up to kick a field goal, have it blocked, and then that leads to points for the opponent? It is a total negative experience for your team. Usually blocked kicks lead to big plays for the opponents.

One other situation that I think is extremely important is committing penalties that deny you possession of the ball. If it is fourth-and-three and you jump offsides trying to block the punt, that act denies you possession of the ball. Roughing the kicker or running into the kicker are penalties that can deny you possession of the football.

When we get a chance to gain possession of the football through a punt, our major focus is on catching the ball. The second goal is to enhance our field position with a return. If we can get ten yards on the return, that is one less first down our offense has to get.

We want to make plays in the kicking game when the opportunities present themselves. We want to have returns and blocks in our package to take advantage of the opportunities when they are there. The pooch kick has an important use in the kicking game. We were fortunate to have a punter who could pooch the ball. He knew the importance of getting the ball over the line but keeping it short of the end zone. Giving the opponent the ball at the 15-yard line is better than kicking it into the end zone.

Field goals are tremendously important in today's football planning. There are so many games won with field goals today than ever before. Last year, we had a tremendous field goal kicker. We were number one in the SEC with red zone efficiency because of this kicker. He transferred after the recruiting season, and we were left without a kicker. We went from first to next-to-last in red zone efficiency in one year's time. All those types of things make a big difference in what you do.

You have to believe in your kicking game as a staff, because you have to commit the personnel you need for those teams. The punt is the first play of defense for us. If that is the case, we need to have the best players on that team. The kick-off return is the first play of offense for your team. You need to commit good offensive players to that team.

When I first became a head coach, I gave lip service to the idea about committing the proper personnel to those teams. I didn't do it, and it cost me some games. The second thing you have to do is commit the practice time to work on the special teams. We have two different sessions in our practice schedule each day to practice some aspect of our kicking game. When we are practicing those special teams, those teams have the focus of our entire staff. When we are working on the punting game, we have six coaches working with that team.

We divide up the front line among the coaches. We have a coach working with the snappers. We have a kicking coach working with the punter. We have someone watching the protection. We have to commit to the kicking game. If we don't commit to the kicking game, the players will know it. We record and document our success or failure and show it to our players. Our punter last year was not nearly as good as the one we had the year before, but our averages were about the same because we improved our coverage.

I am going to go over our punt protection. We have been using this protection and formation for six years, and we have yet to have a punt blocked. It was pretty consistent, and we ended up having a good net punting average. Our number-one goal when we punt is to get the ball off.

In our formation we lined up unbalance to the side on the punter dominant foot (see diagram). We had a left-footed punter and our unbalanced was on the left side. If you have a right-footed punter, the four man side is to the right of the center. Toward the two man side we put two wing backs to that side. The personal protector is to the punter's dominant side. We feel like we can do a good enough job with our zone blocking scheme to take care of anything the rushers give us.

Some ideal situations do occur within a game, where we can get one-on-one blocking. That lets us release quicker, be more aggressive, and cover better. It also gives a built-in wall for our punter and gives him more confidence. We are going to give two calls every time we go out to punt the ball. We make one call for the kicking side and one call away from the kicking side.

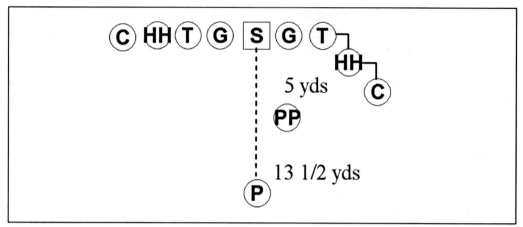

Punt formation

The center is extremely important on your punt team. We have an outstanding coach working with our centers at Vanderbilt. He is one of the best technique teachers there is coaching that position. Robbie Caldwell is our line coach, and he does outstanding work with the center. Whatever stance the center needs to get the ball back there is fine with us.

The punter aligns at 13.5 yards deep instead of 15 yards. The ball arrives in .72 to .75 seconds. The key men in the protection are the two guards. Their stance is extremely important. What we are going to try to do is make sure we don't get anyone up the middle. They are going to be bunched in on the center. The guards are foot to foot with the center, with their inside toe aligned on the heel of the center. They are staggered back from the center so they can interlock with him after the snap. We want the stance of the guards very narrow. On the snap of the ball, the guards are going to hop back and interlock their legs with the center and the tackle. They can't interlock before the ball is snapped.

The personnel we put in those guard positions are big defensive end types who can run. We don't ask the center to do a lot. We may ask him to lean one way or the other, but mostly he is going to snap the ball and try to get big. The tackles are foot to foot with the guard. The tackles are in a normal stance as far as their width. Their heads are up and their tails are down in a good football position.

When the ball is snapped, the tackle steps down the line of scrimmage and punches with both hands outside. He can't go backward. If there are two men in the gap, he has to punch hard enough to go through the first man in the gap to get to the second man. It is extremely important that they do not move their inside leg. The guard is interlocking with his inside leg. If he moves it, a big hole is opened up to the inside. The personnel we use for the tackles are fairly big guys in the linebacker type category.

The head hunter is the outside tackle in the unbalanced side to the punter's leg side. He does the same thing the tackle does. He steps down the line of scrimmage and punches outside with his hands. The head hunter could be a safety type. The contain man to the unbalanced side is in the end position. He hinges back and makes sure no one from the outside comes inside of him. He punches everyone outside and makes them run the hump. In the contain position, we could use corner backs.

To the side away from the punter's kicking leg, the head hunter is off the line of scrimmage. He is one foot outside the tackle's outside leg. He is slightly turned to the outside and cannot give ground. On the snap of the ball, he takes a step up and takes on everything inside out. He can't allow anyone inside of him. The contain man to the away side has his inside foot on the outside foot of the head hunter. His relationship is exactly like the head hunter relationship to the tackle. He does the same thing the head hunter is doing. We make everything to that side run the hump outside the head hunter and the contain man.

The personal protector is at a five-yard depth. He is responsible for up the middle first, to the leg side next, and the back side last. He has to keep his head on a swivel looking for seepage in the line. The punter is at 13.5 yards and punts the ball in two steps. Since we have gone to this protection we have never had a punt blocked.

If the rushers overload to the left side by putting six rushers left of the center and three to the right, we ask the center to lean left. The guards will tell the center which way to lean. Everything else in the zone protection scheme is the same, with the center helping the left guard because he has a man inside and outside of him (see diagram). If the overload were right, the center would lean to his right.

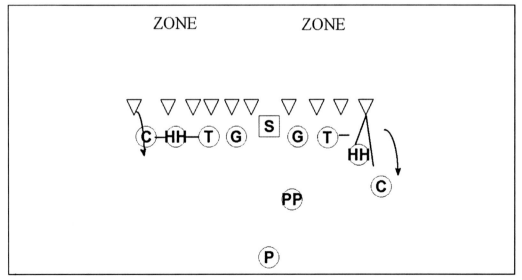

Zone/zone

It is important for the punter to know the strongest side of the protection. He wants to punt the ball behind the strongest side of the protection.

If the situation fits itself to the scheme, we want to build a stronger side for the punter.

If we have five men to each side of the center, we give an overload zone call (see diagram). That means we are going to identify the outside rusher to the left side and let him go free. The contain man, head hunter, tackle, and guard can get a hat-on-hat to their side. The left guard tells the center he has only one man inside him, and the center can lean right. The right side blocks zone like the normal punt blocking scheme. The personal protector takes the outside man to the leg side.

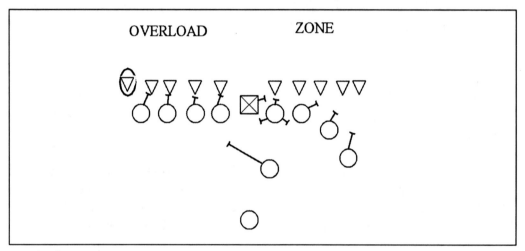

Overload zone

There is one thing that is important about this formation. The reason we have the two wing players to the right side is to give us two eligible receivers to that side plus the personal protector. That makes three receivers who could run patterns to that side. For that reason, we very seldom get pressure coming from the side with the wing set. If people are going to try to block the punt, they will come from the other side.

Since we don't retreat on our protection, we can be more aggressive on our coverage. We can jam and punch the rushers, stop their charge, and get down the field.

Let me show you what some people try to do against us with their overload schemes (see diagram). They put six rushers to the left and four to the right. We still can overload the left side with our call. That means we identify the outside rusher and let him go free. The left guard knows he has two rushers in his gap. He tells the center to lean left and hit the man in the gap. The left guard is interlocked and gets big to jam up the inside gap. The tackle punches his man outside. The head hunter blocks the man to his outside and the contain man blocks his inside gap. They can control their men and get downfield in a hurry. The outside rusher is released, to be picked up by the personal protector.

OVERLOAD

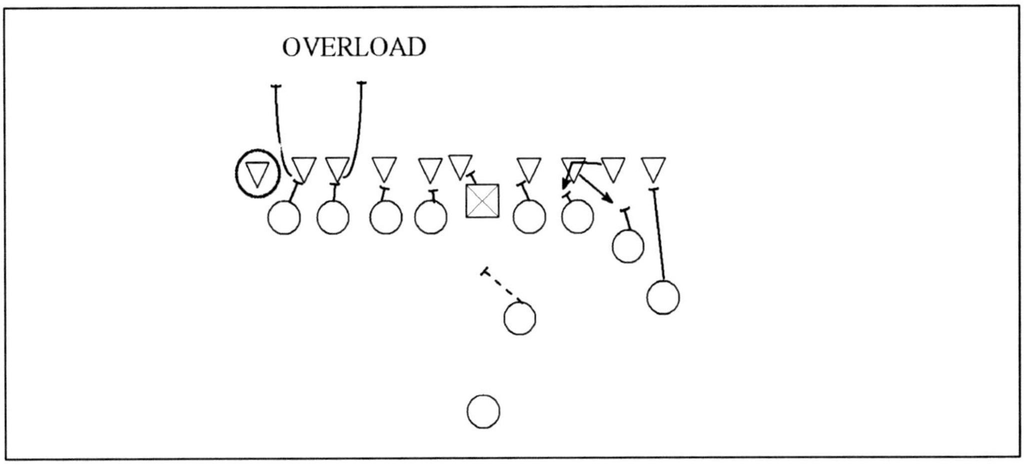

Overload man

To the backside, they are blocking a man scheme with zone principles. The reason they do that is to pick up any twist stunt that may be run to their side. The tackle is punching out but not moving out or dropping back. He can pick up an X stunt coming from the outside. The head hunter and contain man are stepping up and protecting inside.

If the rush overloads to the wing side, we can do the same thing we did the other way (see diagram). To the left they are blocking man-on-man. The center leans to the right side. The right guard interlocks and gets big. The right side tackle punches out through two men if he has to. The head hunter and contain man protect inside and make the rushers run the hump. The personal protector steps right, looking for seepage

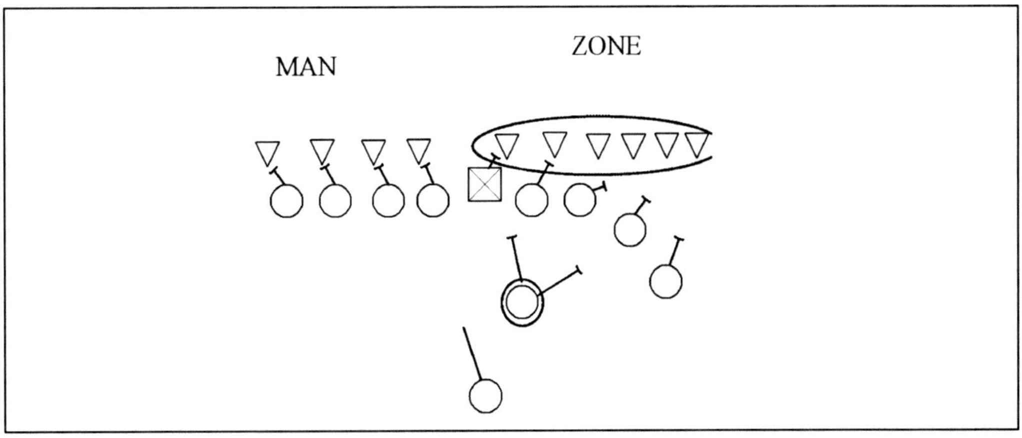

MAN   ZONE

Overload right

over the guard gap and working outside. We are blocking zone right and man blocking left. On the left side, we are blocking a man scheme with zone principles. That way we can pick up any stunts.

If we have a great return man to defend, we split our head hunters in our formation (see diagram). We split him into the wide side of the field. Our protection doesn't change because the defense has to cover the head hunter, and that means one less man inside.

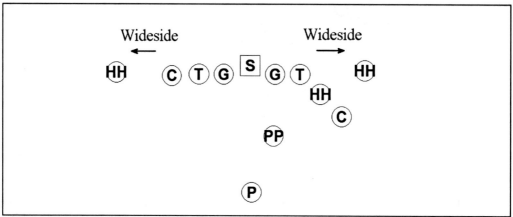

Split head hunter formation

When we are going into the opponent's territory and have to punt the ball we often use the pooch kick (see diagram). In this formation, we split both head hunters. We drop the contain man to the leg side into the wing set, where he becomes eligible as a pass receiver. We usually man the protection and try to get down and down the ball inside the ten-yard line. On the pooch kick, the head hunter will release past the return man. If he is giving a fair catch signal, we run by him and get between him and the end zone.

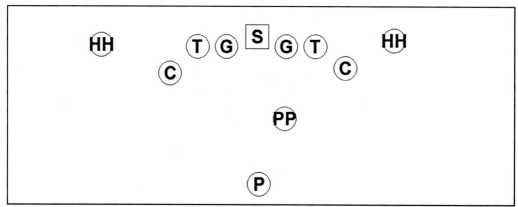

Pooch formation

After you protect the punt, you have to cover the kick. The punt coverage lanes will be determined by where the ball is caught, not where it is kicked from! We will use field landmarks to set the coverage lanes for each defender (see diagram).

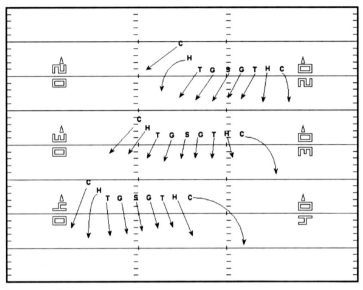

Coverage lanes

As each punt team member releases from the line of scrimmage, he must do four things. He has to fan out and cover the field for the first 10 to 15 yards. He has to realize where the ball is being caught. We key the return man to find out where the ball is being kicked. You may peek for the ball, but don't look for the ball unless you want to get lit up. When he sees where the ball is going, he adjusts his lane in relationship to where the ball is being caught. He squeezes to the ball and breaks down to make the tackle.

The head hunters are going directly to the ball, and the contain men are fanning out to keep the ball inside of them. We practice punting the ball off of each hash mark and from the middle of the field to get the coverage lanes exact.

If the ball is caught in the middle of the field, the snapper is going down the middle of the field (see diagram). The tackles are covering two yards outside the hash marks. The guards are half the distance between the center and tackles. The distance between the snapper, guards and tackles is about five yards. The contain men are covering down the top of the numbers. They are keeping everything inside of them.

The head hunters are going straight to the return man if they are not held up. If they anticipate being held up, they give a switch call to the contain man. The contain man changes responsibility with the head hunter. The head hunter covers on an

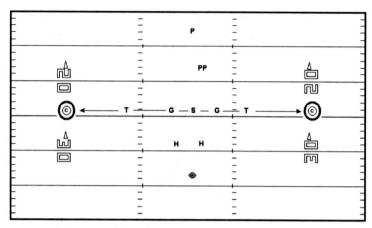

Coverage lanes middle

outside-in angle. The halo rule doesn't apply anymore, so the head hunter has to time up his hit on the return man so as not to arrive before he touches the ball.

The personal protector covers five to seven yards behind the first wave of coverage. He mirrors the ball. If the snapper, guard, or tackle gets pushed out of his lane, he fills in for him. If he sees a wall forming as he leaves the line of scrimmage, he gets behind the wall and covers at full speed.

The punter covers 15 yards behind the coverage wall. He mirrors the ball as he comes downfield. He tries to force the ball out of bounds.

If the ball is caught on the hash mark, the snapper is splitting the distance between the hash mark and the middle of the field. The boundary side guard is two yards outside the hash mark and the field side guard is up the middle of the field. The boundary side tackle is down the top of the numbers and the field side tackle is five

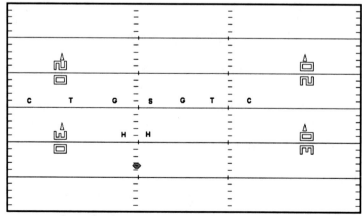

Coverage lanes hash

yards outside the field side guard. The boundary contain man is between the sideline and numbers. The field contain man is two yards outside the hash marks. The head hunters, personal protector, and punter have the same rules of coverage as they did on the middle coverage (see diagram).

The quickest way to give up a punt return is for the coverage team to turn in to the ballcarrier. They have to keep their pads square as they cover. They want to squeeze the ball, but not turn their pads to chase the ballcarrier. If the return man starts inside and breaks outside, the coverage has to stay square on his movement.

The snapper covers down the hash mark. The boundary guard is between the numbers and the hash mark. The field guard is halfway between the middle of the field and the hash mark. The boundary tackle is on the bottom of the numbers. The field tackle is cover down the middle of the field. The boundary contain should be three yards from the sidelines. The field contain-man covers down the field hash mark. Rules for the head hunters, personal protector, and punter are the same (see diagram).

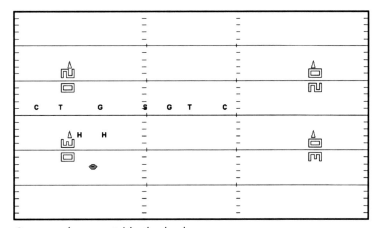

Coverage lanes outside the hash

As much as we practice the protection of the punter, we practice our coverage lanes. One man out of position can result in a touchdown. Most times we are using defensive players on our punt team. That means they are getting tackling practice every day. They have to apply their tackling-in-space rules in their coverage.

I want to show you our kickoff return before I run out of time (see diagram). It is extremely easy and you do the same thing over and over. We align our front line across the field at the 47-yard line. That is two yards over the free kick line. We distribute them across the field to guard against any onside kick situation. You can go back to 15 yards from the ball, but that leave you vulnerable to the onside kick.

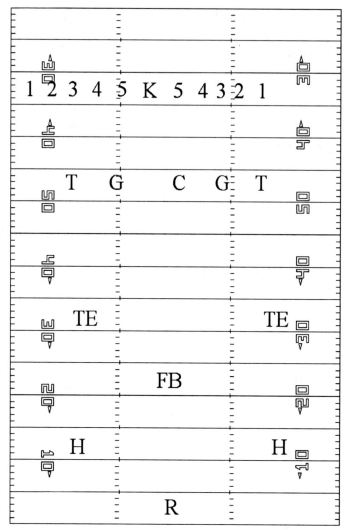

Kickoff return formation

The ends are aligned on the 30-yard line just inside the numbers. The fullback is in the middle of the field at the 20-yard line. We have two halfbacks who align inside the numbers between the 10- and 15-yard lines. The return man is aligned on the ball around the goal line ready to go.

The front line is playing the onside kick. The tight ends are going to play the bloop kick. They never back up to catch a ball. If the ball is over their heads, the halfbacks make the play on the ball. The halfback never backs up to catch a ball unless the return man tells them to take the ball. The fullback never backs up to catch a ball. If the ball goes over the fullback's head, the return man has to get the ball. If the ball is moved to the hash mark to kickoff, we adjust accordingly.

No matter what the coverage teams do, our return rules will stay the same. We are going to run a double wedge (see diagram). When I was at Furman, we ran this one return all year. We led the nation in kickoff returns, and our return man leads the nation in kickoff return average. We ran the same return for the eight years I was there.

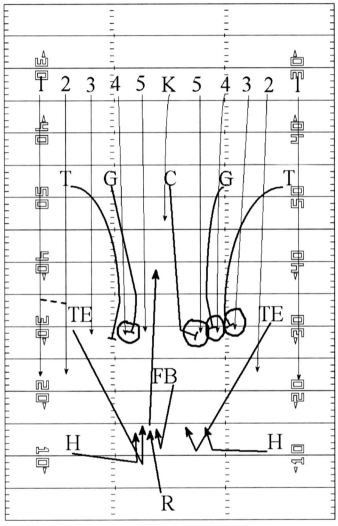

Middle double wedge

Our tackles are going to ensure the kick and run toward the football to around the 30-yard line. They are going to turn and block the first thing coming outside of them. Most of the times in coverage, the two men on the outside of the coverage team are contain men or some kind of safety backs. We don't block them at all. The good thing about the tackle's block is they don't have to be vicious blocks. All they want to do is move the defender outside. It is like pushing a rusher past the quarterback in a pocket.

The guard does the same thing by dropping inside and blocking outside. They block the first man inside the tackle. The center drops to the wedge and blocks one of the two defenders coming down the middle of the field. If the front five can stop the charge of the coverage, we have a chance to return the ball all the way.

The fullback sets the second wedge 12 yards in front of the ball, wherever it is kicked. He never takes the wedge outside of the midpoint between the hash and the numbers. The fullback has to set the wedge exactly at 12 yards. If he doesn't, the outside defenders will get behind the wedge and blow up the return man. The tight ends have to hustle their butts to the fullback and get shoulder-to-shoulder with the fullback. The two halfbacks come inside and get shoulder-to-shoulder with the tight ends.

The return man gets the ball and starts up field. As soon as he has momentum and feels no one can get behind the wedge, he calls "Go." The wedge has to move. They can't stay there and catch people. When we were at Furman with 12,000 people in the stands, you could hear the "Go" call. At Tennessee, with 109,000 people in the stands, the fullback has to anticipate the call because he can't hear it. At home we might be able to hear the call, but on the road we have to anticipate it.

As the wedge moves forward, the halfbacks are going to block the first thing that comes outside of our offensive tackles. They have to block the crazy guys who are trying to knife through the wedge. The fullback and the tight ends are going to lead the return man to the promised land. If we are lucky, we will have 10 men blocking on seven. Kickoff teams are coached to stay in their lanes. We let them stay in their lanes and run by them.

The return man has to be fearless. He has to take the ball and run as hard as he can and trust the back wedge. He is depending on them to protect him from any screamer that is coming down that field. With any luck at all, the return man is going to run right off the fullback's block, and everyone else will be past him and down too deep. That is what we do every time on our kick-off return.

If the ball is kicked outside the hash mark, the fullback never takes the wedge outside the midpoint between the hash marks and the numbers (see diagram). The return man has to bring the ball back to the wedge. It is his job to get the ball back to the wedge. If the screamer is coming down the sideline into the corner where the ball is kicked, it is the halfback's job to make sure the return man gets back to the wedge. He may have to leave the wedge to do that.

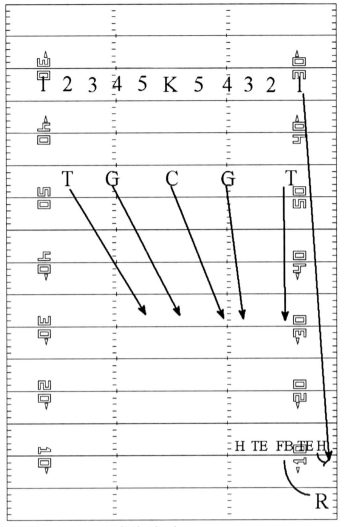

Double wedge outside the hash

The Southern Conference and the Southeastern Conference are a little different when it comes to the athletes in the league. When we went to Auburn they sent a 6-7, 300-pound athlete who could run like a deer down as a wedge buster. He almost killed our fullback. We felt like we had to have an answer for that kind of play. We decided to put in a side return to help us out (see diagram). When coverage teams stays in their lanes this return will not work. However, since we have been at Vanderbilt, people send everyone to attack our wedge.

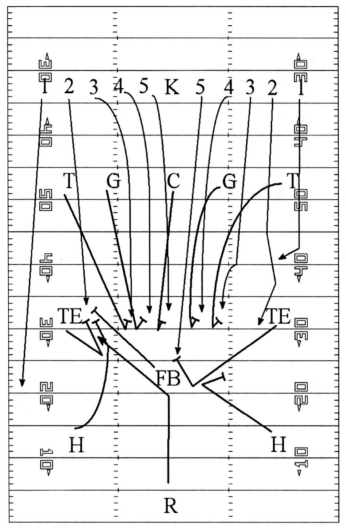

Right or left return

We tried to make everything look the same as the double wedge return. Everyone in the front wedge is going to block away from the side of the return. The halfback to the side of the return kicks out the contain man to that side. The fullback and tight end to that side are going to double-team the second man to the outside. We are not going to run this return if the number 3 man in the coverage is staying in his lane. If he is cheating and going for the wedge, we are in Fat City. The offside tight end takes the missile coming down the middle. The offside halfback makes sure the return man gets into the sideline by cutting off the outside.

I am out of time. I appreciate you being here. Thank you.

8

Special Teams Organization

Carl Johnson
Jenks High School (Oklahoma)
2009

Let me tell you what a privilege it is to be here. I have been going to Nike clinics since I was a young coach right out of college. I used to be one of those coaches who did not care about special teams. I was more concerned about my individual time because I was coaching the defensive line at that time. My players were not involved in special teams, so I did not pay much attention to it.

In 2001-2002, I was a graduate assistant at the University of Houston. One of my responsibilities was to work with the special teams. I got to work with Coach Joe Robinson who is now the special teams coordinator at LSU. When I worked with him, I found he was one of the top two or three special teams coaches in college football.

I learned a great deal from him. I learned not only about schemes, but also a great deal about organization. One thing that impressed me was his passion for special teams and how he enjoyed that aspect of the game. It rubbed off on me, and I have been the special teams coordinator for five years at Jenks High School. I learned from Coach Robinson, so I gave it a shot.

I enjoy coaching the special teams. For many coaches, it is a headache, but I view it as an opportunity. I have a head coach that gives me a lot of freedom to take the ball and run with it.

I am going to talk about some different areas today. I will talk about the keys to our success. I will cover how we organize our coaching staff, how we handle our installation schedule in the fall, and how we divide what we are working on. I will talk about our practice schedule during the week and how we game plan for an opponent.

Nothing that I do is original material. It is something that I got from someone else. I will be more than happy to share it with you. I want to start out by giving you the keys to success.

KEYS TO SUCCESS (PART ONE)

- Have a designated special teams coordinator. Sell the head coach on yourself and your passion for special teams.
- Organization is key. Have no wasted time or reps.
- Involve the head coach as much as he wants to be involved.
- The special teams coordinator is responsible for all schemes but will involve all other coaches with the exception of the coordinators.

I have been on staffs where the special teams were divided up among the coaching staff—there was no coordinator. I feel, to be successful, you need a coach that oversees the entire kicking game and is the coach where the buck stops. I am that guy at Jenks High School. When I got to Jenks, I had to sell the head coach, Allan Trimble, on my organizational skills and my passion for coaching the special teams.

There is only a certain amount of time every day to get everything done. I am fortunate because I have 20 minutes a day to get everything done. That is not counting pre-practice and postpractice kicking. I want to make sure when the clock starts ticking, I do not waste any time. That takes a great deal of organization. I do not want to waste any reps, and I want maximum effort throughout that 20-minute period.

I also feel you involve the head coach in the special teams as much as he wants. Some head coaches are involved with the offensive or defensive staffs. The head coach goes through all the hassles during the day. When it comes time for practice, that puts him at ease doing what he loves to do and that is coaching. Coach Trimble wants to be actively involved with the special teams. He coaches at least one of the positions on every one of our special teams.

As special teams coordinator, I am responsible for all of the schemes, and I will involve every coach on the staff in coaching them. The exceptions are the offensive and defensive coordinators and the quarterbacks coach. The rest of the staff will be involved in special teams in one aspect or another. Some coaches will be more involved than others—it depends on how much a coach feels comfortable with and how much he wants to be involved.

KEYS TO SUCCESS (PART TWO)

- Try to eliminate as much of the work for the other staff as possible.
  - ✓ Meetings/film sessions
  - ✓ Opponent scouting/film breakdown
- Play as many offensive and defensive starters as needed in order to be successful. Sell those kids on being difference makers.
- Build your special teams philosophy throughout your program (junior high, youth programs, etc.).
  - ✓ Make yourself available to those programs and coaches.

When I involve the other coaches, I feel it is my job to eliminate as much of the work for them as I can. They have their own position groups, teaching schedules, and their families to think about. I do not want to burden them with the work that is involved with coaching special teams. I want to take all the responsibility away from them that I can.

I take the film breakdown and scouting report responsibilities on myself. I am a member of the defensive staff, and I have a very understanding defensive coordinator who allows me the time to work on my special teams responsibilities while we are working on defensive game planning. I coach linebackers, and while I am working on the special teams breakdowns, I am contributing to the defensive staff meeting. That lets me make the plan for the upcoming week.

I feel, to be successful, that you need to play as many offensive and defensive starters as needed in order to win. Coach Trimble feels if we need to rest a player, we rest him a couple of plays on offense or defense. We are not going to rest him on a punt or a kickoff return where one play can determine the outcome of a game.

Some players may be hesitant about covering a kickoff, knowing they have to turn around and play defense. I involve the other coaches and try to sell those players on being difference makers. You may have a player who is not being recruited heavily. If you can sell him as a great special teams player, it could improve his prospects.

I try to build a philosophy throughout our program at all levels. I do not handcuff our youth programs to do what we do, but I want them to have a sound scheme. They do not have to use our schemes unless they want to. I want them to know the importance of the special teams. We do the same thing with the youth leagues in our area. I try to make myself available to them, and we conduct a clinic in the summer for them. The kids that are playing in these programs are the same ones that will play for us down the road.

The thing I tell those coaches, and the message I have for you coaches today, is that you need to make it fun for them. There are coaches out there who are trying to rehash the "glory days" when they played—they are serious about it. In some cases, they are too serious for the kids they are working with. A good youth league coach or a bad youth league coach can make or break some of those young players. In our program, it is all about numbers. We want as many players coming into the high school program as possible.

KEYS TO SUCCESS (PART THREE)

- Head coaches must believe in the importance of good special teams play.
- As staff, you must do several things.
  - ✓ Sell it to your players.
  - ✓ Place importance on selecting personnel.
  - ✓ Understand that special teams involves more areas of the field than offense and defense.
  - ✓ Get the most out of your practice time.
  - ✓ Emphasize special teams in pre-season camp.
  - ✓ Special teams time can be combined with conditioning—it will help win early games.
  - ✓ Remember, there are many facets of special teams play to be covered prior to the first game.

The head coach has to believe in the importance of good special teams play. It cannot be lip service. Our head coach is involved with every special team, and he coaches at least one position on each of those teams. In the special areas, there is a lot to learn before the first game. It is my job to make sure we do not go into the first ball game without having covered a certain kicking situation. I have a checklist that I go by to make sure I do not forget anything before we play.

We are a 6A football program in Oklahoma and are fortunate to have a large staff. We have 13 coaches on our staff. I give this sheet to our coaches in our staff manual before the beginning of the season. This is an example of one phase of the kicking game.

Punt Return/Block	Coaches
2-5 techniques	Johnson
6-9 techniques	Trimble
Corners	Calip
Return	Riggs
Scout Team	Johnson

Jenks Trojans Special Teams
Coaching Responsibilities

Also listed on the chart is a breakdown of coaching assignments for punt cover, kickoff coverage, kickoff return, PAT/FG block, and PAT/FG team. We are fortunate to have a coach who takes care of all the scout teams. When we get to the point-after team, we divide that up by offensive positions. On the point-after- and field-goal-block teams, we divide that by defensive positions.

On game day, we try to break it up so we have our eyes on every part of the field at all times. We have coaches in the box and on the field watching what is going on in the kicking game. That way, we are getting feedback on every situation that happens in the game. The first year I was special teams coordinator, I was on the field. I liked it for the excitement of the game, but I got no feedback because everyone was involved with their own particular position. The next year, I moved up to the box and it has worked out better. I can see the entire field, and I am able to make the adjustments in the scheme.

Every season, we have an installation schedule. We have a calendar of the day when all the aspects of the kicking game are to be installed. On the first day of practice, we have a team meeting and our media day. We take pictures and take care of those types of activities. On the first day of actual practice, we put in the punt team. After that, we try to install two special teams a day. From August 18 until our first game, we work on two special teams every day. We try to work 10 minutes on each team.

I have a kicking game depth chart that helps keep up with the players. That chart can fluctuate during the week. I start out on Sunday night with one version of the chart, but by Thursday or Friday, it may be entirely different. It could be affected by injuries, grades, or whatever might come up. On our punt team, I try to go three deep on the depth chart, working as many young players into the chart as possible. We have a Trojan punt team we use when backed up. We take out the bullets on the outside and replace them with additional blockers on the inside. I have a copy of the depth chart in the press box; the head coach has a copy; and two assistants on the field have copies.

My scout teams coach is my box coach on Friday nights. We have a box set up at the 50-yard line. It runs from the plus 47 to the minus 47-yard lines. On third down, anyone on the punt team comes to that box. The scout teams coach calls, "Punt team alert!" He has his depth chart and makes sure we have everyone accounted for and any injured players replaced. On fourth down, if we have to punt, we go straight out onto the field.

On the depth chart, we have the replacements on the "punt safe team." If you are not sure the offense is going to punt the ball, you can leave your defense on the field. However, most of the time, you take out your safety and replace him with the punt return man. The defense stays on the field, and we bring in the player who usually catches the punts.

We have a two-point chart on the sheet that tells us when to go for two points instead of kicking the point after.

Go for two points if	
behind by	**ahead by**
2,3,10,(12),16,	1,4,5,11,12,
17,18,21,(25),26	19,22,(25)

PRE-SEASON INSTALLATION

- A two-deep special teams depth chart, along with a scout depth chart, will be posted prior to day one.
- Meet with the two-deep special teams for 30 minutes before practice during the first four days (base calls/emphasize SAKR).
  - ✓ Day one: Protect/cover punt
  - ✓ Day two: Punt return
  - ✓ Day three: Kickoff return
  - ✓ Day four: Kickoff cover
- Scout team will also meet on the first day and on an as-needed basis.

We go through that routine the first week of practice. At those meetings, I usually show them some kind of drill tape of actual film footage of what we should be doing. The notation SAKR is an acronym for stance, alignment, key, and responsibility. We also have a scout team depth chart to make sure we have every position filled. We want to evaluate players on the scout team and possibly move them up into special teams positions. We want to know if a player can block a punt, be a wedge player, cover a kick, or if he has a special talent we can use. We are trying to find places for the young players to play.

Each meeting will consist of the following:

- Review of depth chart/personnel
- Goals of unit/expectations
- All teaching is done by using PowerPoint® presentations and video
- Breakdown of each position of unit (SAKR)
- Stance
- Alignment
- Key

- Responsibility
- Drills are explained and demonstrated

When we show the video, the players will see good examples that they can model themselves after.

On the first day of practice, the only special team we work on is the punt.

PRACTICE #1: PUNT PROTECTION AND COVERAGE

- Stance/alignment/key/responsibility (SAKR)
- Man protection
- Communication
- Breakdown by position
  ✓ Left side: Step-and-jolt technique
  ✓ Right side: Step-and-jolt technique
  ✓ Bullets: Release/breakdown on receiver
  ✓ Snapper and personal protection: Recognizing solid protection
  ✓ Scout team: Organize/explain the look we want to see

We place emphasis on stance, alignment, key, and responsibility. We start out with a man-protection scheme. That requires the players to communicate because they will have to switch some of the blocks. We break it down by positions. We start out in small groups. One of the coaches takes the left side, and another coach takes the right side. They work on step-and-jolt techniques.

We have another coach take the bullets and work on their releases and breaking down on the return man once they get to the ball. I take the snapper and personal defenders and work with them. We do 10 minutes of individual drills the first day. We work five minutes of individuals against the scouts. We work the left side and the right side on the step-and-jolt techniques.

The last five minutes of the 20-minute period, we bring all the parts together. That gives us a look at the big picture. We have the snapper snapping the ball live to the punter. The left and right sides work on their protection techniques.

On the second day of practice, we emphasize the SAKR principles. We install our zebra protection, which is hinge protection. That is a zone type of scheme. We also put in our punt return on the second day. We break down the teaching into individual parts as we did with the man-protection scheme. The difference between man protection and zone protection starts with the splits in the formation. We cut our splits down in the zone scheme. All the coaches work with their individual groups as they did on the previous day. The last five minutes of the punt drill is a team period against the scouts.

We have 10 additional minutes to work on our punt return. The first five minutes we walk through the return and talk about everyone's responsibility. We do that in two-deep groups from the depth chart.

On the third practice, we work on the hinge or zone protection and punt coverage lanes. On this day, we introduce our kickoff return and our alley scheme, which is a man-trap scheme. During this day, we reinforce all the skills we taught the first two days. We work with our bullets on a double-team block and how to escape it. You see, each day we are reviewing the previous day's work.

The fourth day is our first day in pads. On that day, we work on the punt for five minutes in group and five minutes against the scout team. We spend 10 minutes introducing the kickoff team. We kick the ball deep middle and to the right and left.

On the fifth day, we have our first scrimmage. The punt is the only live kick we have that day. We have six live kicks at various places during the scrimmage. We have four with the first team punt and two with the second team punt.

During the season, the first thing we do on Mondays is to have a team meeting. We go over the kicking scouting report before the players go to their offensive and defensive meetings.

The first thing we do at practice is work on backed-up punting. We punt the ball from our three-yard line and have to protect it. The worst thing that can happen is having a punt blocked inside your five-yard line. I put 12 defenders trying to block the punt. I have put as many as 18 defenders trying to block the punt. The second part of the kicking practice is punts and kickoff returns.

On Tuesday in pre-practice, we work on our point-after-touchdown and field-goal teams. We also install a fake based on what we have seen on film. During practice, we work on our punt and kickoff. During the kickoff period, we install the onside kick. We work on the onside kicks live so we can get the kicker and coverage personnel timed up. We put scout team personnel to receive the kicks, but we practice precaution with them—we do not want to get anyone hurt.

On Wednesday morning at 7:10, we have a special teams meeting for the two-deep kicking members. We review the scouting report and watch cut-ups of the opponent. In pre-practice, we work on the field goal and the point after blocks. We cover fakes and swinging-gate formations and adjustments. In practice, we work on punts, punt returns, and kickoff returns. We also work on an emergency field-goal kick at the end of a two-minute offense.

On Thursday in pre-practice, we work on punt safe with the defense. We go over the punt formation with the defense and alert them to the punter and personal protector groups. They have to see any addition of the quarterback as the punt or in the protection wall. They have to notice if the punt team has inserted a running back as the personal protector. The reason they are on the field is to stop a fake punt. They have to cover all eligible receivers and not get faked out. In practice, we work our game script on all kicking. In the postpractice session, we walk through the hands team routing, and I give a tips and reminders sheet. This tips sheet comes from our game with Union High School (Tulsa).

UNION SPECIAL TEAMS TIPS 2008

Kickoff

- We must do a great job of staying in our lanes. Use great ball get-off and stay in your lane—if you get knocked out, get back in your lane as soon as possible.
- Remember, kick left/avoid right, kick right/avoid left.
- It will be of the utmost importance for us to establish field position with our kickoff cover team.

Kickoff Return

- We will use double wedge and alley check this week.
- On the wedge, we must do a great job in getting to our wedge and make it very tight. Block head-up to outside.
- On alley, we will run to the hash they are kicking from. In the middle, check to double wedge.
- Front line needs to make sure that they see the ball kicked off the tee cover; any onside kick and work to protect your teammates; expect fiddler.
- Ends should be ready for a sky kick. You can call for a fair catch if needed.
- Be alert for kicks over your heads into a dead zone. We must cover all kicks. All kicks are live once they have traveled 10 yards.
- Know your squib kick rules.
- Hands team must be ready and alert.

Punt

- We will be in spread punt unless we are inside our own five-yard line. We do have substitutions in Trojan (backed-up) punt.
- Spread/over punt calls will be automatic zebra. On a zebra call, cut your splits down and punch the inside man to block outside. Take care of your gap responsibility. Protect first, then cover.
- We will directional kick.
- Expect to jump and try and draw you offside.

On Friday, I meet with the players two hours and 15 minutes before game time. I go through the roll call of each team so they know when they are supposed to be on the field. After pre-game and we return to the locker room, I go over the depth chart one last time. I call them by position, and we have players respond verbally.

On Saturday morning, we come in and lift. After we lift, we watch the game film as a group. We try to be constructive as coaches with the film session. I try to be as positive as I can and encourage them to get better. The films are graded, and grades are passed out to the players on Saturday.

The one thing that is true and consistent in our practice is the punting game. We work on punting the football every day. The biggest swing of momentum in a game occurs when there is a punt block. It is an instant chance for the defense to score. If the punt is blocked behind the line, there are more defensive personnel there than offensive personnel. Touching the ball does not constitute a possession. Everyone on the defense tries to scoop and score. Even if the offense recovers the ball, they lose the ball.

After the game on Saturday, I start putting together the scouting reports of the upcoming opponent (Figure 8-1). I take the film we have and tag their kickoffs. I get all the cut-ups, watch them, and look for similarities in the way they kick off. I record the numbers of the players on their kickoffs and identify the safeties. I chart the depth and height of the kicks as well as the directions of the kicks. This is one of the forms I use in our scouting report.

Base Alignment	Base Coverage Lanes

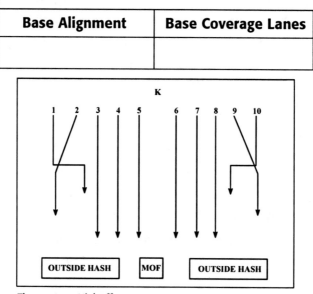

Figure 8-1. Kickoff coverage

Other schemes and alignments	
Leg strength of kicker	
Safeties	
Who is the first downfield?	
Miscellaneous	

I do alignment charts for all their kicking teams and coverage teams. I draw them up so I know where to kick the ball. I want to know where their stud is on all kicks. I want to kick away from him whenever I can.

The most frequent kick in a football game is the punt. We want to do a good job of analyzing their punter. I want to know the quality of his punts and the timing of the kicks. I want to know if he is left-footed or right-footed. I want to know how many steps he takes to punt the ball. I want to know the protection scheme and who their best cover people are. The most important aspect of the punting game besides the punter is the snapper. He is the one component of the game that has to function right every time.

On our block teams, I try to list the weak link on each team, and that is who we try to attack. On their extra point and field goal teams, I list their most dangerous rusher and have an alert for his alignment (Figure 8-2). We have to be aware of his position and make sure we block him on every play. That is the biggest thing you can get from a scouting report. In the diagram, we have their kick-blocking scheme. Following is an example of our field goal defending sheet.

Base Scheme	Base Protection Scheme

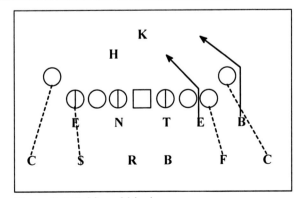

Figure 8-2. Field goal block

Most dangerous rusher	
Number of Safeties	
Which is the blockside?	
Fakes we will run	
Miscellaneous	

One of the best things I have done was to develop a participation list. It lists the positions, player's name, and the special teams he plays on. If a player gets hurt, he has to be replaced. However, we need to know how many special teams he plays on. You can find that out from a participation chart. If you do not have a participation list, you have to go through the entire list of depth chart sheets to check for his name. Following is an example of one entry. We do this for all positions.

This shows you the teams he is on and the position he plays. Jones is on the kickoff team at the left 5 position. He is the end on the punt-return team, and he plays on the kickoff return. It keeps you from looking through your depth charts to find his name.

Participation List

Position: Defensive End	Special Teams
Jones	KO/L5, PR/E, KOR,
Smith	FG/T PUNT, KOR/T
Phillips	Punt center

We have a goal board posted in our locker room. We list the goals in the left column of the board and keep a running total of how many goals we achieved each week. Across the top of the board, we put the name of the team we played. In the boxes under the team name, we put a Trojan sticker for each goal we accomplished.

GL   **Teams On Schedule**

	A	B	C	D	E	F	G	H	I	J
1										
2										
3										
4										
5										
6										
7										

Following are listed the goals which go in the first column on the goal board.

SPECIAL TEAMS GOAL BOARD

- Win
- Opponents average less than 10 yards on punt return
- Opponents average less than 20 yards on kickoff return
- Trojans average 15 yards on punt returns
- Trojans average 25 yards on kickoff returns
- 100 percent on PATs
- No penalties in the kicking game
- Disrupt one field goal, punt, or PAT

We went 12-2 this year. We lost to Union High School (Tulsa) in the second game of the season, and we lost the last game of the season—they were loaded. That was probably the best collection of talent I have ever seen in a high school. We did well in the other categories except on kickoff return. We had three Division I players on the return team. Anytime they touched the ball, they were a threat to go all the way. No one would kick the ball to them. We had only two games where we averaged 25 yards on the kickoff return.

I hope you got something from this. I have all kinds of material I can send you if you will email me. Thank you for your time.

9

Punting, Kicking, Snapping, and Holding Tips

Amos Jones
University of Cincinnati
2000

The first thing I want to do is to thank Coach Paul Bryant for the time he spent with me and for what he taught me about football. A guy by the name of Paul Davis taught me what I want to pass on to you. As coaches it is important to go back and give credit to the people you learned from.

I am going to break this talk down into three segments. I want to talk to you about the punter and the placekicker, and the kickoffs, and the snapper. Along with the placement, I will talk about the holder. I have been in coaching 21 years and four of those years have been in high school. I think it is important for you to coach your punters and kickers. The best way how to coach them is to find out all you can about those techniques.

I am not going to use the X's and O's much here. I am not going to get into schemes. You protect the punter the best way you know how. We are going to start with the mechanics of coaching the punter.

There are a couple of things you look for in a punter. First, you must look for a great athlete. If your quarterback is the best athlete on the team, I would try to make him the punter. I would make his backup a punter. They are the types of players that are going to be able to handle the football. Handling the football is something the punter has to do consistently.

I am a firm believer in teaching the two-step punt. I do not even talk three steps. It is the same with the placekicker. I teach him to kick the ball off the ground. I am not going to give a scholarship to a kid that kicks off a tee. First, it takes too long to change from the tee to the ground. Second, it gives him a chance to kick from a wider surface. And third, it gives him a chance to watch the techniques used on TV on Saturday and Sunday. If you have a two-inch block and you love it, I am not telling you to change. I am telling you what I like to do.

Mechanics of Coaching the Punter

I. Stance – Balance is the key.

For coaching a punter in the two-step method, I will cover the stance first. Balance is the key to punting. I have heard Coach Bryant and Coach Davis say that a thousand times. By balance, I mean the same as if you were teaching a lineman or a linebacker. You must have balance. We want a little weight on the inside of our feet. We want the feet shoulders' width apart and squared up toward the snapper. I want to be squared up to the center. There is no need to do the angle snaps or the angle punts. You will get more out of the kicking game if you will let your center snap the ball straight and let the punter kick it straight. The hips are the key to punting, as well as the stride. The stride should be normal. We want a slight bend at the knees. We want the shoulders over the toes. Many of you coach another position and you will tell your other players to get a slight bend in the knees.

We want a slight bend in the knees. The reason is for the high snap. That is the reason for the weight on the inside of your feet, that is, so you can push up. Having your feet spread helps keep the balance. I do not like to see punters that have "ants in their pants." They are always wiggling. I do not like movement. It is a sign of anticipation of the snap. Watch film to see what happens. Watch your punter as much as you can to see what problems he has. A punter that is moving his feet or dangling his hands has a nervous twitch. Before he ever makes the catch of the snap, that twitch is going to stop. He is going to come to balance. He is going to come to a pause. We do not want them to sit there and move around. We want no movement. Once they get their feet set, stay set.

I am going to teach the two-step punt. I have a left-footed kicker. I can't demonstrate for him very much. Everything has to be transferred back to him because he is left-footed. Some punters will stagger their feet. I like for them to be squared up, toe to toe. If I have a player that takes a false step, I will have that player put more weight on the foot that he takes the false step with.

II. Catch – Focus is the key.

We all use some kind of signals to let the snapper know that we are ready to go. The personal protector usually gives that signal. We may say, "set," or we may say, "ready." Someone tells the snapper and punter that we are ready when they are. We have to have some type of communication.

On the catch, you want the punter to catch the front stripe of the football. It is no different than what it is for the receiver. The difference is the punter catches the football going *away* from him. The punter has to catch the ball coming *toward* him. We want to see the front stripes of the ball from the center's release to the hands on the catch. We want him to focus in the area through the center's legs. He needs to extend and lock his elbows to get the football quicker. It is just like teaching the receiver to reach out and catch the football. You teach the punter the same thing. When the ball is coming, he extends his arms. He does not have to lock them out completely, but he wants to be able to get to the ball faster. The quicker he gets the ball, the better the punter is going to be. The get-off time from snap to punt for the punter is going to be 1.8 seconds to 1.7, or 1.9 at the most. You are still dealing with 2.2 seconds of operation time with a 14- to 15-yard snap.

We want the punter to get his pinky fingers touching together to form a cup. We do not want him in a situation where his hands are open. We want to firmly squeeze the ball with both hands. We talk about a grip and a control hand. If I am a right-footed punter, I catch the ball and immediately put the ball in the V of my right hand. I want the laces pointed north. I want to control the football with one hand. That firm grip is all I will need on the ball from the standpoint of going through the progression of my steps and dropping the ball on the punt. I want to stress getting the control hand up on the ball. The higher on the point of the ball you hold it, the more problems you will have with the drop. You want the back elbow to be at a 35-degree angle in the bend. We want the shoulders in square. Keep the feet and hips square just like you were playing linebacker or end. Keep the control hand to make sure you keep pressure on the football to keep it on the ball in the V of the hand.

III. Footwork – Maintaining an upright torso.

Again, let's talk two steps. If you have a three-step punter, how do you get him to become a two-step punter? I tell him I am going to step on his foot so he can't take that first step. That first step is just a comfort step. Most three-step kickers take a first step with the off-foot first. They take the second step and then the third step, and they punt the football if they are right-footed. The only way a player is a three-step punter is because we let him be.

The first step is a normal stride pattern (right). It is with the punt foot. That first step has to be a normal stride because I want to keep my torso erect. I want to stay tall. We love a tall punter. You do not have many of them. You love a tall punter because that is the guy that has the leverage on the football.

The second step will be slightly elongated (left). The second step is longer because the hips will have to come through to the football. The body will tell you what to do. It is okay to make the second step longer because the next step through is going to be your hip. It is going to be the strike step. The strike step is the contact point. It is the foot up in the air. The finish phase is the key to your distance.

Now you start talking about the drop. The more the punter pulls the ball into his body, the harder it is going to be to get a good drop to his foot. He must keep the ball extended.

One thing you cannot do is to allow the punter to turn his toe toward the sky. You are talking about locking out the heel to point the toe straight. Don't let him point the toe upward, which punters like to do.

IV. Ball Management – Use both hands until the release point.

Grip the back one third of the ball and maintain the extension with the control hand. Kick the ball high and above the waist. We are not talking about high above the head. We are talking about high above the waist. As long as the ball is above the waist, you will not run into a problem kicking on a windy day. The drop will not be a problem if it is consistent. Where you make contact with the strike is about hip high. Film the punter from the side and watch him.

The control-hand release is maintained until the last second. The drop should start above the waist and the ball needs to be tilted.

V. The Strike and Finish – Allow hips and shoulders to help you.

A 45-degree bend in our grip-hand elbow is a major factor. Keep your shoulders square throughout the entire process. Allow your balance foot to be naturally lifted off the ground. Learn to keep your hips and feet underneath you at all times. Keep the strike foot locked out throughout the entire time. The bottom line of all of this is that it starts with balance. It is important to end up on a balanced stance.

I have a couple of film clips of a punter that I want to show. You are not going to see everything perfect. We were 12th in the NCAA in net punting and a lot of if was because of our punter. (Film)

I have a specialist tips sheet that I want to cover. It covers the phases of the kicking game. I did not invent the wheel, but I really believe in these things. The first part is for punters.

Punter's Creed

- Have a balanced two-point stance with every step planned.
- Total concentration on completing a perfect punt – every time.
- Total confidence in your snapper and protections.
- Keep eyes down on the ball after the catch and use good follow-through.
- Be sure to use directional calls to alert the catch and use good follow-through.
- Get in front of the bad snaps. Handle it as a good shortstop would.
- Work on punting the bad-snap situations and when one occurs in practice take advantage of the experience it gives you. Punt all snaps. Remember to bring the tip of the ball into your view and get your hands in front of you as quickly as possible.
- When punting on or near the end line, always have at least one full step from it. Know the situation so you can make the correct decision regarding an intentional safety.
- Your most effective punts will take place in situations where you have a chance to use our sky punt call. Remember, the best punters in football are those that display distance, height, and skills when punting the football in the plus field.

Punter's Warm-Up

All punters will start 45 minutes before every practice time with the goal of being ready to go full speed when our specialty period starts. During this time you are responsible for jogging two full laps around the field (as a group with the other specialists) and for the stretching that you need (as a group with the other specialists) before you touch a football. This warm-up phase will be done every day of practice so you can get your timing down for our pre-game procedures as well. Your warm-up with a football will consist of the following drills that should be done on a line:

- Pedals – Five minutes of one-legged pedaling to increase leg strength and balance.
- Reach – Ten leg swings to ensure that you reach your highest leg elevation with your foot pointed.
- Drops – Four times across the field on a line. Done properly, ball should come back to you.
- Pass Offs – Ten reps to ensure that you see how the ball should come off your foot.

- No Steps – Ten no-step punts to a partner 15 yards away.
- One Step – Eight one-step punts to a partner 25 yards away.
- Full Steps – Eight full-step punts to a partner 40 yards away.
- Goal Post Punts – Ten reps from 10 yards away with a snapper to ensure punts are reaching their highest elevation.

Punters' Individual Practices

As a punter, you must make sure that the following schedule is done on a weekly basis for you to be a successful punter:
- Stretch at least two times a day (four during two-a-days) and three days of distance running (one mile per day.)
- 30 minutes of balanced pedaling at least three times per week (Monday, Wednesday, and Friday).
- 50 catches per week including the following snaps: good, high, low, left, right, and wet ball.
- 75 drops per week (does not include teamwork). Two days of setback with a partner (works your sky punt technique). Two days of punting into the sideline net. 30 of the following punts on your own: normal, hash mark, coming out, sky, raw (no catches and no returns), and corner.
- Three days of horseshoes for at least five minutes that include the following punting situations: hash mark, coming out, sky, raw (no catches and no returns), and corner.
- At least three punts: after a safety or penalty, wet ball, and end line.

Mechanics of Coaching Placekickers

The next part of my lecture will cover placekickers. This refers to the PATs and field goals. I do not equate them with kickoffs. We are talking about a person kicking for points. Again, it starts with the Stance.

I. Stance – Balance and setting the 90 degrees are the keys.

The feet should be shoulder's width apart with a slight stagger. The feet cannot be square. How many of you have had a straight-on kicker before? The last one I had was in 1984. I loved him to death because he won two big games for me. We don't have those straight-on kickers anymore. Now we have the soccer-style kickers. They are going to have a stagger with their feet. It does not have to be elongated. They still need an erect torso. The knees are slightly bent and the shoulders are over the toes. The real bend comes in the front knee. I do not want the back leg locked out, either. We want them to keep the back heel flat on the ground and the left foot flat on the ground. The arms should hang to the side. We do not like for them to swing the arms. We do not like the kickers that have happy feet that keep moving their feet and arms.

II. Focus Point – We need some type of signal to get all three on the same page.

How many of you use some type of signal for the center to snap the ball on the PATs or field goals? Joe Paterno did it for years. I could give you our signal at UC but I would have to shoot you before we leave here tonight. Come to practice one day and watch us. We do have an indicator. The worst thing you can do to a high school kicker is not to tell him when to go. "When do I start the kick, coach?" Give him an indicator. It could be the center saying, "set." It could be the holder saying the snap count. It could be a little hand signal, or it may be something else. We want the center, holder, and kicker to all be on the same page. The kicker must see the big picture and then focus on the job.

The thing that hurts these three positions is when the coach cannot be with them. When they kick on their own in the summer, that is when bad habits are formed.

III. Approach – Maintaining an upright torso.

The first step sets the direction and he must do something with it. It should be a short step. Don't let him lift the first step and put it back down on the same spot. A lot of kickers will not use the left foot. They do not do anything with the front foot, provided they kick right-footed. That is okay. He is a natural two-step kicker. Don't change him. I tell the kicker he has the two outside rushers. I tell him I can't move him back in the cup if his operation time is bad. If it is slow, the man will block the kick from the corner.

The second step gets the tempo started. That is why I do not like bare-footed kickers. I like a kicker that has a cleat on his off foot and his kicking foot. The second step is going to get his momentum going.

The third step is the key to the ball's direction (plant). That is the step that is going to take the ball through the goal post.

The strike must be consistent and it must come with force. In the tips for specialist, you will see butt kick. It has been around a long time. We still have them do it. We have them do the one-step, the no-step kicks. But, the kick must come with force. The main point here is to be consistent. If he is not consistent, find out why his tempo is not the same.

IV. The Strike and the Finish – "Control the leg – Don't let the leg control you."

The strike must come from the waist down. We want to get the foot through the ball as quickly as we can and then get it down as quickly as we can. Once a kicker plants his non-kicking foot, and meets the football, what does he become? He becomes a straight-on kicker. That is all he is. Once they get to the strike spot, they become straight-on kickers. They do not believe it, but that is what they are.

They must contain a consistency with their width of the plant foot from the ball. They must learn to keep the weight equally distributed at all times. They must firmly stick the plant foot and control their torso. Film the plant foot. That is going to tell you what he is doing. It may be too close or too far away from the spot. He has to learn where that spot is and he must be consistent. As the plant foot becomes secured, ensure that your strike foot is pointed downward.

On contact, allow the kicking leg to fully complete its swing. Try to avoid any pivoting or lateral sliding by the plant foot. After the strike, learn to force yourself to walk through to the finish. Follow the kick.

The contact point is important. We chalk the toe to see where they are hitting the ball. That will let you know if they are hitting the ball in the sweet spot. The only two panels of the ball are the two on the bottom, and with the laces on top. You have to work like crazy with the holder to get the laces pointed up. The natural flight of the football is controlled by the laces. The more the laces are off from being straight toward the goal post, the more chances of missing the kick. Most long field goals missed are probably because the holder did not get the laces pointed toward the goal post. That is, if it is a solid kick. You kick the PAT and field goal the same way. You may back up a little more. Kick it firm with good tempo.

Kicker's Creed

- Have a balanced two-point stance with every step planned.
- Total concentration on completing a perfect kick.
- Total confidence in your ability to land kickoffs in the hit zone, and complete faith in your holder, snapper, and protection.
- Keep your eyes focused on your strike spots and a good controlled follow-through.
- Your most effective kickoffs will come in those kicks where height, distance, and accuracy are the objective; effective placement kicks will take place in situations where we are in the plus field, so we must be accountable for every kick

Kicker's Warm-Up

All kickers will start 45 minutes before every practice time with the goal of being ready to go full speed when our specialty period starts. During this time you are responsible for jogging two full laps around the field (as a group with the other specialist) and for the stretching that you need (as a group with the other specialist) before you touch a football. This warm-up phase will be done every day of practice so you can get your timing down for our pre-game procedures as well. Your warm-up with a football will consist of the following:

- Butt Kicks – Four times across the field, ensure that every rep has a heel to butt emphasis.
- Reach – Ten leg swings to ensure that you reach your highest leg elevation with foot pointed. Ensure that with every rep you maintain good body balance.
- Push Drill – Ten reps to ensure that you see how the ball should come off your foot. Ensure that with every rep you maintain good body balance.
- No Steps – Ten no-step kicks that are done within eight yards or less of the goal post.
- One Step – Eight one-step kicks that are done within 8 yards or less of the goal post.
- Full Steps – Eight full-step kicks that are also done within 8 yards or less of the goal post.
- Goal Post Kicks - Ten reps from 10 yards away with a snapper to ensure kicks are reaching their highest elevation.

Kicker's Individual Practices

As a kicker, you must make sure that the following schedule is done on a weekly basis for you to be successful:

- Stretching at least two times a day (four during two-a-days) and three days of distance running (one mile per day).
- 30 minutes of balanced pedaling at least three times per week (Monday, Wednesday, Friday).
- 30 minutes of abductor work on the field for the inner and outer thigh (two times per week).
- Two days of hurry-up kicks with an emphasis on your accuracy and distance (no timeouts).
- Two days of kicking into the sideline net.
- 20 of the following kicks on your own: PAT, +four-yard line from L. ML, MR, and R/L hash marks.
- Three days of horseshoes for at least five minutes that include the following kicking situations: normal, left and right, tackle over from the middle left and right, and from left and right hash marks.
- Two days of at least 10 kickoffs from following: M/M, M/L Deep, M/R deep, high Floridas, must onside, surprise onside (lob).
- 20 bag kickoffs, to reinforce your height and hand times.
- At least five kickoffs: after a safety or penalty, and wet balls. (FG steps)

Mechanics of Coaching Placements

My big thing with the snapper is to approach the football. Do not let them take the football from an up position and spot it on the ground. Make them approach the football every time they come up to snap the football. Make it realistic for them. It all starts with the feel. This is what we work on.

I. Stance – Weight needs to be equally distributed.

The feet should be wider than your shoulders and squared up to the punter. The heels are slightly tilted inward and the knees turned outward. It is not an easy position to play the way we coach it. I want the center to be able to squat, and then hold it. They must get the knees out. They have to force the knees out.

II. Hands and Ball Positions – Hands should be firm and secure.

The ball should be in front of your nose and the grip hand should be able to control the ball. (Work the laces to the ground.) The guide hand should have a light touch on the ball. (Don't bear it!) You can use the weighted ball to develop the strength needed to snap. Use the medicine ball if you do not have a weighted ball. We do not want the ball extended too far out in front. I do not want the ball turned up on the point. I want the ball flat. I want the ball pointed toward the holder or the holder's hip. If they get it up on the point, the next thing they do is to develop the forward hitch. Hold the ball flat. The thumbs should be up. They need to shoot the thumbs through on the snap.

III. Focus Point – You need some type of signal to get all three players on the same page.

You must see the big picture and then *focus* on the *job*. Go on the indicator.

IV. Pull and Release

As you snap the ball, start to rotate your hands to create a natural spiral that is caused by the rotation of your hands. Reach up and through your legs and allow full extension of the arms. As you release the ball allow momentum to pull you backward.

I want to talk about the holder. Let me talk about the laces. The same things apply for a holder on a field goal. I thought everyone snapped the ball with the hands on the laces. I had a kid at Tulane that did not put his hand on the laces to snap. It taught me something. He got the ball to the holder with the laces perfect every time. I left him alone. Coach Bryant said it best: "Coach those that can't play; don't worry about those that can."

For years Coach Bryant practiced the field-goal snap and the punt snap as the same. He said a punt snap was a PAT snap that went through the holder's hands. I do not use the same snapper on both anymore. I like a bigger snapper on the field goal for blocking.

Snapper's Creed

- Total concentration on placing the snap where it is needed.
- Keep your eyes on the target and vary the rhythm that you use in your snapping so that the opponents will not be able to focus in on our snapping keys.
- Always approach the ball separately each time you snap in practice situations. Do not stay in one spot and merely get in a groove. You want to provide yourself with as many game-like situations as possible. Remember to always take at least 10 minutes to warm up (heavy ball if possible) and never, ever snap without pads.
- Have a balanced two-point stance with the following characteristics: The feet should be evenly positioned slightly wider than the shoulder width (no built-in staggers). Make sure the legs are spread sufficiently to allow for proper follow-through of the elbows. Work on keeping your heels slightly tilted inward to help you on forming an apex with your lower body—an example of this would be a man sitting on a horse. Your butt should always stay nearly level with the shoulders. Weight needs to be distributed evenly; balance is key.
- Have a firm two-handed grip on the ball with the following characteristics. Grip hand should grip the ball with your dominant hand in the same manner as if you were going to throw the ball (fingers on the laces). When spotting the ball, you want to have the laces facing downward and the seam opposite the laces is facing your.
- The guide hand comes next. This hand needs to have your middle finger on or close to, or near the seam of the ball as it faces you. By placing your middle finger on the ball, you have helped yourself increase the rotation and spiral of the snap. Also, at this time, on both the long and short snap, you can start to learn about cocking the wrist of your grip hand more in an effort to start having your snap arrive to the Holder or Punter with the laces up.
- Be consistent with your release and have good follow-through using the following guidelines. Ball release and follow-through is the next progression in the snapping phase. With the wrist properly cocked around the ball, you should get a spiral when released with the correct follow-through of the hands. As the ball is pulled through, rotate the palms outward with the thumbs pointing up at completion. The overhead release drill is the best way to start practicing the ball release and follow-through motion. In this drill you should spread your feet to the proper width of your stance and then grasp the ball with the correct grip placement. Bring the ball overhead. Then bring the fire arm forward and release the ball with the palms rotating outward and

the thumbs pointing down on completion. Concentrate on developing a tight spiral through proper grip, release, and follow-through. Your target should stand 10 yards away. Try to keep the ball aimed and release at the partner's belly button.

- Maintain good speed on the ball by using the following tips to aid in the hip flexion needed to get velocity on the ball. Hip flexion is where most of the velocity in the long snap comes from. It is a result of your hip and lower back flexion. To begin the motion of the snap, the hips are contracted moving the butt down and in slightly. Form this position, the hips explode backward providing the immediate impetus to the ball. (This action must be instantaneous in order to keep the rushers from timing their takeoffs.) As the hips explode backward the arms should move simultaneously to coordinate the major muscle groups of the snap. The total explosive effort of snapping should then cause the snapper to slide backward just slightly creating separation from the rushers. Our hip flexion drill will help you get a more realistic practice progression going for this. Again, as in the ball release and follow-through drill, you should spread the feet to the proper width apart and grasp the ball correctly. Bend at the ankle and knees to get yourself in position to see the catcher and while suspending the ball in the air sight your target and execute the proper release and follow-through. This drill forces the snapper to use his hip flexors and lower back muscles to propel the ball.

Snapper's Warm-Up

All snappers should start 30 minutes before every practice time with their goal of being ready to go full speed when our specialty period starts. During this time, you are responsible for jogging two full laps around the field (as a group with the other specialist) and for stretching that you need (as a group with the other specialist) before you touch a football. This warm-up phase will be done every day of practice so you can get your timing down for our pre-game procedures as well. Your warm-up with a football will consist of the following:

- 10 – 15 overhead releases with a partner from 15 yards away using the heavy ball.
- Five overhead releases with a partner from 15 yards away using the heavy ball.
- 8 –12 long snaps with a partner from 10 yards away, using the heavy ball (if only a short snapper, do it from six yards away).
- 10 – 15 positional snaps from regular depth (14 yards away if long snapper, and six yards and two feet if short snapper).

Snapper's Individual Seasonal and Off-Season Practice Schedules.

As a snapper, you must make sure that the following schedule is done on a weekly basis for you to be a successful snapper:

- Stretch at least two times a day (four during two-a-days) and three days of distance running (one mile per day).

- Squat drills at least three days a week for five minutes at a time to stress the importance of having flat heels and maintaining good balance.
- Thrust drills for 15 yards at a time to ensure the heels are being shot backwards. This is for you to have the lower body follow-through needed to help the ball have good velocity and to create the needed separation between you and the defenders. (Drills should be done on a line or hash mark at least eight times per practice day.)
- Hand slaps done to ensure the feel of getting your hands through for good follow-through. Do at least eight sets of three per practice day.
- Stadium steps run two days a week to help promote the ability to get your knees up.
- Heavy ball to help in the development of your upper body strength and the reinforcement of your follow-through. You should always use the heavy ball in your warm-up phase. On those days when you do not wear shoulder pads, you should only snap the heavy ball. *Never do more than 10 at a time. Start out seven yards from the catcher and work back.*

Also responsible for following specialized snaps per week:
- Wet Balls – Only if weather conditions warrant.
- Tight Punt – We consider any snap from five-yard line going into the end zone to be a tight punt snap.
- Flank Punt – Snaps that are 10 yards away.
- Quarterback Exchange – In case we use the freeze play.
- Man Over Me – Snaps that occur when the center has a man over the ball.
- Non-Rhythmic – Snaps that destroy our tendencies.
- Snapping – Working with the punters, kickers, and holders based on their schedules.

Holder's Creed

All holders should start 15 minutes before every practice time with their goal of being ready to go full speed when our specialty period starts. During this time, you are responsible for jogging two full laps around the field (as a group with the other specialist) and for the stretching that you need (as a group with the other specialist) before you touch a football. This warm-up phase will be done every day of practice so you can get your timing down for our pre-game procedures as well.

Holder's Warm-Up

- Three Sets of Finger Push-ups.
- 15 up-to-spot practice holds on air (using your finger key).

- 15-20 holds with Kicker without Snapper.
- 10-15 holds - Kicker and Snapper before Specialties start.

Holder's Individual Practice Schedule

As a holder, you must make sure that the following schedule is done on a weekly basis for you to be a successful holder:

- Catch work vs. high snaps, low snaps, inside snaps, outside snaps, and wet ball.
- Fire passes, left and right.
- Shuffle pass work going left and right.
- Blocking work for snaps that get into the kicker's hands
- Coverage work from middle, left, and right.

The opt time is very big for us. We want the snap back to the punter in 0.75. The total opt time is 2.0. You have to develop a tempo. We use a lot of naked rushes with our field-goal people and our punter. If the snap and the hold are there you should get the kick off against the rush.

We do not tilt the ball on the hold. We want it straight up with the laces pointing toward the goal post.

Men, I am glad you came tonight. Most of the time when you start talking about the kicking game at a clinic, a lot of coaches get up and leave. Did we have a good time? Good! I enjoyed it. Thank you, it has been my pleasure.

10

Special Teams Organization

Rick Jones
Greenwood High School (Arkansas)
2005

Thank you. I am happy to be here. Today, I am going to talk about special teams organization and preparation.

After 25 years of coaching, I felt that I did not really understand punt protection. As a result, I decided that every off-season I would do something to improve myself as a coach. Three years ago, I decided that I needed to learn more about special teams.

As a result of that decision, I began to ask college coaches who they thought was the best special teams coordinator in America for me to visit, to learn about that particular part of the game. Eventually, the name I got was Joe Robinson, who was then at Houston. He is now at Arizona. He is creative and a great resource. I visited with him at Houston for four or five hours and learned a lot.

At our school, I am the head coach, and I prepare the practice schedule. If you looked at it, you might think that we devote too much time to special teams, but that is the first thing you have to decide. How much time will be devoted to special teams practice? It can make a lot of difference.

Then, you have to decide how multiple you want to be. You start by writing down all the special team situations that you think you need to cover. We look at the situations that relate to special teams. Every so often, we will cover each of these situations in the kicking game. In no particular order, the following is a list of the looks that we cover with special teams.

SPECIAL TEAMS CHECKLIST

Punt:

- Regular punt (spread): We teach man, zone, and a combination
- Right or left over: The wings go to the wideside of the field
- Rugby punt: Run right or left and punt
- Tight punt: Bring the bullets in tight
- Blue punt: Hurry up (12-second punt, zone protection)
- Brown punt: Line up with backs to the line of scrimmage and quick punt (zone)
- Gator punt: Trips to the wideside. (We motion the wingback on punts.) We can abort with a "black call."
- Gold punt: Fake with motion
- Purple punt: "Freeze"

Punt Block:

- Ralph/Larry: Florida State 8-man front (four-man rush—two play man-to-man, two hold up); return away from the block
- Gus: Hold up 8-man front (two outside rushers, six hold up); middle return
- Block of the week: Named after the opposing coach; game plan zone; stretch block man; rip and run or twist, overload
- Block 10: Send ten after the block
- Rizzo: Double the bullet to the return side
- Double Rizzo: Double both the bullets
- "Georgia": Butts down, find the ball
- Punt safe: Punt safe, run it

Kickoff Return:

- Conversion right and left: Kick 1; double 2 and 3; Pin 4, 5, 6, and 7
- Wedge right and left:
- Sky alert, sky:
- Hands team: 5-5-1; 5-4-2; 6-4-1

Kickoffs:

- Left and Right Deep: Trap Kick
- Sky right and left: Lob the kick to the 20/25 numbers

- Squip
- Rose
- Set onside
- Surprise onside
- Stack (versus conversion teams)

PAT and Field Goals:

- Green, green
- Pink
- Blue check
- Red

PAT and Field-Goal Block:

- PAT block
- Field-goal block
- Field goal safe

The "pooch punt" is a good example of something that I had not done before. In practice, we put the ball on the 35-yard line and practice pooch punting from the left hash and from the right hash. In addition, we actually practice downing the punt. As a team, we really down punts well, because we specifically practice it.

Tight-punt situations are another example. We are a spread-punt team, which means we have two gunners, two wings, and one upback. In some situations, however, we have to go to tight punt.

We haven't punted on third down that I can remember, but we practice bad-snap situations on third down as well as fourth down, from tight punt, and cover all the possible situations.

We work on blocked punt situations, and we cover when and when not to touch the ball. If the punting team touches the ball after it is partially blocked, is that a "first-touch" situation in which the receiving team gets a "free opportunity" to advance the ball? If the ball does not go past the line of scrimmage, the receiving team should try to "scoop and score," but if it goes past the line, there should be a "peter" call, and the receiving team should avoid any touching.

Other situations that we practice include punting versus the 11-man block, clock punt, quick kick, fakes, and Packard/Panther situations in which we line up in short punt and go for it unless you line up correctly as a defense. You should also practice taking a safety, delay of game situations, uncovered gunner on a spread punt, and punting out of bounds.

Do you know how to teach a punter to punt out of bounds? Do you just tell him to pick out a spot and punt it over there? Well, if you want to punt to the right sideline, you take one step to the left, pick an imaginary spot 30-to-35 yards from the line of scrimmage on the sideline, take the snap, and aim directly toward that spot.

We take a helmet bonnet and place it 35 yards down the sideline. We always do it to the near sideline. We always practice out of bounds punts to both the right sideline and the left sideline. If punting out of bounds to the left, our punter takes one step to the right, takes the snap, and then steps right through it. While we do not like to punt out of bounds, we can do it if we have to.

Defenders who try to draw the punt team offside are "jumpers," and you must prepare for them. You should always cover that scenario when working on the punt team.

You should always prepare for stacks and twists in your punt protection, as well as for "floaters." Floaters are defenders who jump in and out, moving inside and then outside. You can count them in your normal count, or you can check to zone-punt protection. We prefer to sprint onto the field, line up quickly, and punt it away before the defense gets organized. That set of circumstances is what we call a "blue punt," and we use zone protection on it.

If you are a spread-punt team, then you must prepare for "uncovered- gunner" situations. The punter and gunner work together on this. If they "read uncovered," then the punter throws the ball out to the gunner. We have a signal from the sideline to tell them if the "uncovered" read is on. If not, we go ahead and punt the ball, whether uncovered or not. Since there is a risk involved in throwing the ball, we prefer to control that situation from the sidelines.

There are several other situations in the punting game that you should regularly cover, such as downing a rolling a punt near the end zone.

I would now like to briefly touch on the punt block. Any time we call for a punt block, we always have four players designated for coverage, who always cover the eligible receivers on the opponent's punt team. We set it up by design, so that against any punt formation, with any shift or motion, we can cover the opponent's eligible receivers.

In everything we do in special teams, we number each position from 1 through 11. Numbers 2 and 9 in the punt block are responsible for the inside receivers, while numbers 1 and 10 are responsible for the outside receiver to their respective sides. If we see trips, then we just move them over. If we see motion, we cover it in a similar way. That is our base.

"Georgia" is what we call if we see something unusual or crazy. This call is simply an alert that tells our players to get into a hitting position and find the football. This approach has helped us to prepare for any fakes the punting team might use.

Other punt-block situations that should be addressed include receiving the "bunt," "peter," and a "live ball touched by the kicking team," which I've already discussed. In a "bunt" situation, we normally place our return man on the 10-yard line. However, on the new field turf, we put him on the eight-yard line, because we have found that that surface tends to deaden the "bunted" punt.

When we prepare our scouting report on the opponent's punter, we want to know what we call the "point"—the point where the punter's foot hits the ball. Regardless of how deep the punter lines up, he should let the ball go somewhere around nine or 10 yards from the line of scrimmage, in order to fit with the protection.

When we scout, we determine the opponent punter's "point." Then, when we practice punt block, we set a bonnet on the point, so our punt blockers know the correct angle to take to block the punt that week.

We are also concerned with how to avoid "roughing." We do not teach the "lay out." We say, "1-2-3, take the ground that belongs to me." In this regard, it refers to the fact that we get into a sprinter's stance, explode, 1-2-3, and take the ground that belongs to me. We then say, "4 and 5, rip, and drive." We then swim, rip, or round the horn, depending upon the player's position. Then we say, "6 and 7, going to heaven," which is a reminder to go to the "spot."

As stated previously, we do not lay out. We try to make a "V" with our hands and put the "V" on the ball. We actually try to take the ball off the punter's foot. If he is a right-footed punter, we tell our players, especially our inside guys, to fade to the left, which helps them avoid roughing the punter. We never leave our feet. If the punter is left footed, we fade to the right.

Our inside block guys are rippers, and our outside guys practice running both "hoops" and the "swim technique." We have also started teaching all of our block guys a one-handed block technique, whether they are rippers or swimmers.

We also cover the rush of the "punter in the end zone," when he cannot take his full depth, and his "point" is closer to the line of scrimmage.

As almost everyone does, we make the standard "punt safe" call if we suspect a fake punt. As almost no one does, we can also call "fair catch/free kick." By rule, the receiving team may elect to take a free kick after a fair catch, and if it clears the goal post, it counts three points, just as a regular field goal. We've done that once in my entire career.

With regard to kickoffs, we cover the squib kick, short and free kick alignment, after safety, surprise onside, set onside, and rough onside. We teach the difference between a muff and a fumble. You cannot advance a muff, but you can advance a fumble. We review fair catch, "holder needed due to wind," and all those other kickoff-related factors that should be covered with your players.

On the punter's "hit sheet," we mark where the ball landed (Figure 10-1), which includes information from our scouting tapes. Every time our opponent punted the ball, I marked where that ball went. It tells me a variety of relevant information, such as whether the punter is a natural shank punter or a hook punter, what his distance is, where the punter's "spot" is, etc. We use this information to help set up our punt returns or blocks.

We also do a hit chart for the opponent's kickoff that shows where the opponent kicks off from and where the ball lands (Figure 10-2). We can set our return based on this information. For example, when the opponent always kicks from the middle and always kicks it somewhere close to the hashes, we like to run a "conversion" return, where we have the "pin" and the "double kick-out." We hit it hard with great success. We really like that situation.

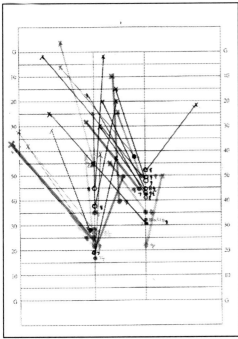

Figure 10-1. Punter's hit sheet

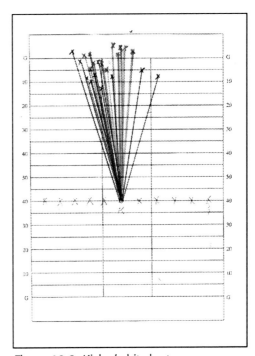

Figure 10-2. Kicker's hit chart

From the information provided by the kickoff hit chart, you can tell if a team is relatively predictable. If, for example, they always kick from the right hash, the only two things we have to prepare for are "deep" right, or "sky" left (Figure 10-3). We would then set up our return by calling "conversion left/sky right."

In other words, if the ball is kicked deep, we go ahead and run our conversion return, but if our opponent "skies" the ball, then we will change what we do on the fly, and run a short wedge. Our front five guys will attack and short wedge to the side of the kick. We want to be aggressive if we get the "sky" kick.

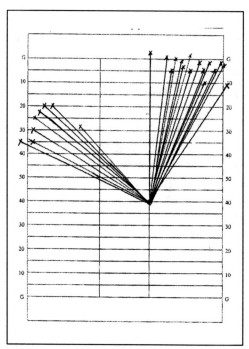

Figure 10-3. Deep or sky

A "sky" kick is anything in the air that is shorter than the 25-yard line. We will try to anticipate a "sky" kick this if we can see how the kicker puts the laces of the ball, and how they may change their alignment on the kick. If we can tell, we will go ahead and call "alert right," and we will go ahead and check "sky." This has really helped us in this phase of the kicking game.

When we scout our opponent in a punt situation, we are looking for what formations they use and whether they use man or zone protection. Using this information, we then set up a punt block, which we refer to as the B-O-W, or *Block of the Week*. We name this play after the opponent's head coach. If protection is man, we try to twist and loop, and attack gaps. If they expect their center to block a man, then we want to attack that gap. If they have a "weak link" in their protection, or if they give up a short corner, we then will attack those areas.

If they are a zone-protection team, which we do not often see, then we will do what we call a "stretch" block. This block involves lining three players up wide, who then go straight upfield ("1-2-3 the ground belongs to me; 4 and 5 rip and drive; 6 and 7 going to heaven").

When we punt, we want to know how many people our opponents are going to rush, and how they are going to rush us. Of course, that information affects our protection and our coverage plans.

We look for certain things when we scout our opponent's kicking game, for example, mismatches, how dangerous their return man is, what fakes we can use, and how they align on "punt safe." Furthermore, do the opponents use a punter or a kicker after a safety? Do they cover differently?

It should also be noted that when we call "punt safe," we also set up a block opportunity with our big men if we can find a mismatch. We look for every key we can find that will give us any small advantage.

One drill that I have found to be particularly effective for improving our special teams play is the "Buccaneer" drill that Tampa Bay uses to teach special-teams skills. In this drill, players are aligned 10 yards in front of big bags in eight lines. On command, the players sprint to the bags and swim the bags, get right back in line, come to balance, sprint 10 more yards, and attack a man holding a shield. They then drive the shield 10 yards. A coach tells the ballcarrier behind the shield to step right or step left.

We attack the shields "thumbs to nipples, elbows in, eyeballs under eyeballs, and chin under chin." This enables us to see which way the ballcarrier is going. The players then rip through to the side of the ballcarrier. It is a great special-teams drill. We try to finish every practice with this drill, and every player does it.

At this point, I would like to shift gears and talk about special teams organization and preparation. On Saturday morning, the kicking-game coach comes in, and we watch game film. Then on Sunday, I meet with the defensive coordinator at 1:10, the kicking-game coordinator at 1:30, and the rest of the staff comes in at 2 p.m.

On Monday, we meet with our players. We meet with our kicking-team players, just as we do the offensive and defensive players, and we think that is important. The kicking-game coach has a cutup film ready for his Monday meeting, so the players will have an idea of what they will see that week. We discuss changes, B-O-W, and all of the preliminary factors that need to be addressed.

Then we script everything for practice. Our normal practice time is two hours. On Monday, we spend one hour and 20 minutes on the kicking game. In addition, we meet a minimum of 10 minutes each day on the kicking game. On Tuesday, we spend 20 minutes on special teams, working on punting and punt blocks. On Wednesday, we spend another 20 minutes on special teams, working on kickoffs and kickoff returns. On Thursday, we come back and tie it all together.

11

Special Team Goals and Punt Protection

Brian Kelly
Grand Valley State University
2003

As the head coach at Grand Valley State, we were very fortunate to win the Division-II National Championship last year. All of you know there is more to winning a national championship than just offense and defense. As the head coach, offensive coordinator, and the quarterback coach, I can tell you a lot of our success is based on our ability to play great defense and play great on special teams. My talk today is not going to be only about special teams. I do not want to lose any more of you that are here tonight to the casino. I will try to keep you interested in what we are doing in our program.

An interesting side note came to me coming to the clinic. Only coaches have the ability to come to a clinic in a casino and think they are going to win. That tells me a lot about this group here tonight. Most people come to the casino resigned to the fact they are going to lose their money. I just talked to a coach before I walked into the lecture hall and he told me he was going to be the one that walked away from here with money in his pockets. Coaches are optimistic.

First, let me talk about *special teams*. It is like all other phases of the game in that you must have emphasis on special teams if you are to get that back from your players.

One of the things we want to do is to let the kids know there are areas where we can achieve certain goals on special teams. Clearly the skilled players want to be on the special teams. They want to touch the football. But the question is how do you draw the interest of the other players on the special team who do not get to touch the football? How do you keep the left tackle on the extra point team interested? We came up with an award for the special team player of the year based on a *point system*. We went out and got the largest trophy we could find. It is about three-feet high. We wanted to get the biggest and gaudiest trophy we could find. We wanted our players to see the trophy every day. The trophy cost us about $100. The bang for our bucks came from the fact that we saw our kids change their attitude on how they could win the special teams player of the year. If you are going to emphasize something you must give the players a carrot, and we did that with the trophy.

In our team room we have three distinctive goals and the goals are displayed on banners. The banners are 12-feet wide by eight-feet tall. They are prominent in our team room. When you walk into our team room it is unmistakable that we have *special team goals, offensive team goals*, and *defensive team goals*. Let me go over our special team goals.

GVSU Special Team Goals

- Win
- Better than average field position after kickoff than opponent
- Better net punt average than opponent
- Score or set up a score
- Give the offense the ball at least one time on the plus -50-yard line
- Never give the opponent the ball on our side of the 50-yard line
- Perfect execution on holds, snaps, and ball security
- Have at least one game breaker – score, block a punt, block a kick, recover an onside kick, cause a turnover, recover a turnover, down a punt inside the 10-yard line, 60 yards of field position change
- No penalties
- Win the hidden-yardage game - kickoff – kickoff return – punt - punt return

---

First is to *win*. That is our first goal. The reason we try to stay away from numbers on the net punt average is the fact there are so many obstacles that may not allow us to achieve these goals. If we get someone who kicks the ball in the end zone or there is a penalty after the kick, it can eschew the numbers relative to better kickoffs for the opponents. What we want is the average. The same thing is true with having a better punt return average than our opponents.

If you break down the film, you will find the special teams set up a lot of your scores. And a lot of the times the coaches do not even talk about that point. You do not build the creditability into your special teams. You tend to lose it in its perspective.

We want to give the ball to our offense at least one time on the plus 50-yard line. There are several ways to make this happen. It could be by a punt, pressure, or on any of our kickoffs. We want our kids to understand what we want in this respect. When we had all of the numbers as goals, such as getting the ball on the 25-yard line, or return the ball 25 yards, they do not remember those things.

On the other hand, we do not want to give our opponent the ball on our side of the ball. We want to have perfect execution on all special team plays. We want to have at least one *game breaker*. The one point here that we think is big is to down a punt inside he 10-yard line. To us, that is a game breaker. If you do the job on defense you will probably set up a score or get into a potential scoring situation.

All of these are great goals. But the one goal that we work on more than any other is the last goal: *win the hidden yardage game*. Let me categorize hidden yardage. Here we are talking about the kickoff, kickoff returns, punts, and punt returns. We use the 25-yard line on kickoff returns and 35-yards net on punts and calculate the yards. Let me give you an example. If we have a team that kicks the ball out of the end zone on us, it means we would start the ball in play from the 20-yard line. This means we are at a minus 5 yards in hidden yards against our opponents. Conversely, if we had a kickoff that we returned to the 50-yard line, we would have a plus 25 yards on the hidden yardage.

We do the same thing on punts. We use 35 as the magic number. If we had a punt that netted 50 yards, we would be plus 15 yards in the hidden yardage. If you keep track of these hidden yards, you will find they make a difference in winning and losing. We have won 26 straight games and we have won 36 out of 37 games, and hidden yardage came into play in every one of those games.

In one of our playoff games we were plus 210 in hidden yards. Obviously we have turned over the field twice. Those numbers are going to come back to you better than some of the other numbers you may throw at your players when you put up your goals. You want to make sure when the players leave the meeting that they know what hidden yardage is. If you can get your players to understand hidden yardage, you are going to win a lot of battles.

We want to put some competitive goals into the special teams, so we came up with a *point production chart*. On the chart we have team points and individual points. We feel it is important if you are on a particular team to have a chance to get points on the special teams. Our long snapper came within four points of winning the award this year. Our left guard was in the top three for the special team award. So we have team points that we give out for punt and extra point as well as individual points. If you do not do this, the skilled players will run away with the award.

	Points		
SPECIAL TEAMS PRODUCTION (TEAM POINTS)	+10	SCORE	
	+10	BLOCK A PUNT	
	+10	BLOCK A KICK	
	+10	RECOVER ONSIDE KICK	
	+10	SUCCESSFUL FAKE	
	+3	STOP A FAKE	
	+3	DOWNED PUNT INSIDE 10	
	+5	PUNT OPERATION	
	+3	FG/PAT OPERATION	
	+2	KOR OF 30+	
	+2	PUNT RETURN OF 10+	
TEAM (INDIVIDUAL POINTS)	+10	CAUSE A TURNOVER	
	+10	RECOVER A TURNOVER	
	+10	60 YRD FIELD POSITION CHANGE	
	+5	GAME WINNING FG	
	+5	INVOLVED IN 15 OR MORE PLAYS	
	+3	DE-CLEATER	
	+3	TACKLE	
	+3	KEY BLOCK ON RETURN	
	+3	EXCEPTIONAL EFFORT	
	+3	4.0 HANG TIME ON KO OR TOUCHBACK	
	+3	4.5 HANG TIME ON PUNT OR 40 YD NET W/ FAIR CATCH	
	+2	ASSISTED TACKLE	
	+1	DOING JOB EVERY PLAY ON A SPECIFIC TEAM	
	+1	VICTORY AWARD	
	-5	PENALTY	
	-5	MISSED ASSIGNMENT	
		TOTAL POINTS	

GVSU point production chart

GVSU Point Production Chart

Team Points (10)
- Score
- Block a punt
- Block a kick
- Recover an onside kick
- Successful fake

Team Points (3)
- Stop a fake
- Down a punt inside 10-yard line
- Punt operation
- Field goal/PAT operation

Team Points (2)
- Kickoff return of plus 30 yards
- Punt return of plus 10 yards

Individual Points (10)
- Cause a turnover
- Recover a turnover
- 60-yard field position change

Individual Points (5)
- Game winning field goal
- Involved in 15 or more plays

Individual Points (3)
- De-cleater
- Tackle
- Key block on return
- Exceptional effort
- 4.0 hang time on kickoff or touchback
- 4.5 hand time on punt or 40-yards net with fair catch

Individual Points (2)
- Assisted tackle

Individual Point (1)
- Doing your job on every play on a special team
- Victory award

The coach who is responsible for that particular team grades the film. There is some flexibility in the system and we do have minus points. If you get a penalty you get minus 5 points. On any missed assignment you receive minus 5 points. The kids are going to see the chart on Sunday. That is the first thing we talk about in our team meeting.

We have the chart in our team room. You can see how we chart the players each week. On the left-hand side of the chart we have all of the players listed. We grade the film and give the players the points they earn in each area. On the left side of the chart are the team points and on the right side of the chart are the individual points. Also on the right outside of the chart we have the players' total points for the last game.

I think it is important to have this information displayed in the locker room so the kids can see how they are being graded on the special teams. We are trying to build some ownership in this team. This chart will help you build your case for special teams.

We have another chart where we keep a running total of all the games. Each week the kids can see where they rate on the chart. They can come into our meeting knowing they earned a certain number of points from the last game or knowing they lost a certain number of points. We think the chart is good because the kids can see where they stand game by game.

I want to talk about the *punting game* because that is the area I coach on special teams. We have been lucky. In 14 games over the last two years we have only punted 84 times. That comes out to about three punts per game. We have not punted the ball a whole lot in the several games. We practice the punt team because we know how important this team is to our special teams. I do not believe there is any other play, other than a touchdown, that garners more momentum than a blocked punt. When a team blocks a punt, it gives them the confidence they need to win the game.

There are so many moving parts to the punting game that it requires the attention to detail that we all look for as coaches. We have the *snap, kick, protection, catch,* and the *coverage.* I take the responsibility for the punting game because I do not want to put that responsibility on an assistant coach. As the head coach I am going to put that load on my shoulders.

We run the *spread punt.* The spread punt is the easiest of the punts to teach. I have enough going on as the head coach and that was easiest for me to teach. We break our spread punt down into the following *five S's of the punt*:
- Split
- Stance
- Set
- Strike
- Sprint

If you can get those five things down, I think you can build your base for putting in the punting game. Here is more detail about the five S's:
- *Split*
  ✓ Linemen split six inches. The wing must reach and touch the hip of the tackle.
  ✓ Personal protector lines up six-yards deep behind the guard.
  ✓ Gunners are 14 yards on the line of scrimmage (check with side or line judge).

- *Stance*
  ✓ Linemen are lined up with their inside foot up. The heel-to-toe alignment is used. Their feet are shoulder-width apart. Their hands are on their thighs. We want them in a comfortable stance.

- *Set*
  - ✓ *Zone or man set* – it is a principle of taking three steps (IOI – inside, outside, inside) that keeps uniformity to the wall as well as possibly maintaining a consistent six-inch split relationship.

- *Strike*
  - ✓ When the enemy is in the strike zone don't overextend.
  - ✓ Strike the hot zone (torso of the body) with the hands (hot - hands on torso).

- *Sprint*
  - ✓ Center and gunners – go to the ball.
  - ✓ Slots – have containment.
  - ✓ Guards and tackles – stay in lanes keeping the ball on their inside shoulder.
  - ✓ Personal protector and punter are safeties. The personal protector goes to the ballside and the punter goes to the opposite side.

Our punter lines up 15-yards deep. You must have a snapper that can get the ball back to him. If we can get the snap and kick away in 1.9 seconds, I feel very good. If the kick is away in 2.0, we have done our job. We break that down on the snap at .8 and 1.1 for the kicker. It is difficult to block the kick if you can get the ball away in 2.0 seconds.

Let me give you the two rules for the center on our spread punt:
- The center blocks away from the punter or to the right or left call.
- If a man calls (3-3) he can release.

The personal protector is expected to count the defenders. He counts from our left to the right. He must declare which way he wants the center to block. Here are the rules for the personal protector on our spread punt:
- The personal protector is responsible for the overload player. The personal protector will always go away from the center on a 44 call.
- A *three* count is an automatic man.
- Only count those players whose feet are on the line of scrimmage with linemen or in a threatening position.
- The personal protector reads left to right.
- The personal protector scans if there is no man to pick up.
- The center is always counted.

The magic number is *eight men in the box*. You see all combinations of eight. We see the 4-4, 5-3, 3-5, and 6-2 look. This is an example of the call 44 [see diagram].

The personal protector calls out "44-44 left-left." We know eight is the number of possible rushers in the box. The number 44 is 4 rushers to the right and 4 to the left side. Left is the direction the center is to block on the play.

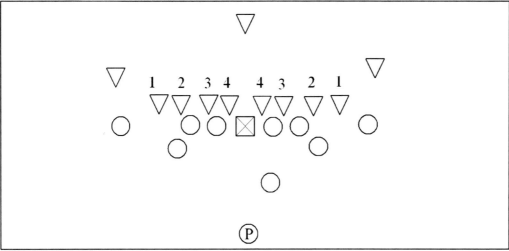

Eight-man combinations (4-4, 5-3, 3-5, 6-2 possible fake)

The center snaps the ball and then steps back to get big or wide to keep a seam from forming. Everyone still takes their zone steps and *IOI* to help the player to his inside. For example, the guards help the center, the tackles help the guards, and the slot helps the tackles. Once the wall is formed and secure, then you drive out on your primary defender. The left slot has the number one, left tackle has number two, the left guard has number three, and the center has number four to the left. The right guard has number three, the right tackle has number two, and the right slot has the number one man. The personal protector has the fourth man to the right side.

If we call *three* it is automatic man blocking. If you are in a 33 protection you can release the center. You have them outnumbered. You are able to block them man-on-man but you never change your steps. It may be conceived as man protection, but you still take the zone steps. If the defense is running a three-man rush on one side, then they are going to try to run some type of game on the overloaded side. If we get a three-man, we communicate it from the guard outside to the tackle and to the slot back. When our blockers hear three they yell twist alert. This is an example of the 5-3 look (see diagram).

Again, *eight* is the call. It is *53-53-Left-Left*. We have five defenders to our left side. We have three defenders to the right side. Left tells the center to block to the left. The center snaps the ball then steps back to get width that keeps a seam from forming. Everybody still takes a zone step (IOI) to help the player to the inside. Once the wall is formed and secure, the blockers drive out on their primary defender. The left slot has number one. The left tackle has number two. The left guard has number three. The center will always have number five in an overload situation. The personal protector has number four to the left. We only count the players who have their feet on the line of scrimmage. We do not count stacked outside linebackers.

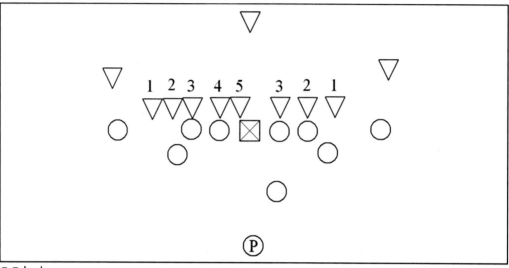

5-3 look

This is where zone and man protection come together. I have made it clear in our special teams meeting if you are on the punt team you had better get your three steps down. You handle yourself relative to the zone element. You must zone the area and stay square. You must use good three-step mechanics. Now, from there everyone is working together. If two defenders come at the blocker he is going to help inside with his hands before he works out to his primary man. The three steps help take the pressure off the man inside. After we take the three steps, then we set up to take on the primary rusher.

Most of the blockers tend to rush the block. Most of the time they want to go get their man. If they do that they leave the inside man on an island. If the slot man goes out after the number four man outside, he leaves the tackle on his own against the number three man. If the number four man comes inside, the tackle has to take on both number four and number three rushers. The tackle cannot let number three go because he has to help out inside. I try to overemphasize the zone steps before we talk about the man steps. If you talk about the man steps they'll want to one-step set and jump their man. It goes against the principles of the three-step set and keeping the shoulders square.

In any of the film I can tell the players their mistakes. "You did not get the third step down and you did not keep your shoulders square." I say this more than anything else. If they turn the shoulders they open up the voids. If they stay square and build the wall and then recognize their man they will have the protection concerns covered.

If a team puts six men on one side of the center and only two men on the other side, that is an *alert situation* for us. If we are ahead 60-0, we will bring a man over to block on the strongside after the snap. If we are not ahead 60-0, we will run the fake punt to the two-man side. We do not want to run the score up on anyone. If we do get the sixth man on one side we call *alert: Fan left – Fan left*. We fan the guard to the left side to pick up the sixth rusher.

Now let me review the coaching points and our concerns on the punt. Another situation we need to cover is when we have less than 15 yards to operate in for the punter. In the spread punt you are working off *geometry angles*. You do not have a block point from the outside because of the set you are in. In theory the punter is supposed to catch the snap and step and strike the ball at nine yards. If we take our three steps, they cannot block the punt at that block point. The rusher cannot bend it inside enough to get the block point at nine yards. If you change the distance, the punter is kicking the ball from a point farther back that allows a potentially straight- line block point. It is less than it would be if the punter was 15-yards deep.

The way we handle the punt when we are backed up on our goal line is with our *gunners*. We will bring our gunners inside to help block. We want to widen the angle out. We will call the gunners inside. They are still responsible to getting head-up on the football. We tell them to make sure they release through their man. That is all they need to do. If they will release through their man the defenders will not have enough time to get to the block point. So we bring the gunners inside if we have less than 15 yards for the punter to line up from the ball. That is how we adjust on the punt when we are backed up on our goal line.

Let me talk about the *center*. The center must block, but first he must snap the ball. This protection will not work unless we get a good snap by the center. I spend a lot of time working with the center, personal protector, and punter in discussing snap location. If we face a 53 look our steps for the punter will change a little. He will work slightly to his right with his first step. If the center pulls the snap a little to the punter's right, it is okay because we want him stepping in that direction. It is not a slide step. It is a directional step. We want the center to know where the overload is so he can make the proper snap. We get that done in drill work. We have our center snap until he hits the goalpost 25 times. We put him out by the goalpost after practice and have him work on the snaps. He snaps at the goalpost until he hits it 25 times. You can put a manager with them to help retrieve the balls. We want the center banging the post on the snaps. We realize this is a tight location but at least he has something he can aim at on the snap.

If you could pick out one thing that I could give you in regards to the long snappers, it would be this: *if they would keep their rear end down and keep the bend in their knees, they will be able to snap the ball on a good line.* This is what I work on more than anything else. If they can keep their back flat and keep the bend in their knees, they have a great chance to get the snap back successful. If their rear end is up high, I can tell them where the ball is going to go.

It is obvious that we all want *two-step punters.* Generally we get two-plus-step punters. The first step is what we call a zero step. That first step is difficult for a lot of young punters. It is hard for them to catch the ball and to take that step to get momentum at the same time. That is why I call it a zero step because most of the punters catch the ball and jab the step. So we talk about no zero step. If we can get this, we are going to have a chance to get the ball off in a good time.

Here is the problem I see in punting. Generally our punters are not scholarship players. They are not real gifted athletes. Most of the punters will start with their hands extended but they always want to bring their arms back inside. They either break their hands down and bring them inside and look at the ball and then bring them back up, or they let the ball come back into their body.

If the ball doesn't hit their hands like a receiver catching a pass with hands like shock absorbers, you are going to have a punter that takes that zero step. If you cannot get him to catch the ball and let his hands act as shock absorbers, he will take that extra step. If he does take that extra step, he is going to deliver the ball later than what you want.

You can get the punters out to kick and some of them have read the book. They look like a million bucks. They will have their arms locked out to receive the punt. You have to teach them to extend their hands so they can catch the ball and use their arms as shock absorbers. If the punter has to bring the ball inside, he is going to change the position of his feet. For most of the details on punting you need to send the punters to camp. But in terms of what you can work on, fielding the ball is one area you can help him with. Teach him to relax his hands just like the receivers do. Have him play pitch and catch with the receivers. Teach him to field the ball and to use the arms and hands as shock absorbers. If you can do that you are doing him a service to eliminate that extra step.

I want to leave you with some things you should keep your eyes on. The following are *six coaching points of concern when punting*:
- The most vulnerable area is between the wing and tackle. In 98 percent of the situations, the tackle is not sinking deep enough or quick enough.
- Drifting by linemen – they need to keep straight vertical set.
- Turning shoulders – they must keep their shoulders parallel to the line of scrimmage.

- If two defenders are on a gunner, he must watch for the inside man to become a screamer off the edge.
- Never follow a twister. We want to take a step back and look for another defender to come into the area.
- On any movement such as stemming by the defense, the personal protector will give a *right* or *left* call to communicate to the center and any possible overload.

If the defense lines up in a 44 and then shifts after we call the set, we just check the move and call *right* or *left*. We are telling the center the direction we want him to block. The communication is important when you have movement. If we are getting a lot of stemming or movement, we have a *red* call that sets our blocking. We get on the ball and everyone gets set. There is no verbal communication by the personal protector. The center snaps the ball right away and we block 44 protection. We just zone everything on the snap. We do not want to get into an *analysis paralysis*. If there is a lot of movement, we call red from the sideline. We run our punt team on the field and snap it on a quick count without any communication. We zone block and punt the football. This takes away the stemming and movement.

I would encourage you to build in an *award system* for your special teams. We call our punt team the *Bomb Squad*. We give them t-shirts with *Bomb Squad* on them. We like to build team pride. The other squads have their names for their teams. I think it is important to give an award to the player who accumulates the most points for the special team player of the year. The more gadgets you can put on the trophy the better. The players really want to win that trophy.

We feel it is important to post all of the grades on the charts. If you want special teams to take a special emphasize within your program, don't just give it lip service. I think goals and production charts will help make special teams *special*.

It is important for the players to understand the *hidden yardage*. If you can get that across to the players they will be able to understand how special teams win football games. This is especially true when the talent level is equal. When the talent level is equal, the hidden yardage is going to show itself in the games. The teams that understand this are the teams that win the close games.

Thank you for your patience. If you want to visit us at Grand Valley State, please give us a call. Thank you very much.

12

Kick Returns and Coverages

Johnny Majors
University of Pittsburgh
1993

I want to talk about the kicking game. I love the kicking game, especially when it is good. First, I want to talk about kickoff coverage. Besides the won-lost record, I like to win the kicking game and field-position aspects of the game. We kept a field-position chart, and we can tell how we are doing in each game. We feel the turnover ratio and the kicking game are very important as far as winning goes in a football game.

Let me cover some points in covering the kickoffs, and then I will show you some diagrams. Stay in your coverage lanes relative to the ball. Sprint full speed on the kickoff. Try to outrun cross blockers. If the wedge comes straight at you, you must take it on as tough as you can. You must take them on above the waist. We want to create a pile. On the sideline return, the outside pursuit must know when to take the cutoff angle. The offside end becomes a removed safety man. Do not overrun the football. Try to converge on the football if you are the wide people.

Basically, we will kick from one part of the field. We like to kick to the narrow part of the field. We like to line up and kick left to left. We have the ball close to the hash mark. We may kick right to right. We have seven men numbered on the line. We have an H1 and an H2 man. They are our hit men. We allow them to freelance. We will change them around from week to week. The other people have to cover their lanes first. We have the safety over on the farside. We want to tackle with the *inside* shoulder.

We have our players on one knee as our kicker gets the ball ready on the kickoff. As the whistle blows, we come up to a sprinter's stance. We want people who will bust their gut to get down on the kickoff. We want players who have speed and desire on the kickoff. We do not want our safety man to pull up too quickly. That creates a soft spot for the return.

If we have a kicker who is erratic or one who kicks the ball out of bounds, we will move the ball over to the center of the field on the kickoff. We will move our coverage over and cover accordingly. We have three men outside the hash marks and four men in the middle of the field. We want people in the middle with some size on them. If we kick from right to right, we will flip-flop our players to that side.

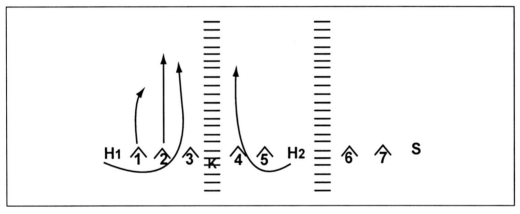

At times, we kick from right to left. When we do that, we want the ball to hang longer to give us more time to get downfield. Again, how much you can do that depends on how effective your kicker is. We work on the kickoff coverage every Monday and Thursday.

We have a squib kick that we use. We kick it down the middle on the squib kick. We change our hit men so we have four men down the middle and three to each side of the hash mark. The kicker lays the ball at an angle. We may kick a deep squib kick. We do this against a strong wind or in bad weather. This type of kick presents a problem for the people receiving the kick. We may use it when we face a great return man and we do not want to kick the ball to the deep man. We use the squib kick and kick it to the up backs. We use the same type of coverage; it is just a different kind of kick. We may use this kick after we accept the 15-yard penalty against the opponent. We may use the deep blooper-type kick after the penalty. This is where we kick the ball high and get our coverage down fast to cover the kick.

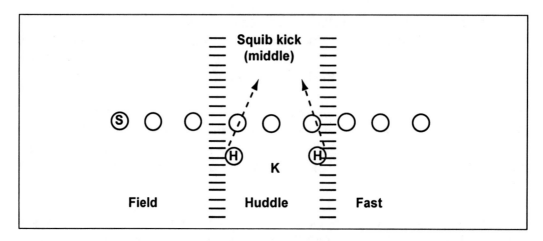

We use a kickoff coverage drill. We will use this drill as part of our conditioning. We may use this drill at the end of practice to get that conditioning in. We use four players on offense and four on defense with a ballcarrier. We will go full speed. We go for only about 10 yards. We simulate game situations. We kick the ball to the back and let him make one move and take a running lane. We work on both the blocking and the coverage on this drill. We will go against the scout team, and then we will go first against first.

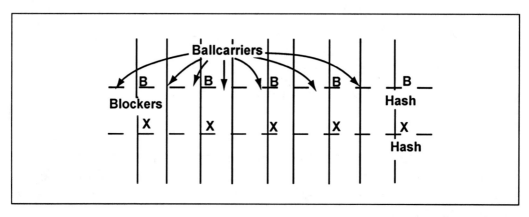

We use two types of kickoff returns. We return the kickoff to the middle and to the side, right or left. First, we have our middle return. We are in a three-deep alignment. I like this because we have a better chance to cover the squib kicks. We have a five-man front.

We number the kicking team from the outside to the inside. We do not number the kicker. We prefer to block from the inside out. If we have a choice, we take the man outside, but we do not get too cute with that. We want our ends to kick the man they are blocking outside. If we do not get there fast enough, we block them any way we can. We want the safety to handle to everything he can. He must call out the signal on all high kicks. If he is going to field the high kick, he yells, "I've got it. I've got it." If he wants the halfback to take the kick, he yells, "You take it. You take it." He calls it two times so that there is no question on the play.

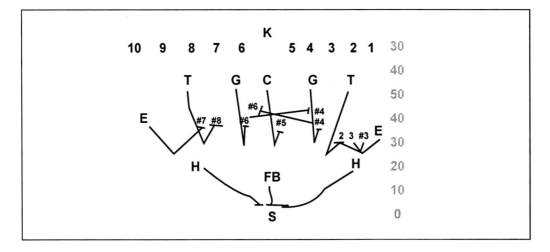

There are times when we will let the guards cross-block on the return. Also, at times we will let the center go after the kicker instead of dropping back on number 5. That is a change-up for us.

The next return is our kickoff return right. If the safety takes the ball, he starts up the middle and cuts it back to the sideline. If the halfback gets the ball, the safety will get in front of the halfback and become a blocker.

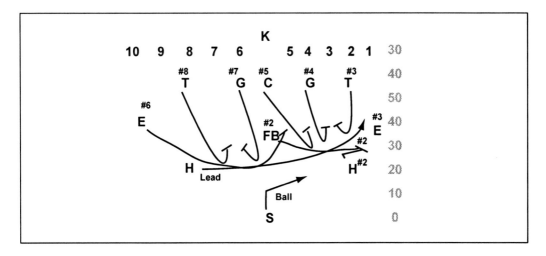

If the ball is kicked short to the opposite side of the field, we will block the best we can and have the man who takes the kick get up the field and get what he can on the play. If it is shallow, we take what we can get and go from there.

Let me move to punt protection and punt coverage. This is how we line up. We have a two-foot split across the front. We like to have speed on our coverage. We will use linebackers and tight ends on this team.

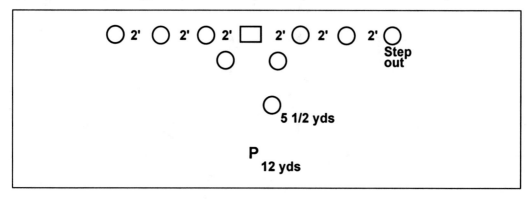

Our fullback is what we call our searchlight. He is five-and-a-half yards deep. He lines up on the side of the punting foot. Our punter is 12 yards deep. We time our punters. We want them to get the ball away in less than two seconds. At 12 yards deep, we strive for 1.9 seconds. We use a two-step kick. The center must snap the ball with some zip on it.

We line up in a two-point stance except for our upbacks. We like to have some decent size in our upbacks. This is where we get a lot of pressure. I know you can't have everything in high school ball, but we need size inside. We use linebackers, tight ends, and, at times, tackles, if they can run in those upback positions. We will allow those upbacks to use a three- or four-point stance.

We use zone blocking on the punt. It is much easier to protect than counting people at the line. Also, you get a lot more opportunities to work on the blocking and coverage with zone protection. On the snap of the ball, the front line steps out and blocks anyone in their zone. They do not move the inside foot. They do not want to leave a gap inside. We can use our hands to stop the rushers. We do not hold; we use our hands inside. If the punter is 15 yards deep, your protection does not have to be as good. You do not have to hold them up as long if the punter is deeper. This may help your coverage more. We want the searchlight to block to the side of the kicking foot. When the ball is kicked, we have both the searchlight and the punter go straight to the ball.

The snap has to be back to the punter in 0.8 seconds. The kicker has to get the punt off in 1.2 seconds. This is a total of 2.0 seconds. We also time our snappers. At 12 yards, they get it back there in 0.7 seconds. We like to get the punt off in 1.9. On the spread punt, we will take it in 2.0.

Let me show you a couple of drills. We use this drill once a week. I like drills, but you must have drills that are applicable to the game. This is how this drill works.

We put two blockers back, 10 yards apart. We put a ballcarrier 10 yards from the two blockers. Then we put two men down deep on the two men who we are sending down on punts. The X's are our punt team and the B's are the blockers. We put a defender in front of the coverage man. They try to hold them up as long as they can, legally. You can do this one or two ways. We can put two men about halfway to hold up the coverage people, or we can eliminate them. We go down and cover the punt. They go down and take on the blockers. The ballcarrier can do one of three things. He can run straight upfield or go to either side. The coverage men play the ball accordingly. We teach him to put his head across the bow. We do not take the ballcarrier to the ground. We come over and get into position to make the tackle. We want them to use the inside shoulder to get to the ball. You can use the drill when you are in shorts. You can have the coverage people tag the ballcarriers. It is a good drill to teach coverage.

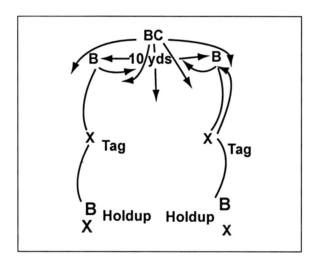

Another drill we like is our lane-coverage drill. We start in the middle of the field. We tell them to disregard the ball on the drill. We may do the drill without the ball. We want the center and the two upbacks to go for the ball. We tell them that for their starting point they are to sprint toward the goalpost. The center goes for the center post, and the upbacks go for the upright post. The guards go one yard inside the hash mark. We want them to spread out and cover the field. The tackles are three yards outside the hash mark. They are going to fan out and cover the field. They are to sprint down and get depth at first. They do not fan out initially as they go downfield. The ends go to the middle of the numbers on the field between the hash marks and sideline. This is how we teach our players to fan out. We can do it without anyone back deep to catch the punts, or we can put someone back there catching the punts. We can run it three-quarter speed, or we can run it full speed. We want to teach them the right angles to use in getting down on punts.

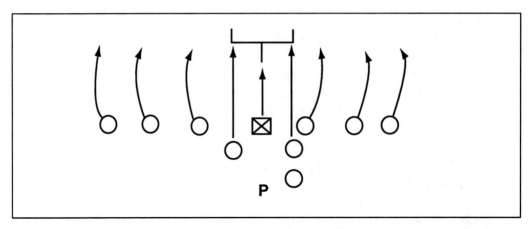

We can kick from the hash mark on the drill. We still have the center and upbacks go at the goalpost. They have to fan out as they get downfield. We do this every time we have our kicking drills.

Another way to teach the coverage is to punt across the field from the sideline. We punt across the field. We put the ball in the middle of the field on the sideline. This lets the players see how far apart they are as they come down on the coverage. Lines on the field give us a good look at our position.

13

Punt Game Protection and Cover Schemes

Matt MacPherson
Northwestern University
2009

I do not know how many of you have seen us play, but we are probably as different as you can imagine. I will go over the reasons we are a spread punt team.

First, we are a four-wide punt team. We have four gunners outside. It mirrors the philosophy of our offense, in that we are trying to spread the defense out. We are trying to create as much space as possible. We are trying to force the punt-return team to show their hand as much as possible.

We are a three-man shield with the four wide. We have a snapper and two guards on the line with the four bullets. We call them the two wings, and the personal protector. Because we use a man-blocking scheme at times, we are going to need that shield to pick up a blocker when the guys up front miss.

We are a man-protecting team. It allows us to be solid on certain players. It allows us to jump them at the line of scrimmage. Also, those protectors can get out into the coverage as well.

We do a traditional punt, which we call zero. This is where the punter kicks the ball down the middle of the field over the center's butt. We will also rugby punt out of that set as well. We can run it either way. We are doing what most teams do on the punt. We are pointing to the defense, and we are counting out loud across the line.

The next thing we do with our punting game is what we call formation variation (Figure 13-1). We move players up on the line, take them off the line, and move them around. We will give you between three and four different formations for our punts in a single game. Yet our rules on our blocking scheme stay the same. While we are giving you four different looks, we are only doing one thing with our kids. You have to practice four or five different things to get ready for us.

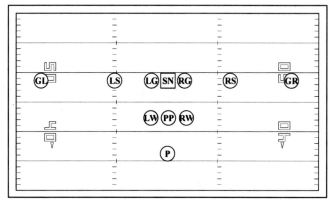

Figure 13-1. Basic spread punt formation—middle of the field

This is the reason we went to this formation. We see several advantages in using this system.

PRIDE ADVANTAGES

- Four skill players covering
- Multiple formations
- Different for teams to prepare for
- Multiple fake options
- Reduces rush looks
- Spray the ball around
- Creates chances for turnovers
- Sky situations

The fact that we can rugby punt from this formation was a big deal for us. The rugby kick, where the ball rolls on the ground, reduces the chances for returns. Two years ago, our net punt average went up 5.5 yards, and last year it went up another 4.5 yards. It gave us the ability to get the ball down the field to gain better field position.

Let me talk about some of the formation variations we have used. We started with the 2x2 look. Next, we went with the 3x1 look (Figure 13-2). We felt if we going to the rugby kick with two gunners, we could rugby kick with three gunners and that would be better. Now, we have three men on the left side as we are trying to directionally kick to our left.

We called the play lake, and it meant a 3x1 formation, kicking from the right hash to the left side of the field. Next, we went with the formation to the left hash and put the three men to the right side (Figure 13-3). Now, we could still rugby to the left side because our kicker was a left-footed kicker. You can kick the ball to either side of the field with this formation.

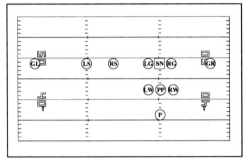

Figure 13-2. 3x1 formation, right to left   Figure 13-3. 3x1 formation, left to right

As we saw that defenses were not respecting us on the pass from the punt formation, we made a few changes to make them respect the pass. We move the right wing up on the line, and moved the right sniper to the slot, and made him eligible for a pass (Figure 13-4). We snapped the ball to the personal protector, and he threw the bubble screen to the right sniper.

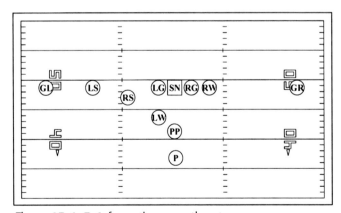

Figure 13-4. 3x1 formation pass threat

To change up the coverage, we came up with a new way to cover the punts. We put the right sniper in motion and had him go to the ball (Figure 13-5). We had the ability to move our players around to prevent the defenders from pressing our best players on coverage.

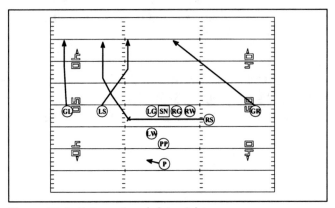

Figure 13-5. 2x2 motion, left to right

We wanted to be able to rugby kick even though we were on the left hash. We put our right wing on the line again. We took the left sniper off the ball and stack him on the right side behind the right sniper and the right gunner (Figure 13-6). Before the snap, we put the left sniper in motion. We do not have to worry about an inside defender coming off on our gunner. We move them off the line of scrimmage and make them eligible for the pass. We have shown you another formation with motion that you must defend.

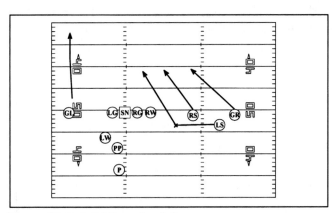

Figure 13-6. 1x3 LS motion left

One advantage I did not list is the fact we are changing the kick point when we rugby kick. In most regular-type kicks when a team punts, there is a set kick point. In this kick, we are moving the kick point three or four yards. With the rugby punt, we are changing the kick point all of the time.

Let me talk about the players we use on our punt teams. I want big and fast players on the punt teams. For the four gunners, we use our fastest and most skilled players.

If I had my choice of who I wanted on this team, I would want an aggressive wide receiver. The reason I say this is because these players work every day getting off the press and getting down the field. Some coaches like defensive backs in these positions because they are used to running people down and making the tackle. I want players who can get off the press.

The three guys up on the line with the ball line up this way. The guards have a one-foot split from the foot of the long snapper. It is not a big split at all. As they get into their stance, we try to cheat them back off the line of scrimmage as much as we can. The rule is that the helmet of the guard must break the hip of the long snapper.

Our wings are back to protect the punter. This is our three-man shield. On the three deep men, we use tight ends and fullbacks. We want the more athletic players in these positions. In addition, we want those players to be able to catch the ball on the fake punt. They all have eligible numbers.

We want them to be able to square up their base stance as much as possible. We can go out after the man, so we wanted to be as square as possible in case we did want to jump outside. We wanted at least a toe-to-instep relationship with those guards. Inside foot up, with the outside foot at least up to the instep of the other foot.

Our deep wings line up 7.5 yards deep. We did change it up during the year. The inside foot could split the stance of the guard in front of them, or they could stack on the outside foot of the guard.

Here is what we tell our players on their coverage:

- Snipers: Inside to the ball always.
- Gunners/outside squeeze players: Keep the ball two to three yards on the inside shoulder.
- Guards/bracket players: Keep the ball four to five yards to the inside shoulder.
- Long snapper: To the ball.
- Wings/contain players: Outside of widest blocker.
- Personal protector/linebacker player: Mirror at second level, inside/out to the ball.
- Punter: Goes to the area based on the game plan.

The reason we want our deep wings at 7.5 yards is because the kick point for our short-body-type punter was at nine yards. We ask the wings to make contact at seven yards. We put the one half yard in for them so they could step into the rushing defenders. We want them to step up and deliver a blow instead of receiving the blow.

The punter lines up between 13 and 15 yards. It all depends on how big he is, and where his kick point will be. For us, we lined up at 13.5 yards, with the kick point at nine yards. This is for a two-step punter.

We do place the personal protector back behind the left wing. He protects the kicking foot of the kicker on the punt. After the snap is made, he steps up into the opening and protects to the side of the kick foot of the punter. The reason for this is when we rugby punt and go to the left, we want the personal protector to stay square shoulders the entire time of the rugby punt. On the traditional punt, the personal protector steps up into the opening and protects the kick leg of the punter. It is important for the personal protector to step up into the opening and not just hop up half a step. We want him up in the opening so the punt will clear him, and so he can block the man without backing into the punter. We want him to step up into the shield.

If we were punting from the middle of the field, this is how we would line up. The gunners would line up by splitting the difference between the hash mark and the numbers on the field. The outer swingmen split the difference between the offensive guard and the outside gunner. This puts them about two yards inside the hash mark.

If we are on the left hash mark, I have him on the outside top of the numbers. Our inside men split the difference between the two gunners. We put our smart players on the outside because they have to learn the rules. The inside men just have to learn to split the difference. It goes back to the old adage, "The closer you get to the ball, the smarter you have to be."

Let me talk about multiple formation in our punting game. By the time you see our scouting report, you are going to find you have four or five different formations to prepare for. Our punt teams get two days to go over the punt information. They have two days to prepare for five or six formations. It is different for them to prepare for our punt game.

We have eight different players that can be eligible for a pass on a fake punt situation. We know we can only have six eligible players at one time. If you are a punt return coach, how much time are you going to spend on defending the play from a punt formation? You are going to spend your time on defending the fake punt instead of working on the return punt.

We punted the ball 62 times. We had two guards and a snapper in the front group to block, and we have two wings and a personal protector to block. We have six men to protect the punter. We saw a six-man defensive rush five times last year out of those 62 punts. We reduce the rush look with this formation. Most of the time, the opponents want you to kick the ball so they can get their offense on the field.

If a team brings seven on the rush, we can adjust the blocking up front and block them. Since we have shown we can block seven, we never see it now.

We can spread the ball around. We are going to rugby punt, we are going to kick it down the middle, and we are going to directional punt. We are going to give you as few chances as possible to return the punt. You do not want some of the return men in the Big Ten touching the football. We want to keep the ball out of their hands as best as possible.

Of the 62 punts last year, 25 percent were returned against us. That means we eliminated 75 percent of our punts from being returned against us.

Many times when we use the rugby punter, we tell him to hit the ground with the ball 25 yards down the field. We want the ball to hit the ground and roll. He is not trying to boom the ball down the field. However, there are certain situations where he will boom the ball down the field. At times, he is trying to get the ball to roll on the ground after he kicks it 25 to 30 yards. When he kicks toward the short guys on the return, he is kicking ball into four players. At times, the ball has hit the opposing players. Teams want to get away from the ball that is bouncing down the field.

The sky situation is what we call our "pooch" punt. We have four men going down the field to try to down the ball for us. It is a big advantage for us. This year we had 16 "sky" punts, and we downed 12 punts inside the opponent's 15-yard line. We had only one touchback, and we had three shanks of short kicks. When we call "sky," we are going to punt the ball high and straight down the middle.

The first point we must consider is the ability of the punter to rugby kick. Can he do it? It is more difficult than you think. To kick the ball while you are moving takes some hand-and-eye coordination. So we must find out if our punter can make the rugby kick and if he can control where the ball is going. The rugby punt does not stay in the air for 4.5 seconds as a regular punt may stay in the air. The rugby kick stays in the air for about 2.5 seconds. If the kicker pulls the ball back inside, where you do not have coverage, it can end up in a touchdown in a hurry. So it is important to understand if your punter has the ability to rugby kick and place the ball where you want it to go.

When the defense is bringing six rushers, we must be able to block them. The long snapper must be able to block man-to-man. Again, the question is: can he do it?

The third consideration is punting when you are back deep near your own goal line. Another way to put that for us is KTW: kick to win. All you have to do is to get the punt away and the game is pretty much over. What are you go to do if you are backed up kicking from your minus-two-yard line? Are you going to change personnel? Are you going to stay with that same punt formation?

This is how we do it. When we are backed up, we keep our same personnel, but we do change our formation somewhat. When we go KTW, we totally change our personnel groupings and totally change our punt.

Next, I want to talk about our guards' protection techniques. We are going to be in a man-blocking scheme. It allows us to be aggressive and physical with rushers

Next, I want to talk about the inside-three protection mindset. This is the inside three men. We are trying to stop a vertical charge by a head-up or by an inside rusher. We do not want the defender to be able to vertically charge up the field. We want to jump him early, and run our feet, and stop him at the line.

With an outside rusher, we want to physically redirect him off of his original course (Figure 13-7). We are trying to stop the vertical charge on the inside rushers, and we are trying to widen the vertical charge on the outside rushers.

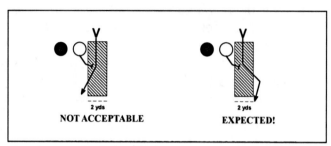

Figure 13-7. Physical redirect rusher

Their technique against an inside rusher, or a head-up, or tight outside rusher is to jump them right at the line of scrimmage. Obviously, the first thing we want to protect is our inside gap. We are going to jump them at the line of scrimmage and run our feet.

Our technique against the wide outside rush is a vertical set keeping inside relationship to rusher. We want to keep the shoulders square as long as possible. We attack inside numbers with the outside hand, then punch with the inside hand. We run our feet to physically red-direct the rusher.

We tell the blockers up front when they make a redirect block, they need to knock the rusher two yards off his course. If you let him stay in the two-yard rectangle, you have not done a good job of redirecting the rusher. We want to force the rusher outside so we can create width for the punter.

The long snapper's technique is to hold his man up at the line of scrimmage. We have him grab the jersey if he has to, but we do not want him to come free. We hold the rusher if necessary, and seldom do the officials call it.

Let me talk about the personal protector and the wing. These are the shield protection techniques. What are those three players trying to do? What is their mindset? The first thing we must teach those three men is patience. Do not chase a rusher outside. Protect the kick point. Make the rushers go to the outside. Do not let them go over the top. The most important thing they do is to protect the kick point. If their rusher is running crazy up the field, the question is: does he have a chance to get to the kick point? If he does not have a chance to get to the kick point, he does not take that man. That is the most important thing you have to teach those men.

We used to tell the wings to keep the inside foot nailed to the grass. What I wanted was for the blocker to stay at home and not chase the pass rusher outside. I will remove the part about nailing the foot to the grass the next time I cover this technique.

He is to attack the inside number with a short jab step. Force the punt rusher outside. Once again, that goes back to the point of protecting the kick point.

The personal protector is to stay square on the inside rush. He must cover the rusher up with his feet. He cannot take a side. He needs to step to contact and do not accept the blow. Against a jumper, he uses the midpoint punch and gets the hands down.

Let me get to the film. If you have questions, let me hear you. We have several examples of each formation.

When we are rugby punting and we are on the hash mark, and we are going to kick in that direction, we tell the punter the ball must be kicked outside the hash mark. If we are in the middle of the field, and we are kicking toward the hash, the ideal position is to split the difference between the hash mark and the numbers on the field. If we are on the near hash and we are rugby kicking in that direction, we tell the kicker it must be outside the numbers or out-of-bounds.

This punting game phase of our special teams has been good for us. It has eliminated a lot of the rush looks, and we have been more productive. We have eliminated a lot of good backs from getting their hands on the ball when we punt.

Thank you.

14

Kicking Game Schemes and Returns

Mark Nelson
University of Kentucky
2002

It is a pleasure and honor for me to represent the University of Kentucky and Coach Guy Morriss. I want you to know that we appreciate high school coaches. We have an open-door policy, and you are more than welcome to come down to visit with us anytime.

The thing about coaching is the fact that it is a continuous learning process. I learned something last night at the sessions and I have learned something today. I am going to tell you everything I know. I do not know a whole lot. I was fortunate enough to play in the Canadian Football League. I was later hired to coach in the NFL. Other people have helped me to learn about special teams. So I have no problems telling you what I know about special teams. If you get better, it is going to make me get better. In football, usually what we know is something we have stolen from someone else. Now what we have to do is to improve what we have taken from others. That is what I am going to try to do today.

In high school coaching, I believe you should win three games a year with the special teams. I really believe this will happen if you spend a little time working on it.

We all know you can outcoach some teams, but in most situations the other team is going to be just as good as you are. So we have to beat them on special teams. That is where the "winning edge" is in football. You have to spend a little more time on special teams to be good. You cannot just talk about the kicking game. We spend time in the classroom and we spend time on the field working on the kicking game. We involve all of our staff in some phase of the kicking. They either work with us or they get the scouting team ready to go against us.

Over the years, the kicking game has been a deciding factor in many football games. It may be the part of a football game that can create the greatest number of momentum changes. Consider these elements of special team play:
- Each play usually covers at least 40 yards of field position. Let's be realistic and say about 35 yards in high school.
- Each play normally involves a change of possession.
- Plays that do not fall into the first two categories involve direct scoring opportunities.

To me those three things are more important than the average plays. An average offensive play is 3 or 4 yards. The average defensive play gives up 3 or 4 yards. More yards gained or lost is determined in the kicking game than on the average offensive or defensive play.

Here are some special team goals that we want to obtain:
- Score a touchdown or set up 6 points.
- Create a turnover; either a blocked kick or a fumble.
- Have a net of 35 yards punting.
- Have no returns over 25 yards.
- Never start an offensive series inside our 20 yards.

The kicking game gains importance when you realize how important a role it plays in determining offensive scoring ability. We already know that the farther away an offense starts from its goal line, the more difficult it is to score. Conversely, the closer the offense starts to its goal line the easier it is to score. The following chart clearly shows this difference.

20	1 out of 30	3% chance to score
40	1 out of 8	12% chance to score
50	1 out of 5	20% chance to score
40	1 out of 3	33% chance to score
20	1 out of 2	50% chance to score
10	2 out of 3	66% chance to score

Here are some other important points to note about the kicking game.

- One out of every five plays, or about 18-24 plays per game (20%), is a kick of some kind.
- 25% of all scoring is attributed to kicking downs.
- A sizable amount of yardage is involved (40 yards).
- There is a change of possession involved.
- A vast majority of all close games are decided by kicking game plays (often in pressure-filled final moments).

I have a tape on the kicking game drills we use. I want to show the tape and let you ask questions at the end.

Next I want to talk about our kicking game schemes. To start out, I want to remind you that it takes a lot of players with a lot of pride to play on the special teams. This is what we tell our players to get them to believe in the special teams.

Champions take *pride* in making things happen positively. Our kicking game is considered an "offensive" phase of our approach to the game of football. We plan to *win* in every phase of our special teams. Our schemes are designed to keep constant pressure on our opponent. The key to success will be *consistency* and *efficiency* executed with your intensity, effort, discipline, concentration, and unequaled enthusiasm.

We have three kicking game strategies. They are the way to beat your opponent. We want to use all of them in an effort to win the kicking game.

Outwork Them

UK will give great effort, physical conditioning, and attention to detail, and practice the results we want in the game.

Outsmart Them

UK will not beat UK! We must be fundamentally sound. We must make wise use of personnel and attack our opponent's weakness.

We are not saying we are smarter than other coaches that we play. But what we mean by that is we are not going to beat ourselves. We are smart enough to know that we cannot do a lot of different things and do them well. We are more concerned about reps on what we do. We want to do a few things well. We will change a few things to get better but we are not going to add a whole lot of new things.

We worked real hard this past year. However, we did not beat anyone with the kicking game. I thought we executed well and we played with confidence. We played with intensity but we will have to turn up the dial to get better next year.

You must have a good attitude to play on the special teams. I tell you how you get a team with a good attitude. You are going to have a core of players on the team. Those players are going to be the backup linebackers, running backs, defensive ends, and defensive backs.

If we had a perfect world, this is how I would pick the players for special teams. I would pick all the starters in this manner. If you are a starter that can run, you would start on two special teams. It would be one cover team and one return team. I think it is asking too much to play on all four defensive special teams if you are a defensive starter.

I know in high school you have players that never get off the field. I am saying this is how we would select them if we were in a perfect world. We would have the linebackers on two teams, one cover and one return. If we cannot have the perfect world we are still going to have a core of players that are going to be on our special teams. We will have about seven or eight of those players involved. It could be 10 or 12 players that play on two or three teams. One or two of those players will play on all four of those teams. I want to take that unit and develop pride in that unit. When they go out on the field on one of the four special teams and they see their buddies on the field as a unit, they take pride in doing a good job. I have to do a better job of developing this unit and the pride in those individuals.

Intimidate Them

UK will *hit* you! Perfect execution! Play with confidence. Play with intensity.

By employing these strategies, we truly believe we can line up against anyone on any given day and win the kicking game.

I want to cover our schemes. I will talk about punt returns, and then I will show some cutups. I have six punts, six punt returns, six kickoffs, and six kickoff returns.

I think we were respectful in the kicking game this past year. We are going to do more next year. I know we have a lot of improvement to do.

That is the name of the game. We must improve. That means we must do a better job of coaching.

I like to involve the entire staff in the kicking game. Some teams give all the kicking game to one coach. I put our material together, but I get help from all of our coaches.

I ask for their input and use them in any way we need them. There are a lot of different ways to attack the game.

I want to start off with punt returns. First I want to talk about the philosophy behind all of this.

The most important single factor in a punt return or punt block is your belief that it will succeed. If you believe it, you will find a way to make it work. If you can't find a way, *make a way!* It is our belief that the punt return/block is our first offensive play in a series. We are gong to make at least one first down with our punt return. This in turn eliminates at least one first down the offense has to get to score. We want to eliminate all of the first downs and score on the punt return/block. *Score on special teams.* Make your effort count. To do this we must eliminate costly penalties.

General

We have three general types of plays on punt returns:
- Returns.
- Safe returns (windy or expecting a fake).
- Blocks and pressures.

We try to combine our return and pressure on the punt teams. If you just have an all-out hold-them-at-the-line-return-the-punt team, they will scout you, and they will release quick and cover the punt. We want to pressure the punter.

Communication

We will usually have a changeover in personnel when we go into a return or block punt. We must hustle onto the field and get the call to those not coming off the field. We will designate individuals going on the field to get the call to our players remaining on the field. We will use key words or signals to communicate our calls. Many teams will not huddle when punting the ball, so it is important to get the call in and get lined up as quickly as possible.

We feel it is very important to catch the football on the punts. If you cannot catch the ball with one back deep, put two backs deep to make sure you catch the ball. In certain situations, we will put two backs deep to catch the punt.

I want to cover a few things before I get to the schemes. First I want to talk about assignments. In order for us to be successful on our punt return team, we must all know and carry out our assignments. Again, we have some goals that we want to achieve related to our assignments.

- On all returns, catch the ball first so we can have great field position.
- No turnovers.
- No penalties.
- Do not give up a fake punt. We must be alert.
- We want to average at least first down on every return.
- Have a momentum changer each game. Examples of momentum changers are: blocked kick, great return that crosses into the opponent's territory.
- No blown assignments. We want execution.

Here are the keys to blocking a punt:
- Get a great get-off. React to the snap and not the sound. Do not be offside.
- The landmark for blocking a punt is five yards in front of the punter to the punter's foot. It is not at the punter.
- Never leave your feet to block the punt. Catch the punt with your hands. See the ball hit your hand. Aim for the sweet spot.
- A blocked punt can be advanced. We want to scoop it up and score.
- Partially blocked punts that cross the LOS belong to us. Make a "Peter" call and get away from the ball. Peter is the safe call to get away from the punt.
- Believe you will block the punt. We call the block for a reason. *Make it happen.*

We believe there are several keys to a good punt return.
- No turnovers. The return men must handle the punt clean.
- No penalties—block high and in front of the man.
- We want a great get-off. Key the ball and react to the snap.
- We want great hold-up at the line of scrimmage.
- We must get to the wall or get the blocks.

Here are our alignments. First is against the spread punt. We are in outside shades. We want to create leverage for our rushers. We want to force the punt team to get depth to block us. We want to be wide enough to stretch the wide punt-coverage people. If the punt team breaks formation, we are going to lock up man-to-man with them. Our outside rushers are defensive backs, and we just play them man-to-man. We have one man off the ball, and his eyes are scanning.

If the punt team lines up in a tight punt, we drop the number 1 rushers on the outside back in the linebacker position between our 2 and 3 rushers. We do not want to change a lot on this formation.

If the punt team is in an open formation with two slots, we move our two outside defenders outside to cover them.

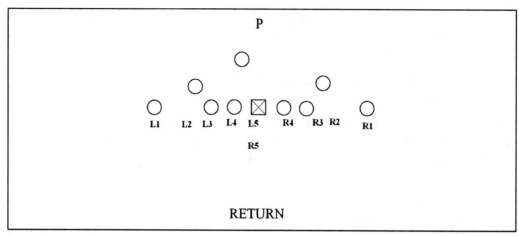

Spread punt rush

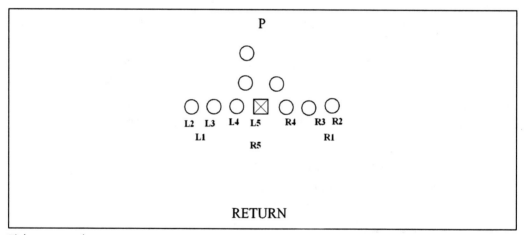

Tight punt rush

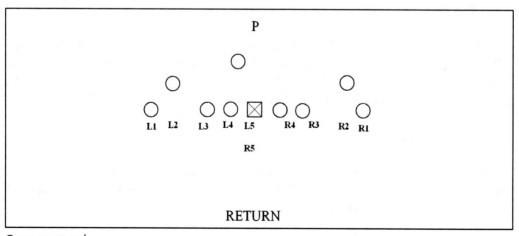

Open punt rush

We use three punt returns. First is Jesse James left.

L1 - Align inside shoulder of the bullet. Bump and run. Do not allow the bullet to get inside.

L2 - Align outside of wing. Key the snap. Burst upfield. Attack wing and force him away from the return. Bump and run downfield.

L3 - Align inside shoulder of wing. Key the snap. Burst upfield and attack the tackle and force him away from the return. Bump and run downfield.

L4 - Align inside shoulder of tackle. Key the snap. Burst upfield and attack the guard and force him away from the return. Bump and run downfield.

L5 - Align head-up on center. Key the snap. Burst upfield opposite the call side to the block point. Block the punt. If you do not block the punt, get to the wall.

R5 - Alignment on movement. Key the snap. Check for the fake on the wing opposite the call side. Make sure the ball is punted. Sprint back and get the return man to the wall.

R4 - Align inside shoulder of tackle. Key the snap. Burst upfield 3 to 4 yards, then to block point. Block the punt. If you do not block the punt, get to the wall.

R3 - Align inside shoulder of the wing. Key the snap. Burst upfield 3 to 4 yards, then to block point. Block the punt. If you do not block the punt, get to the wall.

R2 - Align outside wing. Key the snap. Burst upfield 3 to 4 yards, then to block point. Block the punt. If you do not block the punt get to the wall.

R1 - Align inside shoulder of bullet. Bump and run with him. Do not allow the bullet inside.

Return man - We will have a wall set to the left. If we do not block the punt, catch the ball and get to the wall. *Score*!

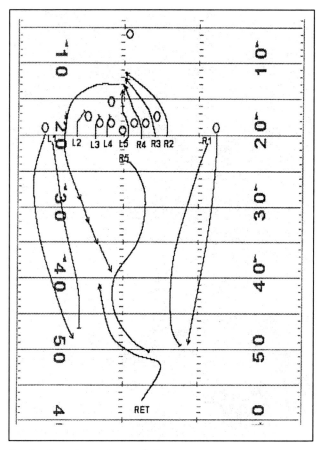

Punt return-Jesse James left

Next is the middle return. We call it Jesse James middle return.

L1 - Align inside shoulder of bullet. Bump and run against the bullet. Do not allow the bullet inside.

L2 - Align outside of the wing. Key the snap. Burst upfield 3 to 4 yards. Force the punt and then block the punter.

L3 - Align inside shoulder of wing. Key the snap. Burst upfield 3 to 4 yards. Attack the wing man. Force him away from return. Bump and run downfield.

L4 - Align inside shoulder of their tackle. Key the snap. Burst upfield 3 to 4 yards. Attack the tackle, and force him away from the return. Bump and run downfield.

L5 - Align head up on their center. Key the snap. Burst upfield to your left. Attack the guard, and force him away from the return. Bump and run downfield.

R5 - Alignment is on movement. Key the snap. Burst upfield to your right. Attack the guard, and force him away from the return. Bump and run downfield.

R4 - Align inside shoulder of tackle. Key the snap. Burst upfield 3 to 4 yards. Attack the tackle, and force him away from the return. Bump and run downfield.

R3 - Align inside shoulder of wing. Key the snap. Burst upfield 3 to 4 yards. Attack the wing, and force him away from the return. Bump and run downfield.

R2 - Align outside of wing. Key the snap. Burst upfield 2 to 3 yards. Stop and check the fake punt. Fall back inside for the fullback. Bump and run downfield.

R1 - Align inside shoulder of bullet. Bump and run against the bullet. Do not allow the bullet inside.

Punt return man - Catch the ball. You must beat the center on your own. Middle return and *score!*

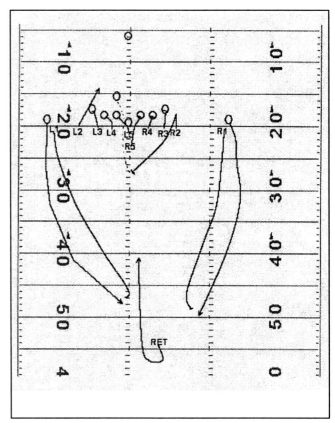

Jesse James middle

We run a return to the right side and it is just the opposite of the left return.

L1 - Align inside shoulder of bullet. Bump and run against the bullet. Do not allow the bullet inside.

L2 - Align outside of wing. Key the snap. Burst upfield 3 to 4 yards, and get to the block point. Block the punt if possible. If you do not block the punt, get to the wall.

L3 - Align inside shoulder of the wing. Key the snap. Burst upfield 3 to 4 yards, and get to the block point. Block the punt if possible. If you do not block the punt, get to the wall.

L4 - Align inside shoulder of the tackle. Key the snap. Burst upfield 3 to 4 yards to the block point. Block the punt if possible. If you do not block the punt, get to the wall.

L5 - Align head-up on the center. Key the snap. Burst upfield opposite the call side to the block point. Block the punt. If you do not block the punt, get to the wall.

R5 - Alignment is on movement. Key the snap. Check for the fake punt if you are the wing opposite the call side. Make sure the ball is punted. Sprint back and get the return man to the wall.

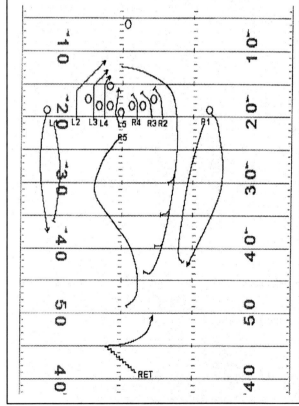

R4 - Align inside shoulder of tackle. Key the snap. Burst upfield. Attack the guard, and force him away from the return. Bump and run downfield.

R3 - Align inside shoulder of wing. Key the snap. Burst upfield. Attack the tackle, and force him away from the return. Bump and run downfield.

R2 - Align outside wing. Key the snap. Burst upfield. Attack the wing and force him away from the return.

R1 - Align inside shoulder to the bullet. Bump and run downfield. Do not allow the bullet inside.

Return man - We will have a wall set to the right. If we do not block the punt, catch the ball and get to the wall. *Score!*

Jesse James right

Let me get to the kickoff coverage. I will cover three kickoffs. Most of the time we are gong to kick from the hash mark to the short side of the field. I will show you how we cover on a deep kick to the left and to the right. Also, I will show you one of our onside kicks.

Kickoff Deep Right

L1 - Middle safety.
L2 - Hard contain - squeeze the outside in to the ball. (9 yards)
L3 - Feather contain between the L-5 and R-5.
L4 - Attack lane - squeeze outside in to the ball. (6 yards)
L5 - Attack lane - squeeze outside in to the ball. (3 yards)
K - Short-side safety.
R5 - Arrow to the ball - inside shoulder.
R4 - Feather contain between the R-3 and R-2.
R3 - Attack lane - squeeze outside in to the ball. (3 yards)
R2 - Attack lane - squeeze outside in to the ball. (6 yards)
R1 - Hard contain - squeeze outside in to the ball. (9 yards)

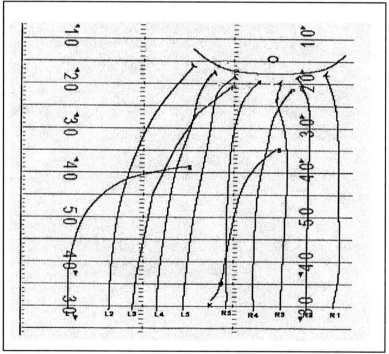

Kickoff deep right

The kickoff to the deep left is just the opposite of the kickoff right. We can always switch the players around on the alignment if we want. The L3 and L4 and R3 and R4 can change places, but L3 and R4 are always the feathers.

Kickoff Deep Left

L1 - Hard contain - squeeze outside in to the ball. (9 yards)
L2 - Attack lane - squeeze outside in to the ball. (6 yards)
L3 - Attack lane - squeeze outside in to the ball. (3 yards)
L4 - Feather contain between the L2 and L3.
L5 - Arrow to the ball - inside shoulder.
K - Short-side safety.
R5 - Attack lane - squeeze outside in to the ball. (3 yards)
R4 - Attack lane - squeeze outside in to the ball. (6 yards)
R3 - Feather contain between R5 and the L5.
R2 - Hard contain - squeeze outside in to the ball. (9 yards)
R1 - Middle safety.

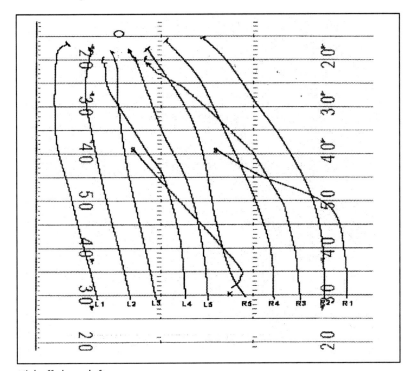

Kickoff deep left

I want to show you one onside kick. We line up the same way. We call it surprise onside kick right.

L1 - Middle safety - cross the 35-yard line, and then sprint back to the deep middle.
L2 - Hard contain - squeeze outside in to the ball.
L3 - Feather contain between the L4 and the R5.
L4 - Attack the lane - squeeze outside in to the ball.
L5 - Feather contain between the R4 and R3.

K - Short-side safety.
R5 - Attack lane - squeeze outside in to the ball.
R4 - Arrow lane to the ball.
R3 - Arrow lane to the ball.
R2 - Attack lane - squeeze outside in to the ball.
R1 - Attack lane - squeeze outside in to the ball.

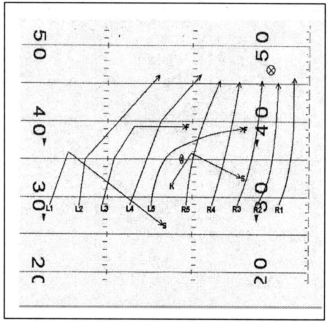

Surprise onside kick right

Next I want to show you a kickoff return to the right and one to the left. The first return is our kickoff return-23 trap left. First I will cover the assignments for each man.

Center - Locate the kickoff landmark. Line up on the opponent's 47-yard line, and offset the ball. On the kick, drop a full sprint to around the 30-yard line, depending on depth of the kick. Your man is the L5. Acquire a good angle, and block him inside.

Left guard - Locate the hash mark as your landmark. Adjust to the center's offset call. Line up on the opponent's 47-yard line. On the kick, drop at full-sprint speed to around the 30-yard line, depending on depth of the kick. Your man is the L4. Acquire a good angle, and block him inside.

Left tackle - Split the difference between the guard and the sideline on the opponent's 47-yard line. Exact position will depend on the offset of the center. On the kick, drop at full-sprint speed to around the 35-yard line. Attack the L3, blocking him inside. (Double-team the L3 with the left guard.)

Right guard - Locate the hash mark as your landmark. Adjust to the center's offset call. Align on the opponent's 47-yard line. On the kick, drop at full speed to around the 30-yard line, depending on the depth of kick. Get inside-out leverage on R5, and block him outside.

Right tackle - Split the difference between guard and sideline on opponent's 47-yard line. Exact position will depend upon the offset of the center. On the kick, drop at full-sprint speed to around the 30-yard line depending on the depth of the kick. Get inside-out leverage on R4 and block him out. Be prepared for R4 and the R3 cross. If this happens block the inside cover man.

Left end - Line up on the 35-yard line splitting the difference between the hash and the sideline. On the kick, drop and move to an outside position on L3. Double-team him with the left tackle.

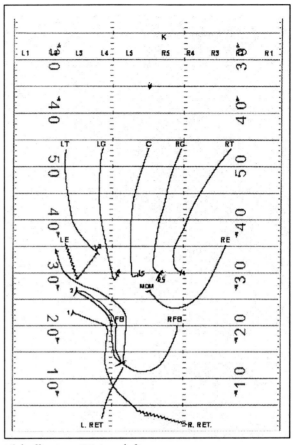

Kickoff return-23 trap left

Right end - Line up on the 35-yard line splitting the difference between the hash and the sideline. On the kick, drop and move to an inside-out leverage position on MDM, and block him out.

Left and right fullbacks - Line up inside the hash on the 20-yard line. On the kick, drop together to a distance of 12 yards in front of the return man that is catching the ball. Listen for the "go" call. Start forward toward the middle of the field before breaking to your left. Double-team L2 blocking him inside out.

Left and right return men - Line up on the goal line 4 yards outside the hash mark. Return man catching the ball calls out "ME, Me, me." Catch the ball and look it in and secure the ball. Start for the middle of the field initially, and then break hard for the alley between L2 and L3. Always find the crease going full speed. The return man not catching the ball calls out "YOU, You, you." He is to be 5 yards in front and to the return side of the return man. Make sure the ball is caught before you give the "go" call to the fullbacks. Start for the middle initially and then break hard looking to block L1 inside out.

Here is a coaching point for the man catching the ball. We want him to catch the ball on the run moving forward.

Here is the same play to the right side. It is "kickoff return - 23 trap right" to us.

Center - Same alignment; check for offset. Sprint back when the ball is kicked, and get outside-in leverage on R5 and block him inside.

Left guard - Same alignment; listen for the offset call. Sprint back when the ball is kicked and get inside-outside leverage on L5 and block him outside.
Left tackle - Same alignment; listen for the offset call. Sprint back when the ball is kicked, and get inside-outside leverage on L4 and block him outside.

Right guard - Same alignment; listen for the offset call. Sprint back when the ball is kicked, and get outside-in leverage on R4 and block him inside.

Right tackle - Same alignment; listen for the offset call. Sprint back when the ball is kicked, and get outside-in leverage on R3 and block him inside. You have a double-team block with the right end.

Left end - It is the same alignment as on the left return. On the kick, drop back and move to get inside-out leverage on MDM. Block them outside.

Right end - It is the same alignment as on the left return. On the kick, drop back and keep outside-in leverage on R3, and block him inside. You must double-team with the right tackle creating a crease in the gap between R2 and R3.

Left and right fullbacks - It is the same alignment as on the left return. On the kick, drop back 12 yards in front on the return man catching the ball. Listen for the "go" call. Start toward the middle of the field before breaking to your right. You are to double-team R2 blocking him inside.

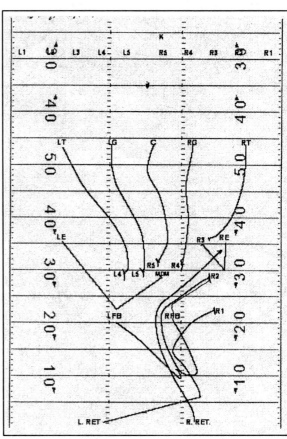

Kickoff return-23 trap right

Left and right return men - It is the same alignment as on the left return. Line up on the goal line 4 yards outside the hash mark. Return man catching the ball calls out "ME, Me, me." Catch the ball, and look it in and secure the ball. Start for the middle of the field initially, and then break hard for the alley between R2 and R3. Always find the crease going full speed. The return man not catching the ball calls out "YOU, You, you." He is to be 5 yards in front and to the return side of the return man. Make sure the ball is caught before you give the "go" call to the fullbacks. Start for the middle initially and then break hard looking to block R1 inside out.

We pick the best players the kicking team has, and we are going to double them. We do not want to ask one of our players to go 1-on-1 against their best players. We are going to give them some help. We will let the far outside people go and double in the middle. We tell them to double the MDM (most dangerous man).

We tell the deep man not returning the ball that he becomes a blocker when he is not returning the ball. We have had some good blocks out of our deep backs on the kickoff returns.

One thing we must do a better job on with the kickoff is timing. If the blockers have to hold their block longer than two seconds, our timing is not good. That is an area where we can improve on. That is something we can work on in the spring.

What we do on special teams is not a lot of different things. What we try to do is to give them enough for them to be successful. We ask our players to do things they can do. We want to help them at the point of attack. If we can do that, I think we have a chance to be successful. This past year we were not good in the kicking game, but we did not hurt ourselves. Now we must take the big step and start winning games with the special teams. We want to block punts, have a punt return for a touchdown, and run a kickoff back for a touchdown. The thing we want to do is to avoid putting our defense back out on the field.

You are welcome to come to see us practice. If we can help you, feel free to contact us or come to visit us. Thank you.

15

Special Emphasis on Special Teams

Steve Ortmayer
University of Kentucky
2005

Thank you very much. It is a pleasure to be here representing the University of Kentucky. My topic tonight is a very specific one. I think it will be interesting to special teams coaches, head coaches, and those who aspire to be head coaches.

Talking about the special teams is a boring topic. I coached special teams in the NFL for 18 years. The beginning of special teams coordinators in the NFL was in 1976, when George Allen was the head coach of the Washington Redskins. I will relay some things to you that reflect what I believe about football in the NFL. That will not be entirely *apropos* to you. However, if you translate what I say, it will be.

I am now coaching special teams in the SEC, which is different from coaching in the NFL to an extent. Coaching the kicking game in high school is different from the college level. Some of the things I consider important, I will relay to you. I think you can get some basic principles from my lecture.

In the game of football, one of every five plays is a kicking game play. I consider the kicking game to have seven levels of special team play. On each play in the kicking game, one or more of these three events take place:

- A direct attempt to put points on the board
- A change of ball possession
- A sizable amount of yardage is involved (40 yards of more)

If you are a good team, the ratio is about one in every six plays is a kicking game play. If you are not a good team, it is one in every four plays. The kicking game plays have the potential for big momentum swings both positively and negatively. Kicking game plays weight heavy as they affect the tide and the outcome of the game.

Many of the big "breaks" in a game occur on a kicking play. Breaks usually happen when a team or a player is unprepared for a situation. When a team is prepared, the chance to capitalize upon a break presents itself at the most opportune time. The kicking game breaks mark the difference in winning and losing.

In my opinion, the kicking game is relative to about 35 percent of the game. If we talk about the kicking game being one in five plays, that relates to 20 percent of the game. The momentum plays and the weight of the momentum in the kicking game is probably as important as the 1/3 offensive and 1/3 defensive plays in a game.

ELEMENTS OF A SUCCESSFUL KICKING GAME

Elimination of Mistakes

Most mistakes made in the kicking game are caused by a lack of belief in its importance. Lack of belief leads to a lack of concentration and from that follows poor protection, poor coverage, and slip-shod application of the complex kicking game rules. *Belief in the importance of the kicking game is the key to elimination of mistakes.*

Intensity

Although intensity is essential in all areas of the kicking game, it is best observed in how you cover kicks. Covering kicks is one of football's great tests of courage. Intensity shows up in the return game in a team's commitment to physical play, yet never at the expense of the yellow flag.

Fundamentals

Kicking involves many precise skills. Time and distance requirements require *precise* skills and constant attention. Precision is attained only through practicing with concentration. Each special team skill can only be acquired through practicing with the speed and intensity of game conditions. There is *never* enough time to acquire all the simulation needed, so focus and intensity must prevail each time a skill is practiced.

It is difficult to practice the kicking at any level of football. It is difficult to do in the NFL because of the intensity with which the players play. It is difficult to do in college football because of NCAA restrictions on time. In high school, in my opinion, the quality of your kicker to an extent will not allow you to practice kicking effectively.

We have a kicking game philosophy that we use at the University of Kentucky. The philosophy of the Kentucky Wildcats special teams is to produce the greatest amount of field position possible on each kicking exchange. We want to use special teams as a weapon for producing this yardage as opposed to merely a unit for smoothly affecting the exchange of the ball in the kicking situation. Because the offense and defense will affect (and be affected by) the kicking teams, offensive and defensive philosophies should determine the specific philosophy of the kicking game.

The offensive kicking game philosophy is to gain the greatest field position and/or to produce the most points possible. *Elimination of penalties is vital to our success.* The defensive kicking game philosophy is to gain field position by limiting our opponent's returns. There must never be a protection breakdown. The punting team must think, "Get the ball out." They must think, "Turnover." The keys are second effort and reckless pursuit.

We consider the punt return and kickoff return to be the first play of an offensive drive. The field goal is the final play of an offensive drive. Defensively, the punt coverage team and kickoff coverage is big parts of the defensive philosophy. The field-goal block team is the third phase of the defensive kicking game.

Each of the teams represented in this room tonight has the right and an opportunity to be good in the kicking game. There is no excuse for us to walk away from each season and not have a good kicking game. The move from good to exceptional requires some things to happen. To be exceptional rather than good, you must have a punter. You need a great snapper. You need to have a good kicker. The fourth element is a classy return man. To be exceptional in the kicking game, you need those four elements in that order.

In my opinion, special teams are a way for lesser or younger players to find a role in your football team. You have to do that in the NFL, but you can do it in college and high school and be comfortable. The one element you cannot sacrifice in the kicking game is speed. You cannot play with players in the kicking game that cannot run. If they can run, they need not be the best or toughest players on your team.

You can get a player to buy into a role in the kicking game and it becomes his special area. Players who are not ready to play on offense or defense will buy into a role in the kicking game.

I want to tell you a story. Probably one of the best players I ever coached in the kicking game played for me in the pros. We do not have this kind of player east of the Mississippi River. The player was a PAC 10 player from the University of California. His name was Jeff Barnes. He was a defensive player in college but could not play defense in the NFL because he never understood what was going on. He was a great special teams player and Jim Plunkett's best friend.

I coached 14 seasons with the Oakland Raiders. In 1982, the franchise moved to Los Angeles. We still practiced in Oakland but played our games in Los Angeles. We had not moved the team at that time and flew to Los Angeles each week for our games. One night we flew back to Oakland. Upon landing in Oakland while we taxied to the terminal, one of the wings of the airplane ran into a food truck on the runway. It jolted everyone on the plane and knocked some players out of their seats. The plane got quiet and from the back of the airplane I heard Barnes say, "Man, I'm glad that didn't happen while we were in the air."

One night we were at the training facility in Oakland and had a horrible electrical storm. It hit the power lines and everything went black in the facility. All the projector and lights went out throughout the building. From the corner of the room, I heard Barnes say, "Ah man, now I am in trouble. I've got a speaking engagement at 6:00 PM and my car won't start."

Those kinds of people can play in the kicking game if they can do two things. If they can run and understand how to get their fits into the particular scheme, they can play on special teams. I am not a big statistic person, but I think we lead the nation last year in blocking kicks. We had a player that blocked seven field goals this season. His name is Lonnell Dewalt and he is a freshman. ESPN ran a poll and they selected him as special teams player of the year.

He is a good player, but is not ready to play on offense. He is a wide receiver and is truly a phenomenal athlete. If you ask him what position he plays, he will tell you he is a kick blocker. Our offensive coordinator will have trouble getting him back as a wide receiver because he thinks he is a kick blocker. That was his role and he became a phenomenal player last year. I believe things like that can happen at any level of football. It is a place for people to find a niche and improve your football team.

There are seven areas of special teams. I will try to talk about six of them if I have the time. The onside kickoff return, or better known as the "hands" team, is the seventh area. I will start with the other six teams and talk about how we put them together.

I believe you coach against what you fear. In other words, you put in offensively what you most fear defensively.

FIELD-GOAL TEAM

The first area is the field-goal team. Our goal for this team is to make every kick we take. We install the field-goal team on the first day of practice and do not change another thing in that part of the game throughout the season. We have only one meeting with the field-goal teams a year. We meet the first day and that is all for the season. From the field-goal formation, nothing ever changes.

We spot the placement of the ball at eight yards from the line of scrimmage. I think it is a mistake to spot the ball at seven yards, even in high school. Kicks are blocked inside by a ratio of ten-to-one over kick blocks from the outside. Unless a team has an exceptional sprinter coming off the outside, you will never get a kick blocked from there. That is of course, if the snap, hold, and kick takes place in 1.35 seconds. In practice, we accept 1.4 seconds. The adrenaline will bring the time down to 1.35 seconds in a game.

We tell our kicker if they are faster than 1.35 seconds, they need to slow down and not rush the kick. If the kicker kicks the ball in 1.35 seconds, the ball will cross the line of scrimmage in 2.0 seconds.

In the offensive linemen's alignment, we ask them to squeeze upon the ball as much as they can. We do not want the defenders to get a big run to the ball. We want the linemen to see the ball. That is not hard for the guards and tackles, but the ends may have a slight problem. The holder calls "set." After that command, no one can move and the center snaps the ball when he is ready.

When the center snaps the ball, the line takes a short set step and gets their cleats on the ground as quick as possible. The next thing in field-goal protection is the target. We are not a man protection team. On field goal, we are a zone protection team. The linemen never move the outside foot. Make sure the linemen *never move forward*. The defender can jerk the offensive lineman forward using his momentum and create holes inside. The eyes tell the offensive linemen to get his pad level under the defense's pad level. That is the entire game in field-goal protection. The offensive linemen get their pad level under the pad level of the defense and deflect the momentum of the defensive linemen upward.

The only way the field-goal protect team can lose is for them to try to block someone aggressively. They have to take their set step and absorb the blow coming from the defense. They can never attack or hunt a defender. They have to hang on for 2.0 seconds. If they hunt a defender, we get beat. You have to convince your offensive linemen to get their pads under the defender and stun him. However, other teams do the same thing we do and it becomes a headache for your offensive line. They will get their bells rung.

In their alignment, we want them with their hand on the ground. The center gets down first and everyone takes his alignment off his stance. We align foot-to-foot with a wider stance than on an offensive play. The guards and tackles never move their outside foot.

The offensive ends on the field-goal team never move their inside foot. He has to stay square to the line of scrimmage because the C gap is the toughest gap to secure. The wingbacks on the field-goal team align at a 45-degree angle with one foot inside the outside foot of the tight end. The tight end drop sets a half yard with the outside foot and does what we call a pivot. When he drops his outside foot, he interlocks with the inside foot of the wingback. He punches the rusher in the C gap and catches the second rusher on his hip. The wingback does a ricochet block. He hits the second rusher coming off the tight end's hip with a punch to the chest and bounces out to get a hand on the outside rusher. In both cases, the block is a disruption-type of block.

This team never changes. From August 8 to January 1, these rules never change. We have a meeting on the first day of practice and do not meet again.

In the NFL, the goal post uprights are as wide as the hash marks on the field. College goalposts are wider than pro posts. Since I came back to college football, I have learned one or two things. We play Georgia, Tennessee, and Florida every year. They have some major athletes that scare head coaches by the way they come off the corner. If you are worried about the wide field rusher on the field-goal attempt, bring the backside tackle over and go unbalanced to the wideside. Teams do not work on the short rush from the outside enough to hurt from that side.

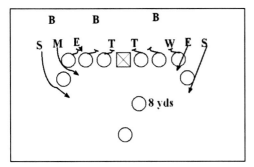

Figure 15-1. Field-goal protection

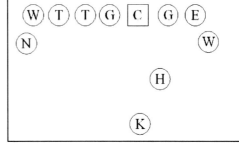

Figure 15-2. Unbalanced to wideside

All they have to do is hold for 2.0 seconds. If they do, the game is over. All we ever talk about on field goal protection is "see the ball, quick set, and pads under." These things have to happen in front of the football. In my experience, in front of the ball is where the kick block occurs. There is a very narrow space where the defense can block a kick.

If the ball is on the right hash mark, the kick comes straight over the left offensive guard's butt. The left guard and tackle must be strong in their set and not get pushed backward. To protect the outside into the wide field, we ask our players to "cheat for inches." If the guard, tackle, and end get four inches wider in their stance, we can put the outside rusher one-foot further outside in his alignment. That means he cannot block the ball unless something goes wrong. Elements for blocking the ball from the outside are time and distance. Unless the defense has a stud speedster outside, they cannot get to the ball.

FIELD-GOAL BLOCK TEAM

Our goals for the field-goal block team are to block one kick or have the kickers not make 50 percent of their kicks. To block the kick, you have to apply the same rules to protect the kick. If we try to block a kick, we want to get ou.r blocker hands in the lane where the kick travels. For the kick to be good, it has to travel in a very small lane. Every kick block is designed for a point on the field where the ball has to travel to score.

Ninety percent of teams spot their placement of the ball seven yards off the line of scrimmage. The NFL kicks from eight yards deep. They know seven yards is too close to the line of scrimmage. We do not rush gaps. Rushing gaps is too hit-and-miss. We rush over a man on the offensive line. We align four defenders in the middle of the kick formation and sprint them as hard and as fast as they can go into the offensive linemen. We want the four players who have the ability to get off on the snap and sprint through someone for two seconds. They want to block the kick with the body of the offensive linemen. In this position, you could use offensive players. They will not block any kick, but they can cause huge headaches for the offensive linemen.

We look to knock the offensive lineman one yard back from his alignment. In 2.0 seconds, the ball crosses the line of scrimmage at a height of 11 feet. If we can knock the offensive lineman one yard off the line of scrimmage, our jumpers can try to block a ball at the height of 10 feet. If we can knock the offensive lineman one-and-a-half yards off the line of scrimmage, they cannot get the kick off.

We tell our jumper to get behind the four sprinters. When the kicking team snaps the ball, the sprinters take off and get as much depth as they can over the offensive linemen. We tell Dewalt that he has two seconds to get as close to the four sprinters as he can and jump. He blocks kicks with his hands and can see the ball come off the ground. He steps into the vacuum created by the sprinters. If they get one-and-a-half yards, he can block any kick. If they get one yard, he has to get into the proper lane where the kick travels.

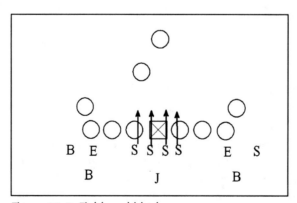

Figure 15-3. Field-goal block

We align two of the sprinters on the inside shoulders of the center and roll him out of line. You cannot hit the center in the head, but we have never been called for this type of charge on the center. The other two sprinters align over the guards and blast them. Our best sprinter is a freshman by the name of Jason Leger. He is a 6' 1" and 283-pound player. He is built low to the ground and has a dynamite take off. He is super quick and tough as a pine knot. His chief goal is to stun the 350-pound guard and drive him back two yards.

That lane changes as the position of the ball changes. The jumper has to move to get his hand position in the proper lane. That is up to the coach to get his player aligned properly on the field. There is nothing more fun than the sprinter's position. The offense line cannot strike back. They absorb the blow, while the sprinters blast them.

Teams got to the point where they did not want to kick the ball against us. Twice last year, we had teams driving deep in our territory inside the last 30 seconds needing a field goal to win the game. It happened against Tennessee and South Carolina. South Carolina was down by one point and Tennessee was down by two points. Neither team wanted to try a field against us. Most teams milk the clock down to nothing and kick the ball as time runs out. They took the chances on scoring touchdowns instead of going for the field goal. Against Tennessee we blocked two field goals and against South Carolina we blocked one.

If we cannot get penetration from the guards and tackles, the jumper cannot get the ball. Eleven feet is too high for the jumper. If we can knock the lineman off the ball, we can get them all. If we do not block the ball, it is because the ball goes through the hands or under them. That is our field-goal block.

You coach against what you fear. What I fear on a field-goal block is a field-goal team that runs a fake. We have six defenders dedicated to defending the fake. We have five players to block the kick. The remaining six players are playing containment and coverage. The only middle of the field kicks are extra points. Everything else usually comes from the hash marks or slightly out of the middle of the field.

Anyone can run a fake field goal if they know where the defense will align. Each week we change the alignment of our six remaining defenders. The only reason I bring anyone from the outside is for the opponent's scouting report. We are window dressing with our six defenders.

The field-goal block team meets every week to talk about the game plan. One reason we block so many kicks is that we identify a weak link on the opponent's team. When we get the opportunity to rush that player, we want to make good. We may only get one opportunity a game to take advantage of that player.

You have to sell your players on your scheme. The secret for the four rushing linemen is to get under the offense's pads. We teach pad under on the block team and pads under on the field goal protect team. Special teams in the NFL are 100 percent match-ups. It is a little less in college because you do not know as much about the special team players. If you can get people matched up on the individual, kicking teams you will hurt them.

Our objective for our kicker is to make every single kick he attempts on the field. We tell our kicker if he misses a kick, to miss short. At least by being short he had a chance. If he is wide, he never had a chance to make the field goal. If the kicker misses a kick, he should miss it short and blame the miss on the coaches.

We have our kickers kick to a point behind the goalpost. We never kick at the uprights. If he is more than three feet right or left of that point, we jump all over him. The kick was good, but it was not good enough. If a kicker makes it in the NFL, he has to be consistent. He has to kick from the 30-yard line, which is a 40-yard field goal, and make 17 out of 20 kicks in the middle six feet of the uprights.

In 1975, when I started coaching in the NFL, there were 26 teams in the league. There were probably 35 kickers in the world that could kick in that league. There are now 32 teams, but the number of kickers has jumped to over 100 kickers. Including this year, there have never been enough punters to outfit every team. Punters are very hard to find.

While we are on the subject, if I were in high school I would never punt the ball. I would placekick the ball. Every school in America can find a soccer player to kick the football. However, you cannot find a punter to serve that purpose. They can place the ball all over the field. I would never punt it again.

Our goal for the punt team is to net 40 yards on the punt. Our goal for our punt-return team is to net 30 yards per punt. Our kickoff coverage goals are to hold the opponent at the 20-yard line or less. Our kickoffs return goals are to return the ball to the 35-yard line.

Assuming you punt six times a game and receive six punts a game, the yardage gained is 60 yards. If you kickoff six times and return six kickoffs, the real estate gained is 90 yards. That amounts to 150 yards in the kicking game or 15 first downs. If you reach your objective in a football game, you can gain between 100 and 150 yards.

PUNT AND COVER TEAM

When the punt-coverage team comes off the field, they know that if the punt nets 40 yards or the ball ends up inside the 15-yard line, they have met their goals. There are time elements involved in the punting game.

The center strives to get the ball back in 0.7 to 0.8 seconds. The risk of getting a punt blocked goes up with each tenth of a second beyond 0.8 seconds. However, a snap that comes back in 0.9 and is accurate is better than one that comes back in 0.8 and is wide, high, or low. The punter must be able to get the ball off within 1.1 to 1.3 seconds. Any time taken beyond this margin is not sound. With the coverage personnel waiting to release with the punt, time is extremely important. They have a clock in their head that says "2.0 equals go!"

Good snappers are like money in the bank. The defense cannot block the punt if you have a good snapper. I would rather have a snapper than a kicker. It is critical.

The "elapsed time" is the combined snap and punting time. With the center getting the ball back in 0.8 and the punter getting it off in 1.2 seconds, the elapsed time will be 2.0 seconds. With our protection and our release, a 2.0 get off time is critical. The "hang time" is the time the ball is in the air. We must keep the ball in the air 4.75 seconds. A punt hanging for 4.65 can be covered and the return held to a minimum with a punt of 45 yards.

Coverage time for a punt can be calculated. Since the punt takes approximately 2.0 seconds to get off, you have approximately 7.0 seconds to cover the ball from the time of the snap. If the punter is facing a 10-man rush, he must get the ball off in 1.2 or less. He may have to use a two-step approach.

To keep the punt cover at net 40 yards, the wide cover men have to get in front of the return man immediately (Figure 15-4). That keeps the return man from catching the ball and getting the first ten yards up the field quickly. They have to make the return man run right, left, or fair catch the ball.

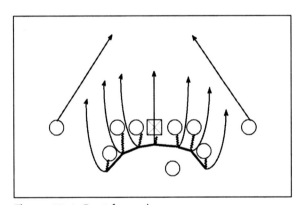

Figure 15-4. Punt formation

If you punt the ball 40 yards and the return man fair catchers the ball, that is net of 40 yards. If you punt 50 yards with not as much hang time and the punt return man brings it back 10 yards that is a net of 40 yards. However, they are not the same situations. The fair catch cannot be returned for a touchdown. The other punt can. Any time the coach gets nervous about the coverage team, kick the ball on the ground. The football is not round and has odd bounces. Make the return man make a play on the ball before he can return it. He will not make all the plays. Do not gamble with a great turn man. Kick it away from him or out of bounds.

College football has a new invention in the punting game. Some teams are using the rugby type punt. To return that ball, you have to get lucky. You could not do this in the NFL because only two players can release in coverage until the ball is kicked. I hate this kind of punt because I am not in control as a punt-return team.

PUNT-RETURN GAME

In the punt-return game, the wide coverage men have to be blocked. We have to do whatever we can to keep them from getting in front of our return man. By blocking the wide coverage men, we are buying grass in front of the return man. If you can buy 15 yards of grass in front of your return man, he will hurt people. If we have to double both the outside men, we will. That means we have five players involved with two defenders.

I will use two blockers on one man, if we run directionally. When we run a directional return, we start everything at a 45-degree angle. We must get the first 10 yards immediately. We never run laterally or backward. I also will double-team the containment man to the side of the return. Every punt coverage team has a player responsible for containment. If they lose their containment man, they are in trouble.

In the punt return game, there are six "don'ts." Don't:

- Be offsides
- Rough the punter
- Clip
- Let the ball bounce
- Let the kicker run the ball
- Field the ball inside the 10-yard line

I think the worst thing you can do in the kicking game is to put your defense back on the field. That is a psychological killer. I do not like to rush a punt on fourth and less than five yards for a first down. If you have a guy who is keyed up to block the punt and jumps offside, that gives the offense a first down.

The same rules hold for roughing the punter. Do not rush the punter in fourth and less than five yards for a first down. If two or three rushers run into one another and one bounces off and hits the punter, you put the defense back on the field.

Do not block anyone when you cannot see the numbers on the front of their jersey. That is a disciplinary thing for the return team. We do not block very much downfield. We tell our return team to find the return man so they know where the return is. They run to a point on the field where the return is coming. We hold up defenders and run to that point, trying to put our bodies between the defender and the return man. All of our returns are man-to-man blocking schemes. We do not run any wall returns.

The return man will beat the coverage coming late. What he cannot beat is the quick speed in front of him. If you let good return men start running upfield at coverage players, they will beat most of them on their own. Teach your return men to run at coverage personnel and make a move. When the return man runs away from the coverage, he puts all of them in the pursuit game. Everyone who can run will run down the return man. However, if he runs at them and freezes the defender, he can get by him.

In my opinion, this is how you should teach punt return. The punt-return team is a brutal special team. If you have a star and want to help him out with special team play, do not put him on the punt-return team. It is sheer hard work. The most important single factor in a punt return is your honest conviction that the play will succeed. Most punt returns teams play as follows.

The first time the opponent kicks, they make a reasonably good effort to return the punt. However, the kick is short or high and no return opportunity develops. This is discouraging. On succeeding punts, their effort dwindles, and they never get in position to execute a successful return. Finally, they do not even try to make a coordinated team play.

If our opponent punts the ball to us five times, we can return one for a touchdown. However, we are never sure which of the five punts it will be. If our head is in the game and our effort is there on each punt, we will make the big play on a punt return. A big punt return can turn the momentum in a game. Your players have to try as hard on the fifth punt as they do on the first one.

The punt return team knows when they come off the field that if the ball is 29 yards from where the ball was punted, they did their job. We want a net 30 yards on every opponent's punt.

KICKOFF COVERAGE

I am going to kickoff coverage. I think I can help you on your kickoff coverage. What we look to do on kickoff coverage is cut the size of the field. Your players can buy into your program and be major contributors in the kicking game if they can run. The kickoff coverage team is the team where that fact is especially true. The kickoff is 75 percent covered before we kick the ball.

We number our personnel from the inside out. Our R5 player is the last man to the right and the L5 player is the last man to the left. Teaching kickoff coverage is almost like the field-goal team. Theoretically, you do not have to practice kickoff coverage after the initial practices at the beginning of the season.

The kicker's steps into the ball will be the same on August 8 as they are on January 1. We kick the ball angled into the sidelines. We hope the ball goes to the numbers on the right or left. We go through entire season kicking the ball to one direction or the other. All we coach to the players on kickoff coverage is to time up their run to the ball.

We do not care where the players line up as they run to the ball. We want them to pick out a spot on the grass. When the kicker passes that spot, they can begin to run a hundred miles an hour and never look at the kicker again. When the kicker's foot hits the ball, the coverage man is within a half yard of the ball. The key to timing up the run is going 100 percent full sprint. If you do not do it that way, the time element changes. If they go 100 percent, they can start the same place for every kickoff and never be offsides.

That is important to the kickoff coverage because the game only amounts to the five blockers on the front line of the kickoff return team. We sell our coverage men on the idea that if they run past the front five blockers, the game is over. No rule in football is as skewed as the kickoff — kickoff return differential. The rules are written so heavily in favor of the coverage team that no kickoff should ever be returned for a touchdown.

As soon as the kicker's foot hits the ball, the coverage team finds the flight of the ball. As their eyes come back to the field, they take lanes on the football. As they cover, a blocker will come into his vision. They should know quickly how to avoid the block, while remaining in the lane. The coverage team should always keep their feet moving to the football.

When the kicker hits the ball, the coverage team is at full speed. The front five blockers stand dead still thirteen yards from the kickers with their backs to where they want to go. By the time the ball crosses the 30-yard line, the coverage team has run 35 yards and the return front has run 22 yards. The coverage team should be running past the front five blockers on the 30-yard line. At that point, the game is over because there is nowhere to run.

The depth of the ball does not matter as long as the kicker can hang the ball in the air for 4.1 seconds. You do not need a stopwatch to check the hang of a kick. If the ball is still in the air as your players cross the 30-yard line, the kick is at least 4.1 seconds. It is that simple.

As the coverage team runs down the field to cover the ball, they must think, "fits." We kick the football to the right numbers (Figure 15-5). We cover with nine men. We cover with five men on the right side and four men on the left side. The L5 is the safety and the kicker comes down on the ball. The R5 coverage man is the outside containment to the right side, but he is almost against the sideline. The R4 comes down the field and is under the first blocker to his side. It does not matter who it is because the R5 is over the top of him.

To the backside, it becomes more critical with the relationship to fits. The L4 is the backside containment. However, he is a hard, go-after-their-butt containment man. His job is to find the last opposite-colored jersey outside his way. He does not cover grass; he squeezes the widest blocker, keeping his outside arm free. Never cover the field; run to blocker in the return game.

If we kick the ball to the five-yard line, the return team will never have more than 17 yards to space to their players. With the coverage team coming down into that area, there are nine coverage players in that area. The return team will have 10 players in the return. That means there are 19 players in that 17-yard area. There is no place to run the ball.

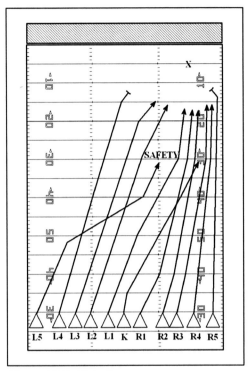

Figure 15-5. Kickoff coverage

The opponent cannot run a kickoff return if the kicker can hang the ball 4.1 seconds and cut the size of the field. The coverage team has to get their fits, and there is nowhere to run the ball. The backside L4 man squeezes the last man to the widest side. The backside L3 man is under one blocker. The backside L2 man is under two blockers. It does not matter who the blockers are. The frontside R5 man squeezes the last blocker to his side. The R4 man covers under one blocker. The R3 man fits under two blockers.

We meet two or three teams a year where discretion is the better part of valor. In those games, there is no reason to kick to certain people. We held teams to an average of the 17-yard line, but we do not play with fire. In our league, there are some super return men. If we can kick the ball deep into or out of the end zone, that stops the return. If your players understand that fit and are timed up, there is nowhere to run the ball.

We do not practice kickoff coverage very much. As a player runs downfield looking for his fits, he has limited options. As he gets to the 35-yard line, it becomes apparent someone is trying to block him. He has only two options. If he feels he will not outrun the blocker, he goes to the blocker. He plays "hands-under-pads" and keeps running. He never uses a forearm. If the blocker is set up, he runs at him to freeze the blocker and avoids the block to the side of the kick.

The thing that kills kickoff coverage is one player avoiding the block to the wrong side. That wipes out every coverage man outside of him. He has to avoid the block to the side of the kick. The coverage team penetrates until they are within five yards of the ballcarrier. When that occurs, they break down and get ready to tackle. Until the ball is at the coverage team, they run their butts off, penetrate, and chase the ball.

We are at the end and I did not get to kickoff return. However, I want to take five minutes and review our kickoff return. When we talk about kickoff return, we think about the other side of the coverage team. The thing the return team has to do is buy grass in front of the return man. The hardest position in football besides the quarterback is the interior blockers on the kickoff return team. They must be good open-field players.

We drop our front line to the 33-yard line in front of the wedge. We ask our open-field players to do one thing. We want him to force his blocking assignment to run over him. We promised them that no matter what happens, there is no laughter when we review the tapes on Sundays. If they force their blocking assignment to run over them, they buy grass for the return man.

I think the middle wedge is a great return scheme. Vanderbilt led the league last year in the kickoff return and never ran anything but the middle wedge. The middle wedge is a great return for high school.

I am completely out of time, but if you want to stay around, I will talk to you about the middle return. I appreciate the opportunity to talk to you. I hope you were able to get something out of this lecture. The best thing I talked about is the kickoff coverage. You have to believe that is the real deal, because it is. If you go to the converse on the kickoff return, it is all about buying grass for the return man. Thank you for your time.

16

Win With the Kicking Game

Steve Ortmayer
University of Kentucky
2008

I want to start off this session with an overview of the kicking game as I know it from the NFL and college football. I will give you the ways I coach the kicking game.

The excitement for the kicking game has to come from the head coach. If the head coach does not make special teams special, they will not be. The head coach needs to be involved in the kicking game. For his own good, he needs to be intimately involved in it. In college football, so many of the big decisions in a game involve kicking-game situations. The head coach is the one who has to answer for those decisions.

Kicking-Game Philosophy

- Produce the greatest amount of field position on each kicking exchange.
- Special teams are weapons for producing yardage as opposed to merely a unit for smoothly affecting exchange of the ball.
- Both the offense and defense will affect and be affected by the kicking game.

Field position becomes important against teams that want to run the ball at the defense. The difference between running and passing teams is how long it takes the offense to make the first 20 yards.

One of every five plays in a football game is a kicking play. It is a significant number of plays in a game. On those plays, there are three things that take place. There is a direct attempt to score points. The second thing that can happen is a change of ball possession. The third thing involves a sizeable amount of yardage exchanged. In most cases, there are 40 yards of field position exchanged in a kick. One or more of those events occurs in a special-teams play.

Kicking-game plays have the potential for big momentum swings. Any play that can score in one play or can gain 40 yards on one play has the potential for big swings. Kicking-game plays can affect the outcome of a game. Breaks in the kicking game happen when players are unprepared for a situation. When a team is prepared, the chance to capitalize on a break happens at the most opportune time. We plan to outprepare the opponent in the kicking game. Therefore, we will get the breaks in the kicking game.

On offense, the kicking teams must eliminate penalties to maximize the greatest field position. On defense, we gain field position by limiting our opponent's returns. There must never be a protection breakdown. Second effort and reckless pursuit are the keys to defensive special teams.

Most of the mistakes in the kicking game are caused by the lack of belief. Having the head coach standing in a kicking-game drill lends creditability to the kicking game. Lack of belief leads to lack of concentration, which causes lack of protection, coverage, and poor application of kicking-game rules.

You must have intensity in all areas of the kicking game. It is best observed in how the team covers kicks. Covering kicks is one of football's greatest tests of courage. Intensity shows up in a game with physical plays, which never results in a penalty. If you can eliminate the penalties on the kickoff and punt returns, you will have a successful kicking game. You have to eliminate the yellow flag and go overboard to emphasize that point.

Every aspect of the kicking game involves fundamentals. It involves time and distance precision. Precision is gained with practicing with concentration. Each skill can only be obtained by practicing with the speed and intensity of game-like situations.

In our kicking-game concepts, we teach from the converse. The objectives for our punting team are to net 40 yards or leave the ball inside the 15-yard line. Our goal for our punt-return team is to keep the net yardage under 30 yards.

There is only one objective on the field-goal team: we expect them to make every kick. We tell them if they miss the field goal, miss short. That way, the kicker can blame the miss on me. If he misses left or right, that is the kicker's fault. It is unrealistic to ask your field-goal blocking team to block every kick, but we ask them to block 50 percent of the kicks or force the opponent to make less than 50 percent. I do not believe you can block kicks off the edges unless there is a snap problem. The way we block field goals is penetration in front of the ball.

On the kickoff, our goals have not changed, but it is harder to achieve them because of the change in the kickoff yard line. Our goal on the kickoff is to net the 20-yard line. We may have to revise those goals unless we come up with a big-time kicker. On the kickoff return, we want to net the 35-yard line.

In teaching from the converse, we tell our punt-return teams that we must have 15 yards of grass in front of the punt-return man. The punt-coverage team has to take that grass away immediately.

On the kickoff return, we tell our return men, if they can run past the front five coverage people, it can be a score. On special teams, we play with speed. We take speed over anything else. The only thing that approaches the importance of speed is accountability.

Outside the punter, the toughest positions to play in the kicking game are the three inside positions on the kickoff-return team. The way we do it, it takes tremendous courage and a will to want to do it. If a defender gets a 40-yard run at the blocker, there is going to be a collision.

I want to go through the six special teams and cover some of the important points. The first team is the field-goal team. I do not have much on field goals. I told you what we expect. The easiest thing to do in college football is to be a holder or kicker. Kicker should never miss. The kick in practice has to be 1.4, which will be 1.38 in a game. If the kicker goes faster than 1.38, he is rushing the kick. If he kicks the ball in 1.4, he makes the kick. The snap is the key to making a high percentage of your kicks. You have to figure out his range, and do not put him on the field until you get to that distance.

The kicker has to see the snap approach the holder's hands. He does not need to see it hit the holder's hands before he starts his move to the ball. The good kickers can wait until it hits the holder's hands. If a team kicks the ball from a depth of seven yards, they are trying to take the outside rusher out of the equation. We kick the ball from eight yards deep.

In the five years I have been at Kentucky, we have had only one kick blocked off the edge. In 2004-05, we blocked 25 kicks with penetration and hands up. If the ball is in the middle of the field, the ball must pass over the area inside the guard-tackle gap on each side (Figure 16-1). The protection has to protect the B gap and the A gap.

If the ball is moved to either hash mark, the critical area is outside the A gap to the C gap on the side of the kick (Figure 16-2). If they kick the ball anywhere else, the kick will be no good. The defense has to get to the point where the kick can be made to block it. We get as many people over the two offensive linemen in that area as we can.

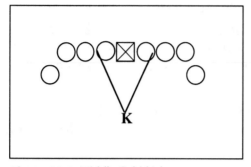

Figure 16-1. Middle-field kicks   Figure 16-2. Hash-mark kicks

In our field-goal block, we want to run over the blockers, get penetration, and put two jumpers at the point the ball must travel. We ask the defensive linemen to run a 10-yard sprint under the offensive blocker's pad level. They will not block the kick. Their job is to penetrate the area the kick passes over. The offense does not work against that type of charge. The jumpers are the ones blocking the kick. We tell our players: the time from when the ball is snapped, the kick is made, and until the ball crosses the line of scrimmage is 2.0 seconds. If we get one yard of penetration, when the ball crosses that point, it is 10 feet off the ground. The jumpers time their jumps based on the 2.0-second count. If we do not have players who can vertically jump and get their hands to a 10-foot height, that is my fault. I put the wrong jumpers in the game.

With the ball in the middle of the field, it is harder because of the rules that protect the center. However, it has been my experience in the SEC, if you do not hit the center in the head, the referees will not call that roughness. We run through the shoulder of the center.

This is why the head coach has to be involved in the kicking game. To block kicks the way we do, we have to commit six players to the block. That leaves us five defenders to play six positions. You have to contain from each side, and they have four eligible receivers. That leaves us one short. I tell the contain players to get on the holder immediately. We do not want to be soft on the containment.

The next part of the kicking game is kickoff coverage. We have two cardinal sins at Kentucky. One is getting a penalty on the kickoff return, and the other is getting a penalty that puts the defense back on the field.

Time It Up With the Kicker

- Sixty percent of the kickoff is covered before the kick.
- Run past the front five.

- Get to your fit.
- Avoid blocks to the side of the football.
- Think: "turnovers."

If you, as the coach, get people on the kickoff team who can flat-out run and keep them onside, you have done 60 percent of your job. Our primary drill in kickoff coverage is timing the run to the ball by the coverage team. Whatever the kicker does with his run to the ball in week 1, he will do in week 15. That will not change. We ask the kicker to kick the ball to the goal line with 4.1 seconds hang time. We want the ball kicked to the numbers on the right side of the field. The coverage team times their run to the ball and does not look at the ball. They use a spot on the ground. Once the kicker hits that spot, they sprint. It is our job to adjust their run-ups. However, he has to go full speed for the coach to help him.

The front-five blockers are 10 to 12 yards in front of the ball. They have to start from a stopped position to run. By the time the ball is kicked, the coverage team is at full speed and closes within five yards of the front five immediately. They have 25 yards to make up the other five yards and get in front of them.

If we run past the front-five blockers, we have nine defenders on five blockers and the ballcarrier. The secret to covering kicks is getting the proper fits. We kick the ball directionally. We do not want our players to cover grass. The left side coverage team starts out on the hash marks, but as they go downfield, they have to squeeze the ball on the right side. They need to redirect their lanes to where the blockers are forming. They want to penetrate until they are five yards from the ball. At that time, they break down and get ready to make the play.

We will give up the distance of the kick to get the proper hang time (Figure 16-3). The R5 cover man is the outside man to the right. As he covers, he leverages the outside blocker in the wall. He plays with his inside shoulder on the outside shoulder of the blocker. That is his fit in the coverage scheme and is a key fit. The R4 man's rule is under one. He is to play under the first blocker he encounters. The R3 runner plays under the second blocker. They play with their outside arm free, squeezing the ball.

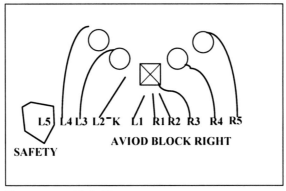

Figure 16-3. Kickoff coverage

On the left side of the field, L5 is our safety for two-thirds of the field. The L4 cover man has the same rules as R5. He contains and plays tight to the outside shoulder of the outside blocker to his side in the return. The L3 has the same rule as R4 on the frontside. Everyone else from L2 to R2 has the same rule. They are to avoid the blockers to the side of the football. If the ball is to the right of the defender, he avoids to the right and continues downfield. If the defender avoids to the left, he wipes out every player outside of him.

That is our entire kickoff coverage. If you look at the tape, there are nine defenders and 10 blockers in a 20-yard space between the hash marks and the sideline. There is nowhere to go with the football. This works as long as the coverage team gets their fits and runs their asses off. When the kicker kicks the ball, he is the frontside safety, and we want him on or inside the 30-yard line. He has to be a player. If the ball ever gets to him, there will not be a blocker with him.

I am going to skip the punt-protection scheme because there are so many ways to do it. As I told you before, when we cover a punt, we want to take the grass in front of the return man away immediately (Figure 16-4). That is the job of the gunners. On the punt-coverage team, you only need four players to play punt coverage. The gunners, center, and the personal protector are the only players who cannot make a mistake. The rest of the punt coverage is very simple. LSU uses their first-team defense as their punt-coverage team. Their reasoning is the first defense knows how important it is to protect the punt.

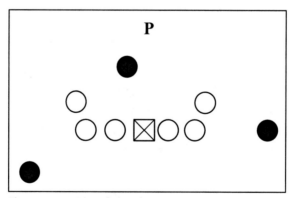

Figure 16-4. Punt formation

On the kickoff, the return team is trying to buy grass in front of them and the ball. We ask the front line players to drop to the 33-yard line and take on the defender square. That means we want them to get "run over slowly."

Kickoff Return

- Disguise your drops.
- Sprint to the set-up, knowing where the ball is.
- Buy grass in front of the wedge.
- Utilize your opponent's responsibilities in blocking a scheme.
- Kickoff is speed.

The return man has to catch every kick. It does not matter where they kick the ball. The worst-case scenario for the return man is leaning in to the ball as he catches it; the best-case scenario is moving forward to catch it. If the return man catches the ball over his shoulder or running away, by the time he gets back under control, the defenders have run 7 to 10 yards. That is critical to kickoff returns. In practice, every field goal or placekick is caught by the return men.

The front-five blockers drop to the 30-yard line and set the wedge in front of the ball (Figure 16-5). If the ball is kicked to the side, the middle wedge blocker sets in front of the ball. The front wedge blockers to either side of the middle blocker drop as long as their defenders continue to come downfield. The further the defenders come downfield, the less of a threat they are, and they block themselves. The front line takes on their blocks and tries not to let anyone cross their face.

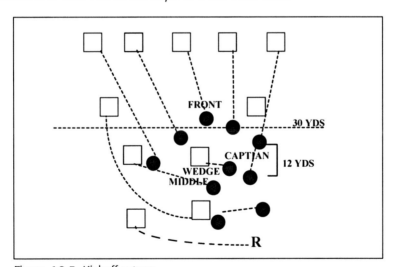

Figure 16-5. Kickoff return

In the kickoff return, the four second-line blockers and the deep back not returning the ball form the middle wedge in front of the kick-return man. They are approximately 12 yards behind the front wedge. The grass we talk about is not between the two wedges. The grass is in front of the front wedge.

If the kicking team kicks the ball away from our directional return, we have rules to handle that situation. On our kickoff return, we have a wedge captain. When he sees the ball kicked away from the return direction, he yells, "Straight, straight, straight." That means the middle wedge closes to the ball. If the ball is kicked deep enough, we still have a chance to return the ball. Our rule for right and left returns is: if the return man cannot return the ball at a 45-degree angle, we do not return into the wedge.

The shorter the distance the ball is kicked and the closer it is to the sideline, the less chance we have of returning the ball into the wedge. We are not going to mess with getting back to the return side. The front-line wedge does not have a chance to move to that side. When they hear the "straight" call, we want them to set short at the 40-yard line. That creates some separation between the defenders coming down the middle and those on the edges. The only thing we try to do with a kickoff return is get back to the 35-yard line. Two of the five years I have been at Kentucky, we never started behind the 20-yard line. The middle wedge players are kicking out on the defenders coming from the outside. The back who did not catch the ball seals the backside.

The apex of the middle wedge is 12 yards in front of the ball. From the apex, the next two players in the wedge are a yard behind and a yard outside the apex player. The two players behind them are a yard behind and a yard outside of them. They do not block anyone unless someone crosses their face. I think the wedge returns in high school are the way to go.

On the kickoff we use an onside kick to the end man on the kickoff line. If the receiving team lines their end man on the front line at the numbers, they are giving you the onside pooch. It takes practice, but the kicker can do it 10 out of 10 times. If the last man on the front line is aligned at the top of the numbers, that is 10 yards from the sidelines. Run the last outside man on the kickoff team down 10 yards, and let the kicker kick the ball to him.

We call the play *fly right and left*. Everyone starts one step slower than on a normal kickoff. Everyone on the team is blocking except for the man who catches the ball. The R4 and R3 players go down and block the end man on the front line. It is harder to go to the left for a right-footed kicker, but he can. If the defense gives it to you, take it.

The same thing is true with the suicide onside. That is the dribble kick in the middle of the field. If you align to kick off near the hash and the opponent adjusts one defender in the front line but not the player next to him, you have 15 yards between the two defenders. The R1 and L1 can block the two inside defenders every time, and the kicker can get the ball every time. Let your kicker work on that, and they can get good at doing it. The kicker can kick the ball so that at 10 yards, the ball bounces up to him.

On the punt, I will do anything to keep people from getting 15 yards in front of the football (Figure 16-6). We double-team the gunners on both sides if necessary. We double-team the contain man on the side that we are running the return. We call that a "whirlwind." We use six blockers to block three defenders. However, we give the punt-return man the grass he needs, and he can make people miss. We give our special teams a buzzword. The punt-return team is the "hard-work team." You can play your starter on the punt team, but the punt-return team is physically hard to play.

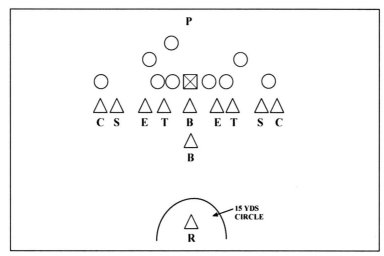

Figure 16-6. Punt return

I want to talk about some fakes before I run out of time. Fakes are something you do not come up with because you are a coach. You run the fakes because they are there. You should never run a fake that does not succeed unless you drop the ball. If you have a player who does not catch the ball or fumbles, you cannot control that. What I am saying is: never run a fake that the defense is going to stop. It is stupid if you run a fake when they are expecting it. On the other hand, you are stupid if you do not run a fake when they give it to you.

You are way ahead of the game if you have a punter who is an athlete. If he can run, that is a big bonus. That opens up all kinds of avenues to you. You cannot return kicks and play fakes. If you are a good punt-return team, you will be vulnerable to some fakes. What I just showed you on our return game makes us vulnerable if someone wants to throw the ball to the inside players. When you design a fake, do it against teams that cannot defend it.

The easiest fake to run is a fourth-and-two, if the opponent cannot defend the area inside the A gaps (Figure 16-7). The simplest punt fake to run is to the kick protector. He walks around and sets the protection as part of his job. He points out overloads and walks from side to side. He simply steps up under the center and takes the ball on a quarterback sneak. If the defense is positioned so they cannot handle that, run it. We call it red alert.

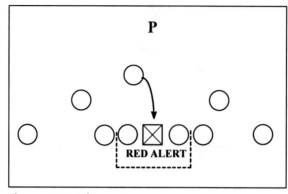

Figure 16-7. Fake punt

The second fake is snapping the ball to the punter. You have to make an assessment. You have to determine whether your punter's running skills are better than the contain defender. If you have a quarterback who punts for you, that is great. In addition to the gunners, the slots are eligible receivers. If teams are beating you up with the return, they cannot play the fake.

There are many instances where a 40-yard punt is better than picking up a first down. That depends on what you believe on field position, and it goes back to integrating the defensive game plan with the special-teams plan.

The last thing I want to talk about is the "hands team" (Figure 16-8). I do not believe you should ever give up an onside kick. It should never happen, even though the ball is not round. In the onside-kick protection, we match up four defenders against their five kick runners. Those four defenders on the kick of the ball attack and block the kickers coming down the field. They want to block them five yards up the field.

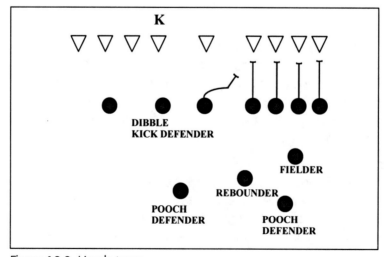

Figure 16-8. Hands team

We align one defender over the ball to prevent the dribble kick and one deep to prevent the pooch kick over the front line. To the side of the onside kick, we have a fielder behind the *rebounder*. The rebounder stands at the top of the numbers. The fielder only fields anything kicked on the ground to the right of the rebounder. He also looks for a deflection from the rebounder if he does not catch the ball clean. We have our punt-kick-return man standing behind the rebounder, playing the ball kicked over his head.

The four blockers have to make sure they do not touch the encroachment line. They sprint as hard as the kickers coming down on them. They want to stop the kickers by using a double hand chuck to the chest of the kickers. We want to square up on them so they have to come over the defender to get to the ball.

It is the job of the special-teams coach to know how the opponent kicks onside to try to get the ball back to win the game.

Thank you, fellows. I really enjoyed it. Come see us.

17

Soccer-Style Placekicking Techniques

Doug Pelfrey
Cincinnati Bengals
1995

The first thing I am going to go through is the mechanics of kicking. There is a lot more to kicking than "keep your head down and follow through." That was my kick training in high school. What I want to share with you is how you can help your kickers. I'm going to talk about the importance of developing a routine. I'll go through what my routine is and make some suggestions for the high school kicker. I'm going over the psychological aspect of the kicking game. I'm going to talk about the importance a coach can play on the kicker's frame of mind. I'll talk about the team and how it should view the kicker. I'm going to relate kicking to golf. The final thing I'm going to talk about is stretching and conditioning.

In the mechanics of kicking, the first thing the kicker has to do is pick a target. It is just like basketball. You know where the goal is and you shoot for it. Don't just kick at the uprights. I always pick a spot behind the uprights and above the crossbar. I am right down the middle. I expect to hit the ball right down the middle. If I'm kicking an extra point, I'll pick a target. It may be a scoreboard, a tree, flagpole, or something to give me the line. It is important in your kicking motion that everything goes through that target.

A lot of kickers go out and just kick. The advice from the coach is kick it high and far. I don't care how you kick it as long as you make it. What we teach kickers in my camps is to be more accurate. It doesn't matter if you have a kicker who can kick 55 to 60 yards. It is important that he be able to make kicks when you put him in. Particularly, the short ones are the ones he has to be able to kick. If you spend time on the kicking game, it will change three or four games in your season.

The second thing I'm going to talk about is the alignment of the kicker. The importance of alignment is to do the exact same thing every time. The kicker faces his target, comes straight back from the tee, and gets to the same spot every time. I take three steps back. From there, I go two steps over at a right angle from that spot. The reason for the 90-degree angle is because of the crown in the fields. We have to kick from the hash marks as well as from the middle of the field. It is important to come over at the right angle because it puts you in the same place every time

The next thing in the kick is the stance. The left knee for a right-footed kick is slightly bent. The chest is out. You should be able to feel the weight on your left knee. That allows the momentum to naturally go toward the ball. You don't want to be straight up and leaning back. If you do, there is a rocking motion in your kicker. The feet should be facing toward the ball. The plant foot is the one that hits right next to the ball. The right lean and weight shift allows the kicker to fall into the proper position of the plant foot. The kicker looks at a spot on the tee. He can't control the snap. What he can control once the ball is placed is that he hits the ball properly. It is important once the ball has been placed that he pictures where on the ball he wants to hit. His head should be going toward his plant foot.

There is no specific place for the plant foot to be placed. If you are kicking from a two-inch tee, the plant step is farther from the tee than if you were kicking from a one-inch tee. Each kicker has his own individual stroke; therefore, the plant foot varies from kicker to kicker. I'm kicking off the ground in the NFL and my plant foot is in front of the ball. That lets you get the proper leverage on the ball. Once the plant foot is placed, it should be facing exactly where the kick is to be made. If the plant foot is open, the ball will go left. If the plant foot is facing to the right, the ball will go right.

The next thing is where the foot is placed on the ball. The proper point to make contact is one-and-a-half to two-and-a-half inches below the widest part of the ball. An easy example for that spot is to cut the ball in half and then cut it in half again. That is the spot the kicker should try to hit. The snapper, holder, and kicker have to be on the same page. When the holder places the ball down on the tee, the ball needs to be as straight up as it can. A lot of kickers like to lean the ball back. They think that gets them more height. What they are actually doing is closing down the sweet spot of the ball. The ball needs to be straight up in the air and a slight lean toward the holder. The reason for the lean is most soccer players have a tendency to rap around the ball.

Leaning the ball away from the kicker exposes the sweet spot and gets the ball away from the kicker. When kickers wrap around the ball the ball rotates like a knuckleball. You want the ball to rotate slowly end over end. That's what you will get by leaning the ball toward the holder.

There are two different approaches I would suggest that kickers make toward the ball. There is a two-step approach, which I use, or a two-and-a-half-step. The two-and-a-half-step includes a jab step. I don't like the jab step because on long kicks the kicker starts to press. They try to kick the ball harder than they should. When that happens, the jab step becomes longer than it should. I use the two-step approach. That is right foot, left foot, and kick. If your kicker is going to take the jab step, make sure it is small. He may pick up the foot and put it right down in the same spot. The jab step needs to be in the direction of the plant foot. For a right-footed kicker the jab step is taken with the left foot. The right foot comes through, and then there is air time before the left foot or plant foot comes down. The kicker is going to engage the ball and he has to cover a lot of ground quickly in that last step. It is important that your kicker doesn't jump up into the air or jump too far. If he is, he is trying too hard and will not be consistent. He needs to stay under control. It is not how hard he goes at the ball that creates the power.

The plant foot on a two-inch tee should be on the instep of the foot. That means the tee should be on the instep of the plant foot. As the ball goes closer to the ground, the plant step moves forward on the spot the ball is kicked from. When I kick the ball off the ground, the heel of my plant foot is next to the ball. The plant foot will be anywhere from nine inches to a foot from the tee. It all depends on the build of the kickers. The great kickers are the ones that can repeat the good kick time after time. They have consistency in the kick.

The next thing is the ball-foot contact. In the kicking position the foot and leg should form the shaft and head of a golf club. The knee and ankle are locked. The foot is locked out. It takes a lot of time and kicks before the kicker develops the proper swing. In the kick there is toe depression. That is where the big toe is pressed down. You want your leg and foot to be solid at contact. The kicking shoe is important to that effect. The eyes and head should actually see where the foot comes in contact with the ball. The shoulders are over the ball but not bent down or back. About 80 percent of kickers at this point will be leaning back. When a kicker leans back, the ball will spray. If you are too far forward, the kick will be weak and low. The hips should be square toward the target. If the hips don't get around, the ball goes right. If the hips are overrotated, the ball goes left. It is important to get a video of your kickers and let them watch themselves. The arms of the kicker are what gives him balance. It is important to stress the arms but don't make them the biggest issue. They are approaching the ball from a harsh angle. The arms act as a counterbalance.

There is a hard bone on top of the foot. That is the point that should contact the ball. I went to dental school, so I don't know the anatomical name of that bone. However, it is the hardest one in your foot. We don't want the ball up on the ankle or down on the toe. It takes time for the kicker to learn to depress his toe and get the foot out in that club like position. The most consistent way to kick the ball is to lock out your foot at the point of contact.

The next thing is the follow-through. This is probably the most important part of kicking. So many people say once you've kicked the ball you can't do anything about it. Everything is going in the direction of the target. Morten Andersen, who is the best kicker in the NFL, kicks the ball and stops. He has no follow-through. But remember, your high school kicker is not Morten Andersen. What we call the follow-through is the skip-through. When the kicker kicks the ball he does not land on his kicking foot. He lands on his left foot or plant foot for the right-footed kicker. The skip is not a long jump. It is about one foot in length. All he is doing is continuing his momentum through the kick. He is not fighting himself. If you want to improve your distance, work on the skip-through.

The timing of when the kicker starts his kick depends on the snapper and holder. The kicker does not look at the center's snap. He is looking at the spot on the tee. When I am kicking for the Bengals, I leave when I see Lee Johnson's left hand go up to receive the ball. For a high school kicker, I suggest that the kicker not leave until the holder has caught the ball. The two most important things as far as frame of mind to the kicker are rhythm and confidence. Establishing a good rhythm will give a kicker confidence. He doesn't want to go too hard or lax going at the ball. He wants to kick nice and easy at a good fluid pace. The kicker wants to be smooth.

Kickers are like any other football player. They need drills to improve their fundamentals. There are so many drills that a kicker can kick his leg out if he's not careful. On certain things kickers shouldn't even use a ball. They can work on their steps and stance. They can work their steps from all points of the field. We let the kickers skip down the line. It is called line kicks. We take a long line, line up the kicker and let him form kick and skip. He should be right down the line. He repeats it again and again going down the line. He can either kick or form kick. If he kicks the ball, it should land on the line 30 to 40 yards down the field. You want accuracy. You don't want that kicker who can kick it 60 yards. Chances are he will be right or left and make about one out of 10. You want a kicker who is consistent. It is important that the kicker can make the 20-, 30-, and 40-yard field goals. That is what you are going to be kicking during the game. After the kicker has worked on the short kicks, he can kick maybe five from 50 yards. You don't need to kick too many balls from far out. This year, I led the NFL with attempts outside of 50 yards. I had four kicks. That was in 16 games. If you are playing 10 or 11 games, your kicker will only get two or three kicks outside 50 yards. That is assuming he is that good. It is not that important to kick a lot of long field goals. It is important to be accurate on the short ones.

Everyone knows where the crossbar is. Take the ball and set it down seven yards behind the goal. The seven yards is the distance from the snapped ball to the kicker. If the kicker can get the ball up over a 10-foot bar, he won't get it blocked by someone jumping at the line of scrimmage. If the kicker can clear the crossbar, he will be fine when it comes to a rush. That is called a ball height drill. The only thing we are working on is getting the ball up. You can even move in to five yards and do the drill. Don't do this drill inside of 5 yards. If you do, the kicker will lean back trying to get the ball up quick and that develops bad habits. We want the fluid motion.

There is another drill called side angle. Go to the five-yard line at the sideline. Move into the field about 10 to 12 yards and have the kicker kick the ball between the uprights. The one thing it does is to narrow the goal. The kicker has to kick at a smaller target. It also works on his angles. It is not important to spend the whole day working on this drill. Make him kick 10 to 15 balls throughout the course of a week. It is something different for him to do. You don't want to do the same routine every day. Go to both sides. It is a lot easier for a right-footed kicker to kick from the left side than it is from the right. On the left side, he can hook it in. On the right side it is tough for him, but you need to make it tough for him. You want him confident and kind of cocky. There are some days where I couldn't miss. But there are also days where I couldn't hit the goal post with a rock in my hand. It varies every day.

A great drill just to get loose is the one-step kick. It is important to do this so he is not out there trying to kill the ball on the first kick. He can gradually get into his kicking. It is like shooting lay-ups before you go out to shoot three-pointers. All you want to do is stay nice and smooth. The kicker kicks straight. The kicker is working on the same spot as the two-step kick. These drills are to get the kicker in the right thought process every time. When a kicker develops his routine and does it the same way every time, you will have a kicker that kicks 80 to 90 percent.

I have used the spot drill. Take 20 or 30 balls, throw them out on the field between the hash mark. The kicker goes to the balls and kicks one ball from each spot. Don't let him kick more than two balls from each spot. In a game he gets only one chance. Keep stats on these kicks. Tell the kicker he gets 20 kicks today. See how many he can make. It is easy to kick once you get in a groove. Don't let him get in the groove. Make him move from spot to spot. Make sure he kicks from every spot on the field. When he goes out to kick during the course of the game, he is prepared to kick. One thing that I know when I go out on that field is, I have kicked from that spot. It doesn't matter if it is 58 yards on the right hash or 18 yards down the middle. I have been there before.

If your kicker has a weak hash mark, make him kick from that hash. Don Riley was my kicking coach my senior year at the University of Kentucky. The one thing he did was to challenge me every day. If I couldn't kick from the right hash mark, that is where we started and finished. Your kicker is going to have a strong hash mark that he likes to kick from. It is important to kick from the center, right, and left. Try to make it so he knows he doesn't have a weakness. When it is coming down to the end of the game and a game-winning field goal, the coach can ask the kicker which hash he prefers. But the kicker knows it doesn't make any difference. I remember this year against Seattle. We haven't won a game all year. Coach Shula asked me which hash I wanted to kick off of. It didn't matter to me. I wanted to kick from the middle but it doesn't matter. The kicker has to know he is going to make the kick.

There is a drill called around the world. I start out on extra points. That is to get me loose. Kick five to eight extra points to get loose. I move to the 12- to 14-yard line on the left hash and kick two balls. Then I move to the right hash at the 16- to 18-yard line and kick two balls. You keep going right, then left, and every now and then throw one in from the middle. You circle around the field but always end up on a close kick. If the kicker starts out close and ends up at 65 yards, I don't know if he is going to be ready to kick that 30-yard goal during the game on his first attempt.

When I was in high school I was trying to kick 100 to 200 balls a day. That is crazy. I kicked four or five field goals in three years of high school. I kicked so many balls, I was kicking them in my sleep. I learned how to kick. When your kickers are learning how to kick, let them kick as many balls as they want. Make sure they are kicking four, five, to six days a week when they are learning. In my red-shirt freshman year in college, all the kicking finally clicked. I went from kicking four or five good balls in a row to kicking all good balls. That is when I started to back down the number of balls I kicked a day. I started to kick 75 to 100 balls a day. I only kicked three or four days a week. With the Bengals, I'm lucky to kick 50 balls in a week. Right now, I know what I am doing. If I miss a kick, I can tell you without looking whether it goes through or not. By looking at the rotation of the ball, I can tell you exactly what I've done wrong. That's what you want your kicker to be able to do. During a game, you can't tell him what he did wrong. He has to know. If he misses it left, he has to know why.

The last drill I want to suggest to you is the bag drill. Get a tall blocking dummy. Get someone to hold the bag. The kicker puts one hand on the dummy and kicks it as hard as he can. This helps the kicker make good solid contact. The first couple of times he kicks it, it will be awkward to him. As he works on it and continues to do this drill, he learns to get the foot locked out at the proper time.

Never work your kicker out at the end of practice when he is tired. All he will do is practice bad habits. In my opinion, I think the kicking game should take priority. I think most coaches will agree with me. The Bengals won three games this year and all of them were last-second field goals. The same thing can happen to you. The kicking game can mean about three more wins for you. Every time you go out on the field, your kicker has just established your field position. It may be your punter, kickoff man, or field-goal kicker. Why not take the time to develop a good kicker? It helps your offense and defense so much. When you kick the ball in the end zone, the offense is starting on the 20-yard line every time. If your kicker can't kick it in the end zone, work on directional kickoffs. Kick the ball in the right corner and use the sideline to corral the runner.

Your kicker or punter can change the course of the game if you will use him properly. Train him at the beginning of practice. That is why the specialist is important. You don't need a tired kicker when the game is on the line. Find him. Go over the entire kicking game at the beginning of practice and spend some quality time on it. Don't have a specialty period and let everyone run crazy. Make sure the snaps are perfect and on target. Have your snapper work after practice. Have the kicker and punter work before practice.

If there is a bad snap, we have a fire call. That means something has gone wrong and we want our receivers to run hot routes. Don't let the kicker try to throw unless he can do that. Kickers generally can't throw the ball. As a kicker, I try to get in the way of the defense. I don't try to block anyone. All I want to do is buy some time for the holder to throw the ball. We sent all the receivers to the right. We didn't want receivers all over the field. We wanted it like a called pattern. The wing ran a short pattern. The right end ran a deeper pattern. The left end came across the back of the end zone. We practice this every week with the Bengals. There is going to be a delayed response by the receivers.

If there is wet weather, I don't change a lot of form. Make sure the back cleats are good because that is what is important on the plant foot. I don't go at the ball as hard on wet turf. I try to stay under control. I try to stay over the balls of my feet. Be cautious, but at the same time kick through the ball. If the kicker slips, he just slips. When the kicker presses, he gets that kind of kick that twirls off to the side.

Let me tell you what my routine is for the week. On Monday or Tuesday, I don't kick a ball. We come in on Monday and watch films and come out and condition. On Wednesday, I come in and kick a lot of balls. I kick 30 to 40 balls and maybe 50 depending on how I am kicking. I chart 15 balls on Wednesday and Thursday. That way I know what kind of percentage I'm kicking. I only do 10 to 12 kickoffs a week. The kickoff is the same form as your long field goals, except for a longer approach. On most Fridays, I don't kick. To kick on Sunday, I need my legs fresh. I do the mental preparation so I don't have to kick seven days a week. On Friday, I may kick 10 balls, but I usually don't. On Saturday, the day before the game, I don't do anything. Game day I kick. I kick a lot of balls in the warm-up and a lot during the game. I want to be fresh on Sunday because that's when I get paid to play.

For the high school kicker, he kicks on Friday night. It is important for him to come in on Saturday and break down the film, just like any other player. He doesn't kick on Saturday or Sunday. On Monday he needs to kick a lot. He wants to kick until his leg is tired. On Tuesday he needs to kick a lot but not as many balls as he did on Monday. If he kicked 100 balls on Monday, cut it down to 75 on Tuesday. On Wednesday and Thursday have him do 15 kicks, but generally these are his rest days. On Friday he needs to get enough kicks to be good and warmed up. Work out a plan for him during warm-up. Start out short, work long, and come back to short. I find out how many balls he has to kick to get loose. In college I had to kick a ton of balls to even get loose. Now I can get loose on kicking 15 to 30 balls. You, as the coach, need to find out how he feels about his kicking.

The psychological aspects of kicking are so important. I know you think we are a bunch of freaks. I don't kick on Friday and Saturday because I am doing a lot of visual imaging. I'm seeing myself being successful. If you check the golf circuit, most of the great players are working with a sports psychologist. At the University of Kentucky, we had one. Seeing yourself being successful is so key in kicking. It saves your leg but it works on your preparation. There are different ways to do that. Tell your kicker to get away from everyone for 10 to 15 minutes. Go to some place where it is quiet. Have him sit there and start to visualize himself kicking to the point where he can actually feel himself kicking the ball. That works if your kicker is hurt. Instead of kicking, he uses visualization. This is a great opportunity for your kicker if you can put him in touch with a sports psychologist.

It is important for the coach to instill confidence in the kicker. Coach Curry at Kentucky really did that for me. If I missed a kick, I felt I let him down. I wasn't worried about missing the kick like I was about letting Coach Curry down. Your kicker should feel like the coach is on his team. There is the football mentality. The coach thinks all you do all week is kick; why can't you hit them every time? There is a lot that goes into kicking. The kicker has to feel the coach is really with him and not trying to make him the joke of the team. I know the kickers are always the joke of the team. When I went to the University of Kentucky, I tried to play some other positions because I knew what the rest of the team was thinking about kickers. My sophomore year at UK, I was embarrassed to be the kicker. As I became more successful, I gladly accepted that role. Being in the NFL and being a professional kicker is the best job in America. I work about three days a week and hang out the rest of the time. It is important that the coach relate to the kicker. He has to find out what the kicker thinks. What does he think about his range, routine, workouts, and all the important things to him? The coach wants to be as respectful as he can because kickers are different than offensive linemen. Some kickers are hard on themselves. Some kickers are like your wife. If you say the wrong thing to them, they pout on you. You don't want that. You want your kicker to be ready at the point when it comes to kicking.

It is important that the kicker do all the conditioning with the other guys. Don't let the kicker get out of conditioning. Don't let your kicker kick while everyone else is running. He needs to be in just as good a shape as everyone else. But when it comes to lifting he doesn't need the heavy weight training. Be smart enough to handle him right in the weight room, but treat him like the rest of the team.

Kicking is like golf. There are a lot of different swings on the tour. But they all do the same thing once the club face gets into the hitting zone. Everyone has a different kick mode, but getting to the right spot is where the kick is made. It is important that kickers go to camps. They can see themselves on tape and get advice from professional kickers. Don't let them learn how to kick on their own. If you go to the practice range and hit golf balls, the first couple of hits you loosen up. Then you go through that phase where everything you hit goes to the hole. If you keep hitting balls, you start to duff them or pop them up. Then you start hitting them right and left. You start to wonder what went wrong. That is just like kicking. The first couple of kicks he loosens up. When he starts kicking great, stop him. Don't let him kick himself into a slump. Let him kick and have a routine. Build his confidence. Walk off when he is doing his best.

There are five key places to stretch. The first place is the groin muscle. Because of the soccer-style kick, there is a lot of pressure placed there. The second place to stress stretching is the back. That is the second most frequent injury with the kicker. The third place is the hamstring muscles. Stretch both of them, not just the kicking leg. The fourth place is the calf and Achilles tendon. Just by leaning on a wall, you can stretch that Achilles and develop flexibility in the foot. The last thing is to jog. Before you stretch, run a couple of laps around the field to get your blood flowing.

When I condition, I start with a stationary bike. That is the key thing. It will do wonders for your legs. It builds strength, endurance, and quickness. It doesn't matter what size your kicker is. The strength in the kick comes from how fast the kicker can get his leg through the contact zone.

On the kickoff, it doesn't matter how fast the kicker runs. He can run as fast as he wants but when he gets to the point of contact, he has to slow down. The kickoff is the same angle as the field goal. The approach is just expanded. He is not practicing two kicks. On the kickoff, take advantage of the extra run up but make the kick nice and easy. He wants to build momentum into the kick. Start him off slow and build momentum into the kick. Make sure he follows through when he kicks off. If he takes advantage of the extended run up and doesn't try to kill the ball, he can kick it in the end zone. It is important to stay under control. If you take a picture of me from behind, my follow-through ends up with my foot over my left shoulder. If the kicker stops, the ball will stay low. The follow-through makes the ball come up.

The shoe is important to the kicker. A soccer shoe will bend and lets the foot lock out properly. A football cleat won't do that. You want a shoe that is flexible and made of good leather. You don't want a plastic kicking shoe. I wear a size 10 shoe. When it comes to my kicking shoe, I wear a size 8. I know you think that is crazy. If the kicker wears two or three pairs of socks, he is not getting solid contact. I wear a sanitary sock. You want maximum impact. With two pairs of socks, you are cushioning the blow. Use a thin sock. Use a kicking shoe that is tight. The first couple of times you kick with it on, it should be uncomfortable. When the shoe breaks in, it is not too big. You want the shoe to fit around the foot. Don't try to kick bare-footed. That's crazy.

18

Special Teams and the Punting Game

Jeff Pierce
Ferris State University
2005

Let me give you a little about my background. I have been at Ferris State University for 21 years now. I started my coaching career in the Upper Peninsula of Michigan as a football coach. I graduated from Ferris State in the 1970s and I coached high school football for five years. I understand the things you are going through. It is all about working with young people. It is satisfying for me to see the young people grow up.

I came to Ferris State 21 years ago as a graduate assistant. After that, I became the linebacker coach. Then I became the defensive coordinator. I have been the head coach for the last 10 years going on my 11th season. It is an interesting time for me. It is all about working with young people. I give the high school coaches a lot of credit for what you are doing. We are in the business that molds young lives. We can never forget that point. That is the most important thing. It is rewarding for me to be able to stay at the same school for as long as I have been at Ferris State. As I travel to high schools recruiting, I see former students all of the time. It is great to see them develop, grow, and mature. Do not overlook the impact you have in working with the young kids today.

A couple of other things and then I will get into special teams. I think one of the most important things in coaching is to get kids to play for you. If you expect kids to give you everything they have, you must do that back in return. There are no gimmicks in this business. If you can show attention to your players and if you are there when they need you, they will play for you. You should treat the players the way you would want to be treated. If you do that, you will get a kid that is going to be committed to you and your program.

The next point I want to discuss will lead into my topic today. As a coach, you must be a teacher. You must be a very good teacher to be successful in our business. There is a difference between the teacher in the classroom, as many of you are, and a football coach. Many things are similar, but if the student does not comprehend and grasp what the teacher is trying to get across to him, the teacher flunks him. If the kid does not understand what the football coach is trying to get across to him, they fire the football coach. That is the difference. You must find a way to get the kids understand what you are trying to get across to them.

It does not matter what you know as far as X's and O's. If you cannot get the kids to learn what you are teaching them and display it on the football field, it does not matter. All of the guys that learned the game of football with a Budweiser in one hand and a remote control in the other hand that are your number-one critics, that do not come to football clinics but think they know every thing about football – they will be on your butt.

I am going to talk about special teams. I am going more into how we break the game up as far as techniques are concerned. In addition, I will cover some drills that we work on. I have been involved with the special teams for several years as the head coach. I want those kids to understand how important special teams are. Some teams take special teams very lightly. Some teams put 11 men out on the field, kick the ball down the field, and tell them to go get it. You can turn a game around very quickly with the kicking game. However, you have to coach it and teach it just as you have to coach linebackers. We work technique drills during the special teams sessions. Do you put players on the field and tell them what to do and then look at the film on Sunday to see if the players performed the task correctly?

You must make a commitment time-wise to the special teams. I want to cover an example of a practice plan that we use. Our Tuesday and Wednesday practice schedules are about the same. We are going to spend ten minutes a day before the stretching period on our specialist. This includes sessions with the snappers, kickers, return men, and all phases of the kicking game. In addition, we are going to spend time with the individual drills with the players. We work on the techniques in this period.

FERRIS STATE FOOTBALL PRACTICE PLAN

Game Week Wednesday—Date:_____

Offense	Time	Defense
Warm-Up	3:15	Warm-Up
Specialist	3:20	Specialist
Team Stretch	3:25	Team Stretch
Kicking Game	3:30	Kicking Game
Teach	3:35	Teach
	3:55	
Giant	4:20	Giant
Inside	4:25	Inside
Skelly	4:35	Skelly
Team vs. Defense	4:50	Team vs. Offense
Team vs. Scouts	5:10	Team vs. Scouts
Goal Line	5:30	Pursuit

Comments: The specialist period is 10 minutes.

Special Teams

5 Minutes = X-PT/FG/Block

15 Minutes = Punt, punt return, kickoff, kickoff return.

On Tuesday, we may work with the punters on their techniques. On Wednesday, we may work with the defense blocking the punt. We dedicate 20 minutes to the team portion of special teams. In the first 10 minutes, we go about half speed. We have not stretched at this point in practice. We want to make sure they understand the proper techniques. Later when we get to our 20-minute period on special teams, we can determine what we need to work on. That covers Tuesday and Wednesday.

Thursday is our review day. This is the last day we are on the field because we meet on Friday and play on Saturday. This is what we do on game week Thursday.

Game Week Thursday—Date:_____

Offense	Time	Defense
Warm-Up	3:15	Warm-Up
Specialist	3:20	Specialist
Team Stretch	3:25	Team Stretch
Kicking Game	3:30	Kicking Game
Teach	3:35	Teach
Skelly	4:10	Skelly
Team Passe	4:25	Team Pass
Team vs. Scouts	4:40	Team vs. Scouts
2 Min. X PT/FG	5:05	2 Min. X PT/FG

Comments: Specialist period is 10 minutes.

Special Teams Script - 25 Minutes

THURSDAY KICKING SCRIPT

Extra Point/Field Goal: 6 Kicks (1's)

Spread Punt: 1's and 2's one each vs. scout (full cover, tag off)

Short Punt: 1's and 2's one each vs. air (mirror)

Tight Punt: 1's and 2's one each vs. scout (full cover, tag off)

Punt Rush: 1's and 2's one each rocket vs. scouts (full return)

1's and 2's one each Lazer vs. scouts (full return)

1's and 2's one each missile vs. scouts (full return)

Punt Safe: 1 defense vs. scouts (snoop smoke 5) full return

Kickoff Return: 1's and 2's one each red vs. scouts

1's vs. surprise onside kick

1's and 2's one each Blue vs. scouts

Kickoff return after safety: 1's one time

Substitutes one time vs. air (1's only leave when replaced)

Kickoff: 1's and 2's one each RDM vs. scouts

1's Surprise onside kick

Kickoff after safety: 1's one time vs. scouts

Special onsides kick: 1's vs. air

We are going to cover every situation that is going to happen in a football game.

I am going to spend the majority of my time left talking about our punt team. The punt team is the most critical part of our special teams. If you get a punt blocked, you have a major problem. It can turn a football game around. I am going to put my best players on this unit. I will use starters on this unit. I know you want to play as many players as possible but you must decide if you want to risk a blocked punt or if you want to have the best players on that unit. Let me go over some of our philosophy and general rules on our Punt Team.

General Philosophy

- Put our defense in the best possible field position.
- Protect our punter with a full zone protection concept.
- Fan two thirds of the field in specific lanes to cover the punt.
- Speed and Effort

General Rules

- Either team can advance a blocked punt.
- A partially-blocked punt that crosses the line of scrimmage is the same as a regular punt.
- Coverage men cannot interfere with the free movement of a receiver in his effort to catch any punt.
- The return man gets a two-yard buffer zone in which to catch the ball.
- Neither team can advance a fair catch, and the fair-catch man cannot be bumped or tackled.
- A muffed fair catch is a free ball and belongs to the team that recovers it.
- The punt team cannot advance a muffed punt.
- To down a punt, the covering team man must stay with the ball until the whistle declares the play dead. (If the official does not rule the ball dead, the receiving team can try to advance it at no risk to themselves)
- To down the ball around the goal line, coverage men must not let any part of their body get into the end zone. (This means carrying the ball in or sliding into the end zone with it.)
- When we punt, we go from offense to defense at the line of scrimmage.
- Past the line of scrimmage, the opposing team cannot block below the waist.
- The kicking team is the only team that can be penalized for not having enough people in the game. (We must make sure we have 11 men on the field and at least seven on the line of scrimmage.)

Stance

- Lineman (guards, tackles, and wingmen):
    - ✓ Feet under the armpits
    - ✓ Inside foot up, heel-to-toe relationship
    - ✓ Knees over your toes
    - ✓ Chest out, head and eyes up
    - ✓ Hands resting on thighs
- Fullback:
    - ✓ Feet shoulder-width apart and parallel
    - ✓ Knees over your toes
    - ✓ Chest out, head and eyes up
    - ✓ Hands resting on your thighs
- Shooters:
    - ✓ Feet under your armpits
    - ✓ Inside foot up in take-off position (like a wide receiver)
    - ✓ Hands up in front and open ready take on defender

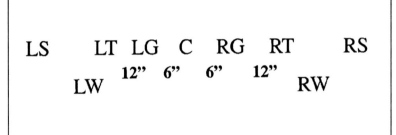

Figure 18-1. Punt team alignment

Alignments

- Center: on the ball
- Guards: six inches split off of C, head on his belt line
- Tackles: twelve inches split off G and at the same depth
- Wings: inside foot behind the outside off foot of the tackle, close enough to his hip
- Fullback: directly behind the right guard, 5 yards deep
- Punter: directly behind the Center, with his toes at 14 yards
- Shooters: on the line of scrimmage, inside the numbers (distance from ball varies by position on field)

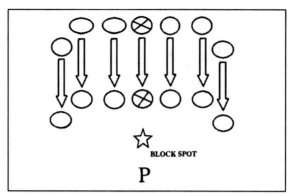
Figure 18-2. Punt-team block spot

Zone Protection Scheme

- Each zone blocker has a specific area of responsibility
  - ✓ Your nose to the nose of the next man to your outside
  - ✓ Block the man or men in your zone
  - ✓ Use inside-out leverage
    - ⇨ Increases his distance to the block point
    - ⇨ Maintains kicking pocket integrity
  - ✓ Meet rushers forcefully so that they cannot drive you backward into the block point.
- Maintain constant split relationships to one another
  - ✓ Drop vertically off the line of scrimmage (straight back).
  - ✓ Give ground as fast as the fastest rusher outside of you.
  - ✓ Continue moving backward until the man outside of you stops.

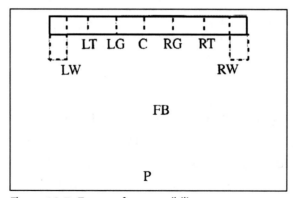
Figure 18-3. Zones of responsibility

The zones of responsibility go from your nose to the nose of the man to your outside.

- Footwork: Kick slide technique
  - ✓ Keep shoulders square
  - ✓ Push off with your inside foot (front foot)
  - ✓ Place outside foot (back foot) firmly in the ground for stability
  - ✓ Slide front foot back to original stance
  - ✓ Repeat until depth is reached
  - ✓ Keep shoulders square

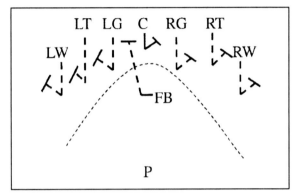

Figure 18-4. Vertical set lanes: "White" call white = fullback right

- Handwork
  - ✓ Hands should raise and be ready to strike
  - ✓ Use outside hand in an extended but strong position to protect your gap (outside zone): big outside
  - ✓ Use inside hand with elbow tighter to body to assist your inside gap only when necessary: little inside
  - ✓ Meet rusher with hands and eyes under his near shoulder pad

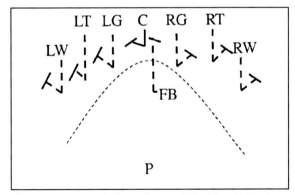

Figure 18-5. Vertical set lanes. "Black" call black = fullback left

- Awareness
    - ✓ Know how many rushers can challenge your zone and the zone to your inside.
    - ✓ Never block inside even if a man crosses your face to the inside.
- Common Rush Schemes
    - ✓ One man in your zone
        - ⇨ Drop straight back to get between him and the block point.
        - ⇨ Maintain inside-out leverage.
    - ✓ Two men in your zone
        - ⇨ Drop straight back to get between both of the rushers and the block point.
        - ⇨ Keep dropping as fast as the outside rusher to use up both men.
        - ⇨ Use your body to inside hand to take the inside rusher.
        - ⇨ Play the outside rusher as you would a single rusher.
    - ✓ Stacked rush
        - ⇨ Pick up the rusher that comes to your zone.
        - ⇨ Pass the inside rusher off to the zone protector to your inside.
- Center zone technique
    - ✓ The number one objective is a great snap.
    - ✓ Get your head up to avoid being caught of balance and pulled out of the center box.
    - ✓ Give ground to fill the area between you and the left guard or right guard.
    - ✓ Release through the gap and any man challenging that gap.
- Coaching points
    - ✓ Expect a block attempt each time we punt.
    - ✓ Survey your zone and then watch the ball as it is snapped.
    - ✓ Move when the ball moves and execute your technique.
    - ✓ React quicker than the man or men rushing your zone.
    - ✓ Block the rusher with proper technique.
        - ⇨ Drive through him
        - ⇨ Force him to restart or redirect
    - ✓ Help your inside gap by maintaining constant split relationships and punching with your inside arm.
    - ✓ Do not allow yourself to be pulled or grabbed by a rusher
    - ✓ Form a solid wall. Work together!
    - ✓ Protect first. Cover second.

COVERAGE

Phase One

- Linemen and wings fan to specific landmarks 15 yards down the field
- Keep the ball on your inside shoulder
- Shooters and fullback go directly to the ball

Phase Two

- Converge on the ball
- Keep the ball on your inside shoulder
- Never, follow another player
- Shooters attack the outside shoulder
- Full Backs play head up
- Wings have ultimate contain
  Coaching Points
- Keep the ball on your inside shoulder (do not let the ball cross your face)
- Start to gather 10 yards away from the ball and breakdown at five yards, continue to find the football
- Continue to close on the ball at all times, keeping it inside and in front
- You must be ready to make the tackle
- If the ball carrier breaks up field away from you, cut toward him and get into a good pursuit angle
- Gang tackle the ballcarrier; first man secure the tackle, second and third men try to strip the ball out.

The punter calls out the direction of the ball. He jogs down the field but he wants to stay on top of the ball. He is the safety man.

We tell the coverage men to fan to their landmark at 15 yards from the line of scrimmage. We set up cones on the field to indicate the lanes the cover team must fill. Here are the landmarks we want the cover team to shoot for.

Center: Go to goal post.

Guards: Go one yard inside the hash mark.

Tackles: Go five yards outside the hash.

Wings: Go to the numbers.

Fullback: Go directly to the ball through his gap.

Shooters: Go directly to the ball.

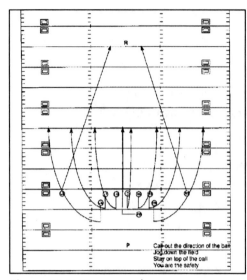

Figure 18-6. Coverage phase one

Next, we kick the ball from the hash mark (Figure 18-7). This is how we cover the kick from the right hash mark. We are kicking the ball down the right hash mark unless we designate otherwise.

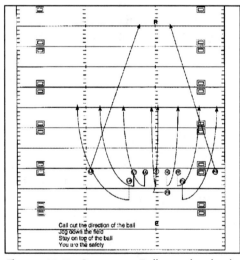

Figure 18-7. Coverage: Ball on the hash mark

Again, we want the cover to fan to their landmarks at 15 yards from the line of scrimmage.

Punter: Call out the direction of the ball.

Center: Go one yard inside the hash.

Boundary Guard: Go five yards outside the hash.

Boundary Tackle: Go to the numbers.

Boundary Wing: Go three yards inside the sideline.

Field Guard: Go to the goalpost.

Field Tackle: Go to upright away from the ball.

Field Wing: Go to outside the hash.

Fullback: Go directly to the ball through your gap.

Shooters: Go directly to the ball.

We want the cover team to go into phase two of the coverage once they have reached their landmark.

We have a plan to cover the kick once the punt is away. If you have a plan, you had better work the plan. If you do not teach the plan and rep the play, it will not happen on Saturday.

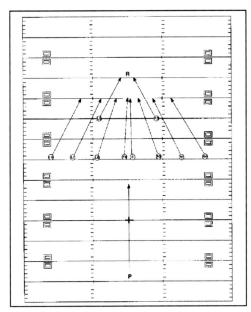

Figure 18-8. Coverage: Phase two

We tell the cover men to get to their landmark first. They must adjust their lanes to close on the return man keeping the ball on the inside shoulder. They must start to gather at 10 yards way from the ball and breakdown at five yards from the ball. They must be ready to make the tackle.

We set up cones to make sure we come down in the cover lanes. We put a coach back to simulate the punt. We do not want a punter back there kicking the ball all over the field. We want to control the punt so we can check the coverage. The coach gets the ball to the return man and we work on the coverage. It is a controlled environment and we get a lot accomplished on the drill.

Let me cover the timetables on the coverage. We cover the timetable from both sides of the football.

On the kickoff, set the standard at a minimum and try to exceed it each week. College and high school kickoffs are at different distances so you have to adjust to those distances.

We feel a good snapper is worth his weight in gold. If you can get a good snapper to get the ball to the punter, it is a big factor in the punting game. If the punter can catch the football and get rid of it in the period we allot, you can have a good punt team.

The importantce of this presentation is this. You want to make sure you have worked on the kicking game so they act as if they know what they are doing in the game.

Our punt drills include the following:

Protection Personnel Drills

- Kick slide: Down the line
- Kick slide: half line
- Individual fit drill vs. Rush
- Kick slide vs. Rush (board)
- Half line vs. Rush
- Coverage lane drills

Shooter Drills

- Fit: Step and swat
- Fit drill: Swat technique
- Foot fire: Swat technique
- Release

Snapper, Protector, Punter

   Team

- Team vs. Air coverage (cones)
- Team vs. Air (phase two)
- Team vs. Rush

Let me see if this tape will fit the VCR. I am technically handicapped. Here we go. (Film)

Hang Time	
Minimum 3.5 seconds / Preferred 5.0 seconds	
Distance	
Minimum 55 yards / We prefer 65 yards	
Minimum goal is inside 30-yard line	

Punt	Punt Block
Total Execution	Block Time
2.1 Seconds	2.4 Seconds or More
Snap Time	**Snap Time**
0.7 - 0.8 Seconds	0.9 Seconds or More
Release Time	**Get-Off Time**
1.1 - 1.3 Seconds	1.6 Seconds or More
Hang Time	
4.5 - 5.0 Seconds	
Distance	
40 - 45 yards from LOS	
PAT Block	**PAT**
Total Execution	**Total Execution**
1.1 - 1.2 seconds	1.3 seconds or more
Snap Time	**Snap Time**
3.4 seconds	0.5 seconds or more
Hold Time	**Hold Time**
0.1 seconds	0.2 seconds or more
Release Time	**Release Time**
0.7 - 0.8 seconds	0.9 – 1.0 seconds
Field Goal	**Field-Goal Block**
Total Execution	**Total Execution**
1.2 - 1.3 seconds	1.4 seconds or more
Snap Time	**Snap Time**
0.3 - 0.4 seconds	0.4 - 0.5 seconds
Hold Time	**Hold Time**
0.1 seconds	0.2 seconds of more
Release Time	**Release Time**
0.8 - 0.9 seconds	1.0 seconds or more

19

Punting Drills and Techniques

Jackie Sherrill
Mississippi State University
1997

I'm going to spend some time going through the kicking game. But I'm also going to talk about the lost art of actually punting the ball. I remember the first job I had as a head coach. I was setting up the staff and doing all the little things. I asked my staff who could coach the punters. There wasn't a person on my staff who could coach the punter. At that time, we had a player that was a great punter. He was an All-Pac-10 punter. I decided to be the kicking coach. I wasn't going to let anybody screw him up.

Great players teach us a lot more than we can actually teach them. Over the years of coaching punters and kickers, I have derived some things. Ever since then, I get every book that comes out on the kicking game. It pleases me to know that what I have been teaching the punter was in all in those books. The techniques remain the same. In the very short time today, I will be able to teach you how to teach your kids to punt. That doesn't mean they will be able to punt. That takes a certain amount of ability.

I have developed the four P's for punters. You *prepare* a young man to do something. You *practice* hard at it. You *position* him to do something that he has to *perform*. If he can't perform, you are not going to be able to do it.

When we talk about motivation and how to motivate people, motivation is a misused term. The more mature players you have, the better football team you are going to have. I've been around probably the best college team ever as far as talent. Every player from our starting 22 played pro football. On the 1980 team that I had in Pittsburgh, we had 27 players; three were drafted in the first round, 11 in the first seven rounds, 18 others got drafted, and 22 went to camp. We went through a span of four years where we went 11–1. If it hadn't been for the dumb-butt coaches, we probably would have won the national championship at least two times. Coaching is just like the Kentucky Derby. All the horses in the Kentucky Derby have a chance to win, or they wouldn't be there. All those horses can run.

What is motivation? The best example I can give you is playing for Coach Bryant. There was no coach in college coaching like Coach Bryant. He forgot more about winning than we will ever know. We were playing Tennessee. It was fourth down, and we had the ball on their four-yard line. Coach Bryant had me by one arm and David Ray, our kicker, by the other arm. He sent us on the field. Suddenly from the press box someone yelled, "Clock play." Stabler came up to the line on fourth down and threw the ball out of bounds. He stopped the clock, but we lost the ball on downs. The game ended in a tie.

We went back to our locker room after the game. The manager had left the keys to the padlock on the door out on the field. Coach Bryant knocked the lock off of the door, and we all filed into the locker room. About that time, all the coaches started coming in. Coach Bryant told all the coaches to get out of the "damn locker room!" Here we were in the locker room with Coach Bryant. He told us that in all his years of coaching, this was the first time he, as the coach, had lost a football game. He always talked to the press. That day he left the locker room, talked to no one, got in the police car, and left. He usually had a meeting with his coaches on Sunday morning to find out who played well. That meeting didn't happen.

On Monday morning, all the coaches were sitting around the big conference table in his office. They were all early because that is the way Coach Bryant wanted it. He looked at his watch and said that he was five minutes early, but he wanted to get started anyway. We were playing LSU the next week, and they had a great football team. He told all his coaches if we didn't beat LSU to pack their bags. He didn't talk to any of them for a whole week and never had another staff meeting. We went to play LSU and won 35–6. They scored the 6 at the end of the game. That's motivation.

Let's talk about the punter. There are two types of punters. There is the slicer and the conventional type. You do not want a slicer. If you are a slicer, you can't control the ball.

Let's talk about the grip of the ball. There are four panels on the football. It doesn't matter how you number the panels. I start with the one to the left of the strings as you hold the ball. A right-footed kicker's right thumb goes on the first panel of the ball. The index finger and middle finger go on the second panel. The ring finger and little finger go on the third panel. On a Wilson football, there is a trademark. It's a circle with an R in it. When I talk about the dot, that is what I'm talking about.

The ball sits in the fingers. Don't palm the ball. It is just as for the quarterback: I want to see air under the fingers. We want the ball back in our fingers so that we can drop the ball down to our side and be able to hold it. It is almost a natural placement of fingers on the ball. I want to be able to place the ball in my fingers and walk, talk, or swing the ball. That means I've got the right pressure on the fingers and no pressure on the palms. Have your punter drop his hands to his sides. Walk up and place the ball in his right hand. It automatically goes in the proper place.

Don't put the ball in the fingertips. To hold the ball in the fingertips, you have to squeeze it with the hand. If you squeeze it with the fingers, you have no control over it. Also, if you squeeze with the fingers, your elbow will go inside, and we certainly don't want that. I have them grip the ball. If I can place my fingers on the ball and take it away from him, he doesn't have control of the ball. If the punter puts the ball in his palm, it is easy to take away from him. The grip is on the back third of the ball.

If he grips the ball, swings it up to the middle, and extends his left hand, that is where it goes. His left hand may be adjusted up on the ball somewhat, but it is a mirror of his right hand. We want a small bend in the back of the kicker. What I am trying to teach you is how to get the ball in the perfect spot every time.

As we swing the ball up and stop it, we can see that the ball is not straight. It is automatically three to five degrees inside and three to five degrees down. If you take the ball in the fingertips, it pulls your wrist and elbow inside, which is not natural.

The next thing is the stance of the punter. We want a parallel stance. That doesn't mean that you won't stagger your stance a little bit. That depends on the punter. We always start off parallel. If the punter is kicking the ball downfield, the only way that can happen is if the body is going downfield. If my hips are pointed outside, I cannot punt the ball downfield. It is impossible to do unless the punter is a slicer. Everything the punter does is going downfield. His shoulders, hips, and feet are all going downfield.

We want no weight on the toe or heel. We want a comfortable stance. We don't want to be leaning forward on the toe. I want a slight bend in the leg. I do not want a straight leg. If the punter is straight-legged, that means his butt is out. He wants his butt forward but a slight bend in the legs. We want him to be relaxed in his stance.

The hands are relaxed. When the punter receives the ball, he does not want his hands locked. I don't want those hands extended forward with the elbows locked. I want them relaxed. After he relaxes, he moves his hands up into position. If he locks his hands, that will force him straight up. He has about four inches between his elbow and his body.

The target area for the center snap is just below the chest and just above the crotch. A good drill for the snapper is the one-man sled. Place the sled at the punter's depth, and let him practice snapping the ball at the sled. A lot of people talk about the speed of the snap. It is not speed; it is accuracy. We talk about 0.7 for the snap.

I've had about five pro coaches call about our punter. I asked them who coaches their punter. The response from all five teams was "no one." The most important play in the game is the punt, and no one coaches it. That doesn't make sense to me. They told me that the punters kind of coached themselves. Every day, I spend at least an hour with our punter. That is pre-practice, during practice, and after practice. I film every time that he punts the ball. I film two angles. I film from behind and the top. He watches those films every day. I want him to understand in the game if I say, "Drop the ball."

When the punter kicks a bad kick in a game, he does one of two things. He goes over and hangs his head, or he wants to know what happened. You, as the coach, better have something to tell him. You can teach yourself how to coach punters just by watching film.

If the hips are turned to the right or left, the first thing that happens when I step is that my foot is going in the direction of my hips. All of a sudden, my hips are pointing to the right, and I want to kick it to the left. That means I have to slice the ball.

I want the conventional style, where the punter strikes the ball and his foot finishes above his head. I want that finish on the right eye with his foot above his head. That is why I take the film from the top. If I don't see his foot above his head, I know he did not finish the kick. If I see his foot to the left of his shoulder or below, that means he had some bad steps, and his plant foot and body were turned.

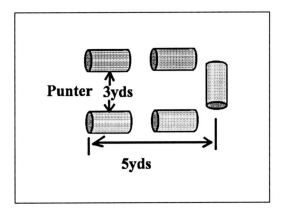

To get your punter kicking down the field, draw a chalk line down the field. Just simply make him step down the line. He is stepping down the line and kicking down the line. We want his foot right on that chalk line. If you don't want to use the chalk line, put him in a tunnel. Form a tunnel with dummies or cones. If you have a punter who is crossing over, he will kick the dummies. That will get him out of crossing over more quickly than you know. If you have a punter who is overstriding, pile dummies up in front of him. However, watch him. They want to stop and jerk their knee up when you do that.

There are two drills that I want to show you really quickly. The first drill is called the seat drill. The punter is on his knees. You can't do this enough. I make our punters do this a thousand times. Have a manager or another punter spin him the ball. The punter catches the ball, seats it, and drops it. They present the ball and drop it. I don't want him to fart around with the ball. The more he adjusts and fiddles with the ball, the less likely he will be a quick kicker. As a punter, you are trying to get your time between 1.3 to 1.5 seconds. I time the punter from the time he catches it until it comes off of his foot. If it comes off in 1.6 to 1.7 seconds, the kick is going to get blocked.

During pre-game, I watch the opponent's snapper and punter. That is when I decide what we are going to do in punt receiving. I watch the center to see how he presents the ball. I watch the punter to see if he can get it off in 1.5. I check to see how many steps he is taking. I look at the distance it takes him to kick the ball. Most punters are 15 yards deep. If the punter takes more than five yards to punt the ball, it will be blocked just about anytime they want to come after it. We can't protect it. That is where I put the dummies to keep the punter from overstepping the five-yard mark. If the punter can't get the kickoff before the five-yard point, the block point is seven instead of nine yards. Even if he can get it off in 2.0 seconds, it will be blocked.

In the seat drill, the punter catches the ball. He grips the ball and presents it. He then drops the ball. If he drops the ball correctly, it will bounce straight up and back to his right. If the nose of the ball is down, it will bounce back to the punter. If the nose of the ball is up, it will go away from the punter. If the ball is turned one way or the other, it will bounce the opposite way from how it is turned. He is not kicking the ball; he can practice these things, and you don't have to be there.

The other drill is called the flex drill. I do this to get the players to understand how to explode through the ball and finish. If your player is doing this the correct way, there will be times when he falls right on his butt. His power will take him through the kick. The punter presents the ball as if he were going to kick it. As he presents the ball, the coach or manager takes the ball, but the punter continues his motion as if he were going to kick the ball. When the plant foot is put down, there should be about a 30-degree bend in the knee. The power leg or punting leg will actually be almost touching his butt as he fires up through the ball. As the leg comes from almost touching his butt to the explosion, contact will be made around the knees. This lets the punter experience the full extension of the leg. This is like swinging a weighted bat. He is really going after the ball, but all of a sudden there is no ball there, so he finishes pretty high.

Next, let's look at the placement of the ball on the foot. When the punter's foot is locked and straight, there is only about four inches of the ball that actually makes contact with the foot. That is because the ball is not flat. The ball is dropped on the laces of the shoe. Because it is dropped slightly down and inside, there is more surface to hit.

I am not concerned about the spiral of the ball. I want the ball 40 yards downfield every time it is punted. I don't care if the ball doesn't shoot out like a gun. We would like to have that, but if it doesn't, that is okay. As long as the punter's mechanics are all right, the ball will go downfield 40 yards. If you want the ball to turn over, the punter has to drop the nose of the ball more. By dropping the nose of the ball, the fit on the foot is better, and the angle is better. If the ball is kicked high, the punter is overstriding and has his weight back.

If the ball is kicked to the right, then that means the ball is dropped on the outside of the foot. If the ball goes left, the ball was dropped on the inside of his foot. When I watch punters from the front, I can tell you by the way the ball comes off of the foot whether it went left or right.

Let me go over some steps for you. Punters are generally two, two-and-a-half-, three-, or three-and-a-half-step punters. You don't want to be a three- or three-and-a-half-step punter. If I am a true two-step punter, I am going right, left, and punt. If I am a two-and-a-half-step punter, I have a jab step to get going. I punt with a right, left, and left step pattern.

What happens if the snap is bad? The first thing that we tell the punter is to get the ball. If the ball is left, he moves his whole body behind the ball. Don't just reach. If we are going to kick the ball downfield, we have to get straight behind the ball. If he doesn't move behind the ball, his momentum will be carried the way the ball is snapped.

Here is a drill to teach a punter how to punt. Get two punters facing each other about five yards apart. Have them play pepper with each other. When I talk about pepper, it is the game you play in baseball. In punting, all you are doing is teaching your punter how to control the ball. Don't worry about the spiral. All I want to do is control the ball. Work on presenting the ball and dropping it. I'm watching the ball. If it goes left, it came off of the inside of my foot. If it goes right, it is the outside. It is a one-step and drop. After we develop some skill with the five-yard distance, we start to increase the distance apart up to 20 yards.

To make a point, I make the punter close his eyes. With his eyes closed, I make him kick the ball. If he can't do it, his drop is not consistent. He can do it if he steps down the line, has a consistent drop, and swings his leg down the line.

During the seat drill, the punter gets so good that he can stop the ball as it is being snapped to him and not have to make any adjustments to it before he kicks. He has to focus and concentrate on the ball, but his hand-eye coordination will let him do it.

We watch the punter's head. We draw a straight line from his head. As he receives the ball, seats it, and steps forward, his head should not go up and down. It should remain level throughout the approach. As he presents the ball, he does not pull it up or down. If the head goes up on the first step, it means his heel is out. I stand to the right of the punter. As he receives the ball and presents it, if he raises the ball up, I'll slap it out of his hands. The ball is not raised or lowered throughout the kick. They work on the level presentation during the pepper drill, also.

The slicer can spiral the ball, but there is no power. I want to kick with power and forget about the spiral.

Next, I want to cover placement of the ball. A regular kick is one that is kicked straight downfield. If I want to directionally kick the ball, there are some techniques involved. Remember, we want to kick down the line. If the line is a directional kick aimed at the sideline, we still use the same principles. If he wants to kick the ball to the right, the punter moves to the left before the snap. The hips have to be turned to the right sideline. If I'm going to kick it left, I move right before the snap. Our rule is he never moves outside the foot of the center. You see some people line up over the guard. If you do that, you are asking the center for an awful lot. We don't punt outside the tackle box. We never punt outside our guard box.

To get the punters to understand height, I make them kick over light poles. I make them walk up within 10 yards of the pole and kick over them.

When they directionally kick the ball, they need a target. If they punt downfield, there is the scoreboard. When they kick for the sideline, I want them to find a target in the stands. It may be a big section number in the stadium or something like that. He can't see the pylons in the end zones. The kicker's target is in the stands.

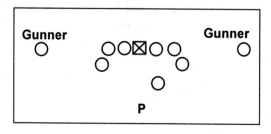

The next type of kick is when you are backed up. Never allow the punter to be closer than six inches from the end line. That has to be practiced. The desperation kick is critical in some games. When the punter has a desperation kick, he has one step to kick it. At the end of the game with 11 people rushing is when the punter has a desperation kick. He gets one step to get it away.

The punt formation we use is the spread formation. We have two gunners on the outside to go to the ball. We have two slotbacks and a personal protector for the punter.

The kicking look for mismatches is just as if you were looking for a mismatch on offense. If there is a weakness in the kicking game, find it. The punter is just as important as the quarterback. The quarterback gets the chance to throw the ball 20 to 30 times a game. The punter gets six times a game to punt the ball. You have to spend time with him. It is the single most important play in any game you play. Don't take it for granted.

20

Kickoff Techniques and Drills

Phil Zacharias
Stanford University
2000

What I am going to do this morning is to talk about and focus on our kickoff coverage. But moreover I want to talk about special teams practice. You have to put time into the special teams and make it more than just something you have to do as part of a football game.

At Stanford, we made a commitment to our special teams and it starts with our head coach. He has given me the freedom and practice time to make sure the kids understood that the special teams are important. He wants them to know we are going to win with our special teams. We were fortunate at Stanford to have a number of coaches on the staff with a lot of special teams coaching experience.

At Stanford all of our coaches are involved with the special teams program. I have a lead coach for every special team. I am the lead coach on the punt and kickoff teams. But I am the facilitator for the special teams program. It is impossible for me to do everything. The coaching staff shares the responsibility for coaching the teams. I basically organize everything and am involved in the personnel on those teams and their motivation.

Special teams play makes up a third of the game of football. We are always going to try to win that phase of the game. We have a special teams meeting a half hour before the team meeting on Friday night. We talk about it, we highlight it, and make sure the kids understand it is important.

One of the things I struggled with when I started coaching the kicking game was how to practice it. What do you do other than running down the field under a kickoff to teach techniques? We began to highlight some specific techniques that happen on the way to covering a kickoff.

What I am going to do is take you through the things we thought about that we felt were important when it came to the kicking game. I'm going to show you how we set up our practice structure and some drills that we use to teach the skills needed in covering kicks. These drill are unique to us at Stanford.

The first thing we have to talk about is focusing on the fundamentals. Alignment and stance is the genesis of anything you do in football. The next things we talk about are time-ups, get-off, and lanes. That is basically your coordination of your kicker, his alignment, how you expand the field, his approach on the ball, and everyone working in unison. When the ball is kicked, we want everyone moving forward. Everyone has defined lanes and we will talk about that later.

The next thing is what we call attack technique. On the way to the ball there are some attack techniques the coverage will be using. We have come up with little words and phrases that speak to that. The first thing we say is the kickoff is a 40-yard dash. It is a sprint. I am expecting our kickoff team to be at the 30-yard line when the ball is caught. The second word we use is avoid. This is a term I use as I am in my lane coming down the field. When someone comes to block me, I am going to avoid him to the right or left. The third thing is what we call two gap. This is a technique, where I have encountered a blocker and I don't know which side the ball is coming. It is shedding the block and making the tackle.

The next technique is called shoot-and-run. This is a combination technique where the cover man is sprinting down the field, encounters a block, gets his hands out, and walks the block back into the ballcarrier. We use the term wedge split, to describe the technique we want used on a double-team or wedge alignment by the blockers. Skins are basically for our outside coverage people. They are coming off of the edges of the wedge. We want them to skin nice and tight and keep their shoulders square.

For any coverage team to be successful, you have to tackle well. We are highlighting these things and we are going to focus the majority of our work around them.

Let's go into our structure in a practice situation. The first thing we cover is our alignment principles and our huddle procedures. Because of our makeup on the defensive staff, I am in the press box on game day. That presents a small problem in the coordination of the special teams. One thing that was a problem before we got there was making sure we had 11 people on the field.

We make a big deal out of our huddle procedures. When we practice, and even in a game situation, we use two huddles. We have an A huddle and a B huddle. The A huddle organizes at the 50-yard line and the B huddle is on the 40-yard line. When the A huddle organizes, if there is a problem we don't know about, we can substitute right from the other huddle. We make a concerted effort to make sure our huddle discipline is there.

On our player count we count from the outside in. The guy on the sideline is number 5 and the guy next to the ball is number l. We have a right and left side. Our right side is considered our strong side. The left side is considered our quickside. The kicker faces the huddle. We have a two-line huddle with the left side on the front row and the right side on the back row.

Huddle alignment

The field is divided into three zones. The right, middle, and left are places we could kick the ball from. We kick the ball either right or left. We don't kick it down the middle. The cover zones are 1 to the right and 3 to the left. An example of our huddle call would be strong right-right-cover 3, run-hit. That means we are putting our strong side right. We are going to kick from the right hash mark. And we are going to kick the ball into the right corner of the field. The run-hit signals everyone to clap and reminds them why they are on the field. If I call strong left-middle-cover 1, our strong side would align left, the kick is from the middle of the field, and the ball is going to the left side. That lets me move my strong side around. That doesn't mean I'll always kick to the strong side. The problem with sending the strong side to both sides is our huddle. If we call strong left, our huddle has to realign for the dispersion of the players. Sometimes that can get confusing. Most of the time where we align depends on what the opponent is trying to do with his return game.

We line up on the 25-yard line facing inward toward the kicker. Our front foot should be on the line and our hands on our knees. The kicker puts his hand up when he is ready. The official will blow the whistle. When the kicker puts his hand down to his thigh, he counts, "1001, 1002, 1003," and then approaches the ball. Everyone should be within one yard of the ball or the 35-yard line when the ball is kicked.

Your alignment comes off of the number 5 men. We want the five guys to align five yards from the sideline and everyone aligns about five yards apart from the outside. That was pretty standard until the rules changed. Now everyone must be inside the numbers until the whistle blows. Because of that our alignments come from the R1 and R2, since we are kicking for the right hash mark on this diagram. The R1 aligns two-and-a-half yards inside the hash mark. The R2 aligns two-and-a-half yards outside the hash mark. The rest of the team aligns off of those guy's alignments. When the whistle blows our number 4's are on the numbers and our number 5's are four to five yards from the sidelines.

I am generally going to kick the ball to my strong side. I put linebacker types on the strong side. The quickside has faster types in its makeup. I am going to take the strong side into the place where I think the wedge or point of attack is going to be. I want to turn the return back to my quickside. If I put the ball in the middle I can use a "check with me" call as to where the ball is going. In that case the ball may be kicked to the quickside.

Let's go into some of our drill work. We came up with what we call a kickoff cycle. We have four coaches involved, with each of them having a particular position. We split the kickoff team into fourths. We have an A, B, C, and D group, which we rotate around to each individual station. We take half the football field. We put two drills on each side of the field at the 20-yard line and two drills at the 40-yard line. When we teach this, there is about three minutes at each station. Once we get the teaching done, we only spend about five minutes for the entire drill. That works out to about 45 seconds at each station and 15 seconds to rotate around. We do it quickly.

The first station is station A. That is our wedge and skin station. We get our defensive line guys to hold some shields. We put four shields up. We put three guys covering the kick. The guys on the outside work on skinning around the shields, and the guy in the middle splits the wedge. We want them to turn the shoulder and take the wedge on with the right or left shoulder.

Never try to split a wedge with square shoulders. They don't drop their heads when they attack the wedge. Once they split the wedge they square up the shoulders once again. We put our extra backs about 10 yards behind the shields. As the guys come through the shield they make a form tackle. The other two guys are working on striping the ball. We rotate around on the skin and wedge positions.

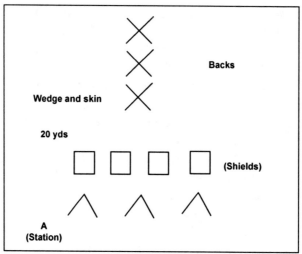

Kickoff cycle – A

The second station is our two gap drill. We have four guys with shields and four coverage guys. They are four ballcarriers behind the shields. The coverage attacks the shields, uses their hands to shed, and goes to make a form tackle. The coach will give the ballcarriers a direction to go, so the coverage guys can shed to that side. When we do this drill, we concentrate on keeping the feet moving. We don't stop the feet to shed.

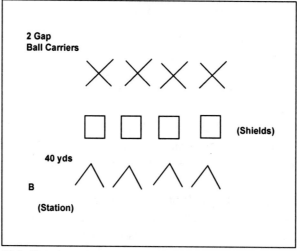

Kickoff cycle – B

At station C, we work on avoid and two gap drill. We use pop-up dummies for the coverage people to avoid. We have people holding the shields. The coach again gives the backs a direction for them to go. The coverage people avoid the pop-up dummies using rip techniques, attack the shields, walk them back, shed, and make a form tackle.

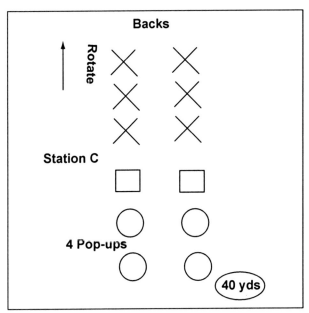

Kickoff cycle — C

The last station is a shoot-and-press drill. We have three people holding shields and three coverage guys. They attack the shields and walk them back 10 yards before they shed them. They work the form tackle and strip techniques in the drill also. Notice in each drill we are working in our tackling techniques. All our kickers take part in these drills also. We expect them to make tackles.

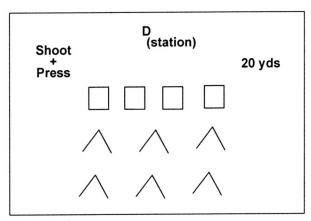

Kickoff cycle — D

The next thing we use is called kickoff gauntlet. This is where we put all the techniques together. We have two groups going. I put groups A and B on one side and groups C and D on the other. We start out with three pop-up dummies. Behind them are the shields. After that we have three tube dummies to step over. At the end we have a cone with a coach behind it. Five yards away on a 45-degree angle we have two stand-up dummies.

The coverage man starts out. He weaves in and out of the popup dummies using his avoid technique. He rips right-left-right or left-right-left. He attacks the shields using his right shoulder on the first group to split and his left shoulder on the second group. He steps over the three tube dummies. In this area, I want them working their hands like a shoot-and-run technique. After that he sprints to the cone. The coach gives him a direction and he performs a run-through and tackles one of the stand-up dummies. These are techniques on the run.

Obviously this takes some time to set up. I only have 10 minutes for my special teams period. While I am working on the punt game or something else, the managers are on another field setting up the cycle or gauntlet drill. We don't use practice time to do that. When we finish whatever drill we were working on and sprint over this field. When we come to the drill it is set up and all they have to do is run it.

When we use the gauntlet, we have anyone who is on any kind of coverage team in the drill. Our punt coverage team is also doing this drill. They have the same techniques that carry over from one to the next. Again, the kickers are in this drill. I grade the drill, show it to the kids, and make a big deal out of it.

The next things I am going to talk about are coverage rules, keys, ball placement, and things like that. These are some general rules and principles we talk to with the kids. Kickoff coverage is an all-out sprint. Speed and desire are important. Speed is important, but we have to have guys who want to be out there. It is not always the fastest guys who are the most effective. It is the guys who understand what we are doing and use their techniques. We want them to stay in their assigned lane if at all possible. If they get forced out of their lane, they want to get back and fill in a vacate lane. If you are knocked down, recover as quickly as possible and get back in your lane. If the man in front of you gets knocked down, try to fill his lane.

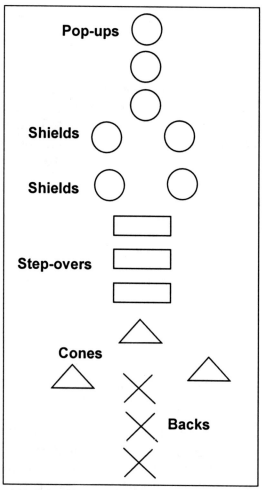

Kickoff gauntlet

It is not a shame to get knocked down, but it is a crime to stay down. To be on the kickoff team, it helps to be wild and crazy. We want people that are kamikaze types. Don't overrun the ball and take proper angles.

Tackles should never be made by one man. We want to gang tackle. Everything starts with a good kicker. The ball has to be kicked where it is supposed to be. It has to be kicked deep with proper hang time. Our goal is to always keep the ball inside the 20-yard line.

A ball that travels 10 yards is a live ball. Never assume the ball is not going to be run back out of the end zone. Anytime we kick the ball into or out of the end zone, our whole coverage team sprints all the way to the goal line. That is something we feel is important. If we see guys not doing that, we are on their butt about it. Our three keys are desire, recognition, and technique.

We have visual keys for all our guys. The inside people, which are our 1's and 2's, keys are going to be what we define as the left and right wedge setters. The 3's, 4's, and 5's keys are the right and left ends, respectively.

If the opponent is using one fullback in the middle as their wedge setter, we call that a diamond set. The 1's and 2's would key him.

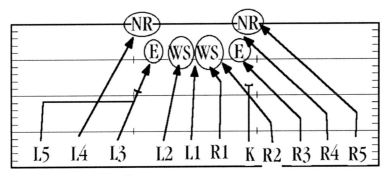

P.O.D. vs. Middle wedge

We want to anticipate where the ball is going. That gets us into what we call points of departure. The point of departure is the point at which the coverage people would hit the wedge. The vision keys take the coverage people to their points of departure. If we were playing a middle wedge, I want to sprint to the 35-yard line before I start to squeeze to my point. If it is a middle wedge, everyone has a point on that wedge that they hit. The R1 and L1 hit the inside shoulders of their respective wedge setters. The R2 and L2 hit the outside shoulder of that wedge setter. The R3 and L3, and the R4 and L4, hit the inside and outside shoulder of their ends. There is an NR in the diagram. That stands for non-return man. If the NR committed to the strongside, the R4 can hit the inside shoulder of the NR to his side because he has an R5 outside of him for contain. If the NR committed to the quickside, the L4 has to play two gap through the outside shoulder of the NR. The R5 and the kicker are on the hash marks about eight yards behind the coverage as the safeties. We play physical and aggressive. If someone breaks, I want our safeties right on him. That is our point of departure versus the middle wedge.

This is all about recognizing on the run. The ball is kicked and I am looking at my visual key. I see the wedge setter and I am working to converge on my point. On the way to his point, he is using the techniques we just talked about.

If we get a right or left wedge, our points change a little bit. Now we end up with what we call single points. As our guys are running down, they have to understand the body language of the returner. Though if the ball is kicked left and the blockers start to form the wedge right, you have to adjust your lanes accordingly. If the ball is kicked to our right, there is a returner and a non-returner. If the non-returner works to the right, R5 skins and contains through the outside shoulder of the non-returner. He uses a shoot-and-run technique through the upfield shoulder. The R4 splits through the outside shoulder of the right wedge setter. The R3 hits the inside shoulder of the right wedge setter. The R2 splits through the inside shoulder of the left wedge setter. The R1 skins the outside shoulder of the left end. The coverage guys away from the wedge direction have a slightly different technique. Hopefully the strong side will force the ball back toward the middle. If that happens, the L1, 2, 3, and 4 uses a run-through technique, where they skin behind the wedge and make the tackle. If the ball, however, has broken to the side, they have what is called a linebacker fold. When the ball breaks to the sideline, they come over the top like a linebacker. The L1 shoots and runs through or uses the linebacker fold. The L2 and L3 run through or use the linebacker fold between the right and left ends. The L4 skins the outside shoulder of the left end and contains. The L5 and kicker keep the ball on their inside shoulders and use their lane progression. The kicker sprints to around the 35-yard line and than presses the area in between R3 and R4. The L5, once he recognizes the return to the right, rotates halfway to the middle of the field. If he needs to he comes over the top to make the tackle.

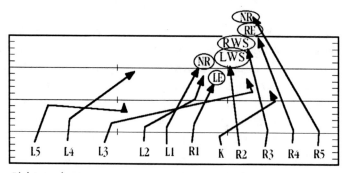

Right wedge

There was a question asked. Do you kick away from good returners? That answer is absolutely. I hate to do it because there are a lot of other variables that come into it. If we have the wind and I think we can kick the ball into or out of the end zone, then I'll kick to anyone. If we are kicking into the wind, I'll probably put the kicker in the middle of the field and go "check with me." Then we directional kick the ball away from the good returner. People that see you doing that line their returners up in an "I" on the goal line. The good returner may get the ball, but he is going to have to run to get it. On our kickoff team, we use our first-line guys.

Here is a coaching point for R4 and R5. We are trying to kick the ball into the right side of the field between the hash mark and the numbers. If we can get it outside the numbers, that is all the better. If we get it outside the numbers, R5 forces the ball back into the wedge. The reason for this is our coverage is concentrating on their points of departure. The coverage is focused on the blocking, not necessarily the position of the ball. When we have bad returns against us, it is because guys are watching the ball instead of their points. Those guys have to funnel the ball into the rest of the coverage.

If the ball is kicked into the right side of the field but the return is coming into the quickside, we have to redirect. The L4 skins through the outside shoulder of the left end or non-returner for contain. The L3 splits through the outside shoulder of the left wedge setter. The L2 splits through the inside shoulder of right wedge setter.

The L1 split through the inside shoulder of the right end. The R1 skins off of the outside shoulder of the right end. The R2, 3, and 4, linebacker fold between the left and right ends. The R5 has to make sure he pushes the ball into the coverage. The L5 keeps the ball on his inside shoulder, uses his lane progression, and presses the area between L4 and L3. As the ball starts to run to the left wedge, R4 and R5 keep the ball on their inside and outside shoulders respectively. They funnel him into the coverage and if he tries to cut back they are playing on his inside and outside shoulder.

Everyone doesn't run the same types of returns. These are examples of what we do each week to play our opponents. People can give you false keys. We work each week on this part of the game. We go over it to the point that we know what we are supposed to do game day. We change the points of departure based on the type of return the opponent has.

When we work on this in practice we kick the ball, but we are not watching it. We are looking at our points. The thing we have to guard against is breaking out of the lanes too quickly. As we come down, we don't have to kill the guys in the wedge, but we want them working to their points.

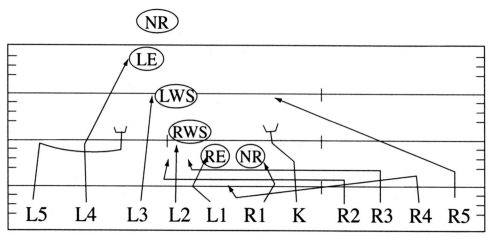

Left wedge

We have a kind of grading system we use on coverage. We have A, B, and F positions. The A position is based on the avoid and body position. If the ball and his key are working right, than his hat should be on the right side. The B position is when the coverage man isn't sure where the ball has defined itself. He is thinking about shooting and running through his man. The F position means the cover guys took a course right and the return and key went left. The A is good, B is acceptable, and F is unacceptable. Sometimes a guy runs the opposite side of the avoid, but I expect to see him skin back to the ball quickly. If I see a guy violate his lane and his key, I know he is looking at the ball as opposed to recognizing his keys.

Hopefully that gives you some insight into the coverage. Maybe you can use some techniques to help with the way you cover. We have won so many games with our special teams. That is the hidden yardage in football.

A lot of times a special team can change the momentum of a game. It can work both ways on you. If you make a mistake in the kicking game it can hurt. How many times have you worked like hell to drive the ball down the field and score, only to have the football run all the way back on the kickoff for a touchdown? In a matter of seconds, the opponent has stolen what it took you so long to gain. If you need help I would be glad to share some of these things with you. Thank you very much.

About the Editor

Earl Browning is a native of Logan, West Virginia. He currently serves as president of Telecoach, Inc.—an organization that conducts football clinics and produces the *Coach of the Year Clinics Football Manuals*. A 1958 graduate of Marshall University, he earned his M.Ed. and Rank I education certification from the University of Louisville. From 1958 to 1975, he coached football at various Louisville-area high schools. Among the honors he has been accorded are his appointments to the National Football Foundation and to the College Hall of Fame Advisory Committee on moving the museum to South Bend, Indiana. He was named to the Greater Louisville Football Coaches Association Hall of Legends in 1998. From 1992 to the present, he has served as a radio and television color analyst for Kentucky high school football games, including the Kentucky High School Athletic Association State Championship games.